D0077177

PHILOSOPHIES OF DIFFERENCE

Also available from Continuum:

PHILOSOPHIES OF DIFFERENCE
A Critical Introduction to Non-philosophy

François Laruelle

Translated by Rocco Gangle

continuum

Continuum International Publishing Group

The Tower Building	80 Maiden Lane
11 York Road	Suite 704
London SE1 7NX	New York, NY 10038

www.continuumbooks.com

Originally published in French as Les philosophies de la difference © Presses Univeritaires de France, 1986

This English language edition © the Continuum International Publishing Group, 2010

British Library Cataloguing-in-Publication Data
A catalogue record for this book is available from the British Library.

ISBN: HB: 978-0-8264-3663-4

Library of Congress Cataloging-in-Publication Data
Laruelle, François.
[Philosophies de la différence. English]
Philosophies of difference : a critical introduction to non-philosophy / François Laruelle ; translated by Rocco Gangle.
    p. cm.
Includes index.
ISBN 978-0-8264-3663-4
1. Difference (Philosophy) I. Title.

B105.D5L3713 2010
110–dc22
                                                            2010019220

Typeset by Newgen Imaging Systems Pvt Ltd, Chennai, India
Printed and bound in India by Replika Press Pvt Ltd

Contents

Translator's Introduction

François Laruelle's non-philosophy marks a bold attempt to think the One, or Real outside of any correlation with Being and without reference to transcendence. It is an arduous and painstaking theoretical enterprise that must skirt the twin dangers of positivism on the one hand and false transcendentalism on the other. *Philosophies of Difference* – published originally in 1986 – appears at a crucial juncture among the dozens of works Laruelle has published from the 1970s to the present day, and because of its specific content and its unique place in Laruelle's far-ranging oeuvre, it serves as an excellent introduction to his thought as a whole. It stands as one of the last works in which Laruelle explicitly engages traditional philosophers in detail and one of the first in which the theoretical workings of non-philosophy are definitively established. It is thus a key work in which readers new to the arcana of non-philosophy may find their bearings.

It is by combining two tasks at once that *Philosophies of Difference* offers an ideal introduction to non-philosophy in general: first, by bringing a new theoretical and critical rigor to bear upon the philosophies of Nietzsche, Heidegger, Deleuze and Derrida, offering powerful and distinctive readings of each but more importantly a collective interpretation of them all as avatars of a common invariant of philosophical Difference; and secondly, by formulating explicitly the new theoretical posture that enables, or rather effectuates this unified, critical reading itself as a non-philosophical theory of philosophical decision. It is with an awareness of these two primary aspects of the text and in view of their ultimate identity that *Philosophies of Difference* should be read. We can do little more than indicate the basic topography here; in any case, there is no need to introduce Laruelle's argument and the organization of his text in detail since he has himself provided for this in the 'Instructions for Use' that precede Chapter 1. It is worth repeating here only that in the 'Instructions' Laruelle singles out Chapter 6 as the 'most fundamental' of the book as a whole. Readers looking for a more detailed synopsis of the thesis and argument of the text would be well-advised to begin with a careful reading of that chapter. We will sketch only the two primary aspects just alluded to.

In the first of its two main aspects, Laruelle's study is a critique of Difference. What does this mean? Laruelle's study examines a quartet of philosophers for whom Difference in one form or another functions as a central concept: Nietzsche, Heidegger, Deleuze and Derrida. Of these four thinkers, Nietzsche and Deleuze are effectively conflated (somewhat summarily) into a single figure, Nietzsche–Deleuze, and particular attention is paid rather to Heidegger and Derrida, each of whom is set off from Nietzsche–Deleuze in a definite fashion. In this way three unique variants of Difference are identified and positioned relative to one another: (1) the Nietzsche–Deleuzean idealist or nonfinite form of Difference in which an essential reversibility of contraries is posited *a priori* in a metaphysics of power, perspectivalism and Eternal Return; (2) the Heideggerean analytic of irreversible Finitude as the essence of ontological Difference and the 'Turning' of Difference in and as the One; and (3) the Derridean deconstructive mixtures of Nietzschean affirmation and Heideggerean Finitude on the one hand and of Jewish and Greek modes of experience on the other that together conjure Differance as a finite and yet interminable form of Difference.

One extraordinary facet of *Philosophies of Difference* is the way it offers coordinated interpretations of these thinkers in a restatement of their philosophies that is illuminating and incisive in each instance without being reductive. But Laruelle's main purpose is broader and more critical. As Laruelle himself emphasizes, there is no attempt to provide a comprehensive summary or analysis of the works of any of the thinkers of Difference; rather, what is primarily at stake is the examination of a powerful generalization of a single structure, or syntax, common to them all. This common syntax is what Laruelle designates and analyzes as *the* Difference, or Difference as such. The individual readings remain subsidiary to a unified analysis of

Difference, which is in turn subordinated or relativized to the critique of what Laruelle identifies as the core invariant of Occidental philosophy, the *coincidentia oppositorum*, or unity of opposites. It is because the contemporary philosophies of Difference are shown to be continuations and fulfilments of this broad, synthetic tradition rather than revolutionary dissenters that the critical analysis of their Difference is capable of bearing its role as an introduction to the more general examination of philosophy as such.

Secondly, then, in his elaboration of the critical analysis of Difference, Laruelle lays the groundwork for a positive and constructive project of much greater scope: non-philosophy as the real, scientific theory of philosophy as such. This project, which Laruelle and others have developed and extended in a large variety of works subsequent to *Philosophies of Difference*, develops naturally here out of the specific form of critique Laruelle mounts with respect to Nietzsche–Deleuze, Heidegger and Derrida. By isolating the core invariant of *Difference* common to these contemporary philosophers and by conceiving this invariant as itself essentially characteristic of philosophy as such, Laruelle sets out a particular set of conditions allowing non-philosophy to be grasped, at least in a broad, preliminary fashion, starting from within the given parameters of current philosophy.

From what standpoint has Laruelle's critical analysis of Difference been made, if not from within the interminable, circular self-analysis and self-critique of Difference itself? What alternative remains to Differential thinking if Laruelle himself conceives Difference to express the very essence of philosophy? Laruelle calls the non-differential and non-philosophical thinking that in fact effectuates (rather than conditions or enables) the critique of Difference, the Vision-in-One. This theoretical modality, this new mode of non-philosophical experience is contrasted most clearly – because most finely – with the essential Finitude of Heideggerean Difference on the one hand and the interminable work of Differance in Derrida on the other. In this regard the final two chapters of *Philosophies of Difference* introduce a pair of concepts – the (non-)One and non-thetic transcendence (NTT) – which clarify exactly where and how non-philosophy breaks with Heideggerean Finitude and Derridean Differance, and in what respect the non-philosophical critique of Difference opens up a theory of philosophy in general as the theory of the radical contingency of philosophical decision. The formidable technical difficulties raised in these chapters come to define the central concerns of non-philosophy up through Laruelle's fully definitive statement *Principes de la non-philosophie* (Presses Universitaires de France 1996), in which the key notions of 'dualysis [*dualyse*]' and the 'cloning [*clonage*]' of the One develop precisely out of this earlier problematic of the (non-)One and NTT. An understanding of the complete theory, or theoretical practice of non-philosophy is thus greatly facilitated by starting from this initial conception as sketched originally in *Philosophies of Difference*.

What finally is non-philosophy? First of all, it is important to emphasize that it is not in any sense anti- or counter-philosophical. It is a broadening or generalizing of philosophy rather than an opposition or antagonism to it. Which is not to say that a strong, critical element, a critical and scientific spirit is not set upon philosophy by non-philosophy in an especially rigorous way.

If non-philosophy is a generalization of philosophy, this does not mean that it makes an example of philosophy or turns philosophy into its own example. In fact, non-philosophy substitutes the Vision-in-One for the philosophical logic of the example in general. For all its ambitions to universality, philosophical thought remains enamoured of its examples, as we see in the philosophers themselves, understood by philosophy not only as its indices but also its instances, as well as in the philosophers' offerings of impersonal and yet fraternal – or perhaps condescending? – aids to philosophical understanding and conviction: the cobblers and craftsmen of Socrates, the asses, whiteness and laughter of the Scholastics, Descartes's wax, Husserl's inkwell, Wittgenstein's slabs, Heidegger's hammer, Quine's rabbit and so on. It is obvious that philosophers make use of examples in highly individualized and often quite telling ways to illustrate their more general theses. Non-philosophy views the use of such examples not as accidental but rather as essential to how philosophy in general thinks.

Non-philosophy does not reject or denounce the essential role of exemplification in and for philosophy, but instead simply treats this as a symptom to be analyzed and adequately understood. Cutting across the diversity of all such examples as well as the diversity of the philosophical views they are meant to exemplify is the form of the correlation itself that *a priori* binds these two sides to one another. In each case, the empirical, worldly and familiar example is used to indicate a general or universal (precisely philosophical) structure that is itself understood to govern *any and all such* examples. In philosophy, the universal is understood in this way always to stand *in relation to* the particular or singular, and in truth this – as seen according to the Vision-in-One – works to the essential detriment of both poles. What philosophy in general takes to be real is the very form of this relationship, what Laruelle calls the 'empirico-transcendental parallelism'. What distinguishes one philosophy from another is merely how this form happens to be filled in for any particular case, how the empirico-transcendental parallelism comes to be specified in one way or another for *a* given philosophy: in terms of Pre-Socratic *archai*, Platonic ideality, essence and existence, experiential-objective constitution, categorial intuition, transcendental subjectivity, ontological difference, etc. In the case of the philosophies of Difference, the parallelism itself is absolutized (in various ways) so as better to ensure its unbounded philosophical (but, in view of non-philosophy, not genuinely universal) functioning. For non-philosophy, however, the *real* universal – the One – does not stand in relation to particular beings at all because it is not in any way correlated to Being (not even through the 'non-relation' of transcendence), and by the same token, real singularities remain finally ungovernable by any philosophical generality or universality. The essential philosophical correlation is thus too narrow and falsely limiting 'at both ends'. Non-philosophy is neither more nor less than what thinking becomes when the axiom of this correlation, the axiom that *there is and must be* such a correlation, no longer operates.

It is necessary to say a few words about the translation. Laruelle's French is almost invariably lucid and syntactically rigorous, even – and especially – when it is at times almost fiendishly difficult to unravel. I have tried to retain the inherent complexity and order of Laruelle's syntax and his sense while at the same time rendering a readable English text. Laruelle's own style is highly varied and is characterized by abrupt shifts from abstract technicality to sharply ironic exasperation to straightforward and ordinary human address that might seem familiar to certain Anglo-American analytic traditions. To be sure there are technical terms in Laruelle, but there is very little jargon. I have aimed throughout at a reproduction of his text that would be as faithful as possible to Laruelle's own rigorous and distinctive movement of thought – its cadences, formalities, stings and surprises.

Laruelle's style involves – for key theoretical, and not merely idiosyncratic, reasons – a rejection of the standard scholarly apparatus of citation and reference. After all, a new form of thought creates its own distinctive conventions and practices. Rather than attempting to overcome or remedy this essential aspect of Laruelle's thought, I have avoided interposing any second-order commentary that would purport to clarify and explain Laruelle's frequent allusions and references. I take it that Laruelle says what he means and means what he says; there is no need to supplement his critical analysis of Difference and his outline of a non-philosophical theory of philosophical decision with additional explanatory notes or commentary. These would only clutter a thoroughly clear albeit difficult exposition. Thus I have in effect duplicated Laruelle's own practice of taking over certain technical terms from the philosophers he engages – Derrida's 'strictions' for example, or the 'historial' in Heidegger – without further discussion. I have made every attempt to use terms in each case that are current in the relevant Anglophone scholarship. Laruelle's claims are explicit and his articulations exact, his argumentation highly compressed and yet nearly always precisely adequate to its sense. There is little room for synopsis or explanation that would not misrepresent or oversimplify (not to say overcomplicate) the real difficulties of the matter at issue. I have aimed at nothing more than providing an English version of *Philosophies of Difference* and its internally consistent textual and conceptual practices.

Several particular points of the translation should, however, be made explicit. One important distinction in Laruelle's work is that of two separate forms of 'duality': to elaborate this difference Laruelle makes use of two forms of 'dual' that exist in French, *duel* and *dual*. Laruelle uses the former (with its connotation of the 'duel' or combat of two parties) to represent the standard philosophical duality in which the opposites are, precisely, *opposed* to one another. The latter form Laruelle reserves for designating the specific non-philosophical duality (or even dualism) obtaining between philosophy and all its constitutive and accidental dualities on the one hand and the One on the other. I have maintained this distinction in the translation in order to highlight this important difference. It should also be pointed out that the 'vertical' metaphor of transcendence that resides in a varied set of Laruelle's terms – among these *lever, relever, monter, surmonter, survoler,* etc. – has been rendered with terms that are in each case suitable to their contexts (*lever* is at times 'lifting', at times 'raising'; *relever* is nearly always 'sublating', and so forth) but that these coordinated terms thereby lose some verbal regularity. I have generally Anglicized Laruelle's occasional neologisms ('enterminable', 'andcosimultaneity', etc.) although with several exceptions, most notably the concept of *enlyse* which he introduces as a critical riposte to Derrida's own *paralyse*. Despite the familiarity of the Deleuze–Guattari notation of the body-without-organs as BwO, I have followed Laruelle's own practice of capitalization and rendered body-without-writing [*corps-sans-écriture*] as BWW. I have not hesitated to restate pronominal antecedents whenever confusion might arise.

This translation would not have been possible without support from various quarters. For scholarly exchange and camaraderie I would like to thank the members of ONPhI (the *Organisation Non-Philosophique Internationale*) as well as the early pioneers of non-philosophy's Anglophone reception and development, particularly Ray Brassier, John Mullarkey and Anthony Paul Smith. Thanks also to Endicott College for awarding a semester course reduction in order to give me time to devote to this work. I am grateful to Sarah Campbell and Tom Crick at Continuum for their editorial support and to my patient readers of early drafts of the manuscript for their thoughts and comments: Joshua Delpech-Ramey, Micah Murphy, Jason Smick, and Willie Young. Finally, I must reserve my most heartfelt thanks for the untiring assistance and support of my wife Margaret throughout the travails and joys of this small attempt at communicative and theoretical reproduction.

Instructions for Use

These studies of a network of contemporary philosophies need to come with some instructions.

Can an introduction claim without a breach of the reader's trust to outline the essential – true, simply the essential – of this philosophy while for the most part explicitly citing no more than three or four of its representatives, even if these are indeed the most incisive among them: Nietzsche, Heidegger, Deleuze and Derrida? A few words of explanation are needed: as to the present book's method; as to its aims; as to the problematic at the interior of which this book means to introduce – in a critical mode – the greater part of contemporary philosophical thought; as to its internal organization.

1. The method in any case is not that of doxography, nor is it that of traditional history of philosophy. No inventories of particular works are to be found here, no presentations of authors, no summaries of doctrinal positions. It will be not so much the names of philosophers that we will uncover as philosophy, and not so much philosophy as its very work of philosophizing. There is a frivolity of doxography from which 'the history of philosophy' does not always escape. It is not a matter here of objects, authors, themes, positions or texts; it is solely the matter of a problematic and of the *reconstruction* of this problematic. Which one? The most enveloping and comprehensive of contemporary thought: that of 'Difference' and its variants. Precisely whenever names are cited, it will be as modes of this invariant that forms our horizon of thinking. Not to exhibit extensively, not to proceed by tracking the diversity of theses and themes, but to dismantle systematically the gesture of 'Difference', the articulation of

its universal moments, the 'syntax' of this invariant and its real conditions of existence. 'Nietzsche', 'Heidegger', 'Derrida', 'Deleuze': these are as much indices, indications of problems that we are striving to demonstrate and analyze in their coherence and functioning; guiding threads for penetrating into a philosophical environment that exceeds them, but the extent, the possibilities and also the limits of which they have made perceptible. Above all Heidegger and Derrida, most frequently 'named'. But Deleuze's oeuvre is constantly included, understood and analysed as appropriate in its specificity, even if it is not treated thematically in its doctrinal variety. Let us offer an example, but this is more than an example; this is the articulation, the construction of the present work: the results we have arrived at have led us to *reconstruct* the essence – what may rigorously be called essence, not some more or less picturesque doctrinal detail – of the most extensive of contemporary problematics from two correlative concepts, those of 'Difference' and 'Finitude'. And yet when Difference is described in its most general structures (Chapter 2), outside of its reference to Finitude as provisionally suspended, one may be sure that this holds principally, and at any rate, for Nietzsche and Deleuze. For Heidegger and Derrida as well, to be sure, but these latter vary it, and in a decisive way, through its imbrication with Finitude.

I thus do not wish, in principle, to devote determined sections to particular authors and to proceed in a monographic way. It is a question of all of the authors in every chapter. At most Chapter 2 treats *more particularly* of Nietzsche and Deleuze, Chapter 3 more particularly of Heidegger and Chapter 5 more particularly of Derrida. Chapters 1, 6 and 7 are more globally 'critical' than 'descriptive' and attempt to introduce a problematic that would no longer be that of Difference. To be sure, the sense of the undertaking requires that these studies, while certainly autonomous, be read in order and their effects capitalized or multiplied by one another. Taken together they hold for all those, among contemporary thinkers, who may be presented under the Heideggerean or Nietzschean, in any case anti-Hegelian, banner of 'Difference'. It is thus also an introduction to Deleuze, *Anti-Oedipus* and *A Thousand Plateaus* included – their problematic rather than their problems – and to an entire oeuvre that is a prodigiously inventive variation of a certain concept – Nietzschean rather than Heideggerean – of Difference. If this oeuvre is not examined thematically but only marked out and designated, although quite regularly, this is also because it is constantly present and active here. Deleuze has produced a systematic internal analysis of 'Difference' and has made appear, by the very excess of the variations that he has operated upon it, its invariant nature. That this analysis remains internal to Difference and is made from its point of view, as is still the case save for certain nuances with all those thinkers who appeal to 'Finitude', is another problem that will motivate a systematic critique of this problematic.

It is thus not a matter of hanging up a winners' plaque of individualities, however inventive and brilliant these may be. But of the major problematic lending its dominant hue to twentieth century philosophy, as 'history' and 'dialectic' did to that of the nineteenth. It is not such and such an oeuvre that we propose to break with here; we are not outlining adversaries or 'positions' in broad strokes in order better to shoot them down. We propose to analyse the most general philosophical horizon that has been ours since Nietzsche and Heidegger.

2. The aims we pursue are complex. How are we to introduce in a 'critical' manner – but we need to be cautious with this term, we will come back to this – a set of philosophies? It is not a matter of scattered local reservations, of personal reticences, of feigned astonishments or settled questions in an analysis that would be finally founded upon an identification with the doctrine examined. Nor even, a habit of the history of philosophy, of somewhat artificially raising problems of doctrinal coherence in order to give oneself the function and the 'benefit' of resolving them. 'There were no contradictions! See how good and clever I am, how I have saved this author!' 'There is an insurmountable contradiction: see how I know the author better than he himself, how I myself am a good author, more Kantian than Kant, more Spinozist than Spinoza!' In order to avoid this Samaritan poison, we will postulate immediately that all these authors are not only systematic but – taken in their totality – coherent up to the point of their sometimes unbridled manner of making Difference play. We will posit their internal rigor in order better to reject them globally . . . More precisely, but this formulation is still not yet intelligible: it is upon the foundation of their global 'critique' that we will affirm their coherence.

What is at issue, at least exteriorly? The regulation of one by the other, as systematically as possible, the introduction into these systems and the exit – if this word still makes sense – outside of them; the exposition of their structure and functioning and their destination, the affirmation of their contingency for man. To recover precisely the dismantling of the systematic and global 'destruction' of Difference – of its pretensions rather than it itself –, this would be the intention that we have set and which, to be sure, has not been able technically to be entirely fulfilled. But even partially lacking, it suggests, by the refusal to take part in things, that it is no longer the matter of a 'critical exposé' so much as an 'analysis' (whatever the form of its argumentation: psychoanalytic, analytico-existential, deconstructive, schizo-analytic, etc.). We will find constantly interlinked with one another the examination of the fundamental problems and gestures of Difference and the exposition of the problematic that allows for this type of examination. Are we working both sides? This technique is well-known to philosophers . . . But here their relation and its law cannot be furnished except through this separate problematic, and they thus do not result – yet already here we have another philosophy and most likely something other than philosophy, other than a philosophical critique of philosophy – from their intermixing.

A critique of Difference in the name of what we call a 'thinking of the One' can no longer be entirely a settling of accounts with a certain philosophical past that would be our own. Philosophy calculates and settles accounts, establishes distributions and draws up balance sheets, recognizes debts and assures its own benefits. There is nothing of that here: this is at once a way of giving notice globally to a mode of thinking that will indeed procure certain affects; and an indirect attempt to recognize in it a positivity that it itself is in no state to recognize. It is the very sense of the critical operation that has changed: although it is *first*, like philosophy itself, when philosophy becomes critical it is here as a second operation and an effect. Why? Because it is rooted in a way of thinking that claims, with its risks and perils, to deliver itself from philosophy, from philosophical Decision itself and not only from Difference, and to substitute for this a thinking that claims, for precise reasons, to be 'scientific': a science assuming in its proper mode the transcendental function that philosophy has captured for its own profit. Upon this new foundation, a critique of Reason-as-Difference, of Decision-as-Difference, ceases then to be the whole of thought and is no longer anything but a result of this science when it is applied to philosophical material.

3. From within what problematic are we playing here as 'against' that of Difference, in view of displacing it rather outside of its own philosophical narcissism, at once *before* it rather than 'in its place' and *for* it, in view of exposing its functioning and its congenital illusion?

These studies are the effect, on philosophy and its history, of the theory developed in *Une biographie de l'homme ordinaire*. They analyze a certain number of consequences that the restitution of his essence to finite man or to the individual imply with respect to philosophy in general, with respect to the philosophical Decision that would deny him this essence. They give body to the following maxim that does not have the sense of a humanist and anthropological revenge against the last 30 years that would have been so anti-humanist: philosophy is made for man, not man for philosophy. In order to illustrate philosophical Decision, it seemed interesting to us to take the case of the contemporary problematic that, most relentlessly, has confounded the necessary anti-humanist struggle with the refusal to recognize in man a specific and positive essence.

It is – to move quickly – truth and truth's *essence*, of which it remains uncertain whether it is able to be converted into the vigilance and the effects of Difference, that is in question as against Difference and against philosophy when it is a question of the finite individual. The essence of truth: not only truth as essence, but what makes its essence, what constitutes it as the fundamentally real *veritas transcendentalis* of science. We experiment here, in the case of Difference, principally of Heidegger and Derrida but of Nietzsche and Deleuze as well, with the 'thesis' that in the One in the sense that we intend, we find the most immanent and most real radical unity of man and knowledge. Radically individual or finite man as finite for intrinsic reasons and as the subject (of) science – this is the content of the non-unitary One and the criterion against which we measure Difference and philosophical Decision in general. Science, so we make of it our hypothesis against its unitary philosophical reduction, is a thinking of two principles: what in *Le Principe de Minorité* we called – in memory of the forgotten martyrs on whose altar Greco-Occidental philosophy was invigorated and reborn – *gnosis*, which is to say, a thinking that recognizes a *certain* irreducibility (still to be evaluated) to the existence of two principles and that separates what the Greco-Occidental fact has always united – here, the One and Being – what, for its account, Difference has tried one last time to reunite, allowing the failure or arbitrariness of this forced unity all the better to be seen. Here, then, is the thinking that we oppose consistently to that of Difference. Without it being possible here to analyze this mode of thinking itself in its internal possibility – we have done so elsewhere –, we are content to invent it as needed in the examination of contemporary doctrines, as the 'presupposed' upon which Difference – which will itself have to a great extent tracked down presuppositions but apparently not its own – is founded without wanting nor being able to recognize it, regularly making use of the two principles that it would have tried in vain to reunite, understanding itself to allow the project of their synthesis for its success, contenting itself with resuming the Greek state of the problem and, instead of dissolving it, elevating it to the state of essence.

Thus in the same gesture we show how the problematic of Difference, including here Heidegger or Derrida, accomplishes and assembles the Greco-Occidental style of thinking, and how this latter cannot constitute itself except through an *absolute forgetting* – more than a 'repression' – of another way of thinking, authentically scientific, that had its effects, *only effects*, poorly engaged and quickly annihilated, in the dualists and gnostics. A forgetting without remainder, without offspring or 'slip', of a mode of thinking that would be specifically 'heretical', or denounced as 'heretical' by ontology and theology reunited. The examination of Difference is made from this point of view that we have elsewhere called radically 'minoritarian'. While contemporary thinkers – those examined here – think it impossible to repeat, in return for adjustments in the *whole* of metaphysics, anything but a gesture that has had antecedents at the interior of metaphysics and which is exacerbated through the appeal to alterity, we attempt a heteronomous destruction, scientific and not philosophical, of the Greco-Occidental style.

It is thus not a question of pursuing the same old game, of proceeding through substitution and proposing the question of the One in place of the question of Being, and in the same place . . . The question of Being has become our horizon because in general Being has rather the nature of a question and a horizon or a finite Cosmos. Yet do we still need a horizon? Are we so infantile as still to wish to be close to or to be good neighbours with the Greeks, to be infantile perhaps like the Greeks themselves in search of their 'locus'? More profound or more superficial than the forgetting of Being (and its contemporary avatars: the forgetting of Writing, the withdrawal of the essence of the Text, the repression of Desire, of Language, etc.) and the forgetting of this forgetting, is there not, at the very foundation of the question of Being and its vigilance, a 'forgetting' of the One that is a much stranger phenomenon, that is not a double, repercussion, or outbidding of the 'Forgetting of Being'? Yet would not the awakening to this, this other vigilance to the essence of truth, be immediately the destruction of the illusions of philosophical decision in general? With the scientific examination of the question of the essence of Being through the thinking of the One there is a way of thinking that is unknown to ontology or first philosophy, even when these refer themselves ultimately to the One, and that dualist and gnostic endeavours have recognized more clearly but only so as to falsify it in the service of religious ends, a way of thinking that asserts itself and demands that we have another go at the task.

4. How is this demonstration organized?

Chapter 1 establishes the conditions of possibility for a real or scientific critique of Difference and of philosophical decision in general. A non-philosophical, non-vicious or non-aporetic critique of Difference is impossible except on the foundation of the One – through what we call the 'Vision-in-One'.

Chapter 2 examines the syntax of Difference. It places the problem of Finitude between parentheses and extracts a schema, a syntactical invariant which holds, save for the modifications that will be introduced by Finitude, by the experience of reality as Other, as much for Nietzsche as for Heidegger, for Deleuze as for Derrida.

Chapter 3 examines the reality of Difference. It introduces the irreducible dimension of Finitude as 'ontic' or 'real'. It makes a precise hypothesis regarding the historico-systematic origin of this theme in Heidegger and opposes Heidegger to Nietzsche.

INSTRUCTIONS FOR USE

Chapter 4 analyses the imbrication of Difference and Finitude and attempts to show that it is this imbrication that in the last instance yields the distinction of Heidegger's project from that of Hegel. It describes the opposition of the *Concept* and *finite Difference*.

Chapter 5 specifies Derrida's work at the interior of the universal schema or invariant of Difference. A few preliminary points on this difficult subject may be useful here. We show that Finitude such as Derrida introduces it also into Difference distinguishes his use of this latter not only from its Nietzschean and Deleuzean usage, but from its Heideggerean usage as well since it is not a matter in Heidegger and Derrida of the same experience of Finitude. At the interior of the common project of imbricating Difference and radical Finitude, a project distinguishing them together from Nietzsche and Deleuze, the one forms a Greco-Occidental idea of Finitude (as real withdrawal of the real in relation to Being, and of what there is of the real in the *essence* of Being), whereas the other plays with a Judaic experience of Finitude (as *inversion* of the primacy of ideality over the relative cut, into the inverse primacy of the cut or inhibition over continuity and relation). Derrida is thus distinguished both from Nietzsche and from Heidegger; he takes over as it were their milieu, borrowing from the former not only the schema or invariant syntax of Difference, but an 'idealist' primacy of the syntax of Difference over its reality; and from the latter the concern for Finitude, which is to say, for an anti-idealist limitation of the primacy of syntax over the real. Given that he constructs 'Differance'[1] on the general syntactical model of Difference, he is no longer able to conceive Finitude as Heidegger does and must proceed to the operation, Judaic par excellence, of the *inversion* of the Greco-Occidental hierarchy that would assure the primacy of continuity over the cut. He substitutes for what is none other than an 'ontic' or at least 'real' finitude, the finitude of an already idealized cut, a real-ideal difference whose primacy over ideal continuity, with the insistence upon the effects of delay/slowing/differance/inhibition that convert this primacy, creates the appearance that it has to do with a 'real' finitude. In Derrida finitude is an ideal effect of syntax, whereas in Heidegger it is the irreducible transcendence of the real (of the ontic and the One) relative to the syntax (that folds Being and beings). Derrida is thus not merely content to extend a Heideggerean apparatus to problems (those of the signifier and textuality) that

Heidegger would have forgotten or even repressed. He modifies this apparatus in an original way and requires, from this very fact, a special examination.

The final two chapters are placed back within the Vision-in-One and undertake the real critique of Difference.

Chapter 6, the most fundamental, endeavours to show that the One in its rigorous or 'non-reflexive' transcendental essence is at once required and denied by Difference, that the proper essence of the One is more profoundly 'forgotten' than the Forgetting of Being, and is forgotten in the very pathos of the 'Forgetting of Being' and Difference. It examines different aspects of the real – the scientific and non-philosophical – critique of Difference.

Chapter 7 opens upon other problems that are more important than those of the analytic of Difference but are not the principal object of the present work. At this work's horizon, there are in effect the problems of philosophical decision in general and of a *scientific theory of philosophical decision*. We sketch this in the following way: all the systems of Difference postulate, even while denying it, a second principle next to and opposite the One, a principle that cannot be perceived from Difference itself, but only from the One as restored in its authentic essence. This second principle is that of the real no longer as One, but as the diversity of an absolute, non-projective, non-horizonal Transcendence, a non-reflexive or *non-positional* transcendence. This diversity is that of a radical transcendence that does not belong to the One, outside the essence of which it is rejected, but which is the effect of its proper act. It affects Being and all the ontologico-ideal structures of Difference with contingency and absurdity. The frame is thus set for sketching *a theory of philosophical decision* and of Indecision as well, of philosophy as Undecidable. A further work will be devoted to this theory of philosophical decision in general and to the transcendental foundation of an algorithm of decision.

Thus is accomplished the analysis of the 'scientific' but rigorously transcendental space in which the modern and contemporary systems of Difference deploy themselves, but where they cannot do so, like the Dialectic before them, except in denying it. This is therefore a thinking of 'two' principles (but it is doubtful that the 'two' and its dualism are specific; it is not the object of this book to nuance this gnosis and to distinguish it from its ancient forms) allowing for a radical critique of the mixture of Difference and its aporetic style, its Greco-Occidental or Judeo-Occidental style. A critique that would no longer be a complement, a rectification, a deconstruction, a supplement, one of these innumerable 'experiences' (through Being, Text, Power, Desire, Politics, Ethics) that the Occident has invented in order to cleanse itself of its congenital defect – to think through unifying duality, through the synthesis of contraries, through the One as All or as unity of contraries, through dialectic and difference – and through which it would be content to re-infect the wound. To think is not necessarily on the order of itching or infection – this is what our research would like to suggest, in particular as against the philosophy that will have known how to conjugate the arts of Job and of Socrates and to carry these to the height of an essence: contemporary philosophy.

NOTE

1 Or any other mark or value destined to relay this.

CHAPTER ONE
Introduction

HOW DIFFERENCE HAS BECOME A PHILOSOPHICAL DECISION

1. One constellation does not dispel another, it installs itself in the gaps of the former, occupies its neighbourhoods and proposes new signs, a new economy of the same places. There was the severely articulated matter of the Dialectic, its astonishing passages from the celestial to the terrestrial state. There is henceforth – for how long? – the cloudy matter of Difference, its dusts, its errant multiplicities, its black and white holes – matter as celestial as it is terrestrial, born apparently from the dissemination of the Dialectic. Difference is the name for the constellation that assembles certain contemporary thinkers in complex relations which remain always those of *neighbouring*: Nietzsche, Heidegger, and those who have accentuated, accelerated or aggravated their modes of questioning, Foucault, Deleuze, Derrida. It is necessary, now that this galaxy retreats from us a little, to say The-Difference as in an older epoch of thought one would say The-Dialectic. The critical analysis of this apparent generality, its evaluation, has become a possible, and consequently urgent, task. As the strongest contemporary research whirls and sinks in this figure, Difference erects itself and casts over us a shadow where to our surprise we recognize once again the oldest spectre of the Greco-Occidental world. It is not 'Being' that will

have come to dominate twentieth-century thought, but finally 'Difference'. Heidegger himself conduces to the decline of the very Being whose rebirth he wished to herald, as soon as he makes apparent in 'Difference' the oldest and most dominant Greco-Occidental invariant. Difference, which concerns neither a category nor an Idea, is, rigorously and despite all the perturbations it introduces, a general syntax and a concrete, invariant type. Heidegger is neither the first – there is Nietzsche before him – nor the last – there are Deleuze and Derrida after him – to have elevated Difference to the state of a principle, albeit in order to affect it in its turn with Difference and to subvert it as 'principle'.

2. Difference is a syntax, a way of articulating philosophical language. It is also a thesis about reality, a certain experience – itself multiple – of the real. As the functional unity of a syntax and an experience, it is a principle, a syntax that is real and not merely formal, transcendental and not merely logical. Philosophical decision engenders philosophical logics – real or 'transcendental' logics – and Difference is nothing but the most recent of these logics, after *Contradiction* ('dialectic'), *Existence*, *Structure*. All these latter 'categories' having received a superior or concrete form, Difference possesses the same signification and the same value they do, the same global power of meaning and truth. In the same way as these others, Difference forms a system (or a semi-system, it all depends) that wishes itself or believes itself to be absolute and with the same right and the same arguments: all these evaluate those that have preceded them and submit them to their critique.

What is the mechanism of Difference? How does it surpass itself to become sometimes a principle (Nietzsche, Deleuze), sometimes a finite Same still more primitive than a principle (Heidegger and Derrida)? How does one pass from the category of difference to the syntax of difference, and from there to the concrete philosophies of Difference?

Difference appears to arise fully armed on the philosophical scene, like a figure at once new and unengendered, lacking sufficient cause in its historical vicinities. This does not merely concern an illusion; it is a well-founded objective appearance: no philosophy or set of philosophies can be born except as orphans. However, from another perspective, more sober but not necessarily any more truthful, Difference is seen to be situated on an empirical and historical terrain, in the midst of certain vicinities or neighbourhoods that determine it without really engendering it: linguistics and differential signification; the necessity of struggling against Hegelian difference and its outcome in contradiction; the phenomenological care for the positivity of spheres of experience, etc. Another decisive neighbourhood: the philosophical practice of the limit. From this point of view Difference is not content merely to reactivate a Greek and then Kantian determination of thought; it is born a second time at the end of the nineteenth century, with Nietzsche and then Heidegger, from the impulsion of the mathematics of cuts in their modern form. This practice of thinking-at-the-limit has filled our philosophical horizon across all the relays it has found in contents such as those of the signifier and textuality, desire and power, metaphysical representation and its 'end', its inscription in the place of 'Limit' or 'End'. Difference is world-historical, historico-textual, historico-desiring – it is also, necessarily, a phenomenon of conjuncture. But like every philosophical conjuncture it gathers in its own way the history of thought. Thus, by another appearance, it seems to continue on the terrain of these pilot-categories. It resumes the traditional functions but with other means and a double supplement – this is its specificity – of critical power and a sense of nuance, multiplicity, positivity. This marks an appreciable variation in amplitude along a long chain, a somewhat stronger discharge in the network of thought. In a very traditional manner – here we see an invariant of all philosophical decision – Difference proposes to close the network upon its own opening, but it does so with this supplement of means in alterity that renders it preferable to previous attempts. It is a particularly plastic and critical instrument; it uses all these sedentary elements as debris over which it builds its empire, imposing its order upon them and making them mutually overdetermine one another.

3. But more profoundly, Difference becomes a real principle or a philosophical decision if one gives to it certain . . . philosophical . . . means:

a. It must cease to be a partial and secondary means, lacking autonomy, for *Contradiction, Existence, Structure.* Subjected to these potent philosophical machines, it remains a simple procedure that must be completed or surpassed by others, an unfinished mode of thinking suitable for beginnings, but whose liberation would be programmed only through its *Aufhebung*, at any rate its suppression. How may Difference become autonomous and give itself a precisely differential form of autonomy? How may it accede to the dignity of philosophical decision? Through the elaboration of its syntactic properties, through giving itself above all a real or transcendental essence.

b. In effect, it must cease in the first place to be a 'category' or even one among the 'transcendentals' ordered to 'Being' and to 'Unity'. A category assumes on the one hand previous ontic givens, a reference to the presence or identity of the present, and on the other hand a transcendental Unity superior still to every category. Difference becomes a concrete principle or philosophical decision when it frees itself from this double subjection and becomes this Unity, capable at once of bringing to itself, in order to determine its syntax, its own 'transcendental' experience of reality, and thus of operating the genesis of empirical reality.

c. Finally, it must thematize its syntactical structure. It is only quite recently that Difference has become as such a problem of philosophical syntax. It is not the contemporary founders of this mode of thinking, Nietzsche and Heidegger, who have developed this aspect however fundamental it may be from the point of view of the technology of thought: it is Deleuze and Derrida. The former has analysed the Nietzschean *'Pathos der Distanz'*, the tele-pathy of the Will to Power; the latter has elaborated a tool specific to the margins of signifying difference, of the Heideggerean *Differenz* and Jewish alterity. It goes without saying that the technology of Difference we present here is massively tributary to these authors without whom Difference as such would remain nothing but a great and yet obscure glimmer. They have contributed to the exit of Difference's syntax from its 'representational' indetermination.

Difference is rescued, it acquires the dignity of philosophical decision thus in the struggle along these three fronts: against its functional requisition as a means or procedure that would be inferior and unfinished; against its solely categorial interpretation; against the state of non-elucidation in which it has remained (since Heraclitus?) from the syntactical point of view. Each of these points may be exemplified through the problem of its distinction from Nothingness. In order for it to acquire its philosophical autonomy, it was necessary that it be able to take from 'authentic' reality an experience that would no longer possess anything of the category of negation nor that of the nothingness-of-beings; neither that of Nothingness as opposed and identical to Being; nor that of the negativity contained in signifying difference, etc. It had to invent the 'nihilating' (Heidegger), *Distanz* and 'hierarchy' (Nietzsche); 'non ? being' (Deleuze); 'Differance' (Derrida); 'Differend' (Lyotard), etc. So many means for sweetening nothingness, rendering it nuanced and positive, 'different' and multiple; pushing it to the margins of representation, of representation's procedures of identity and exclusion, interiorization and rejection. Difference had to shift the terrain, giving up that of beings and Being-substance – its original terrain: ontology – and its inferior status as a category. It had to give itself, as does every genuine philosophical decision through the transcendental operation par excellence, its own terrain, its own experience of the real. From peripheral procedure, servant of Contradiction and then Structure, it has become a problematic, a real principle and even an emotion: yes, an *a priori* emotion, a truly *philosophical or transcendental sensibility* without which philosophy would have perished of Hegelianism or Structuralism, of boredom . . .

4. Two descriptive tasks await us (Chapters 2 and 3) before we may even sketch an attempt at a critique of Difference.

a. What is the syntax called 'Difference' such that it may be distinguished, for example, from 'Dialectic'? This is the problem of Difference as *form of order* or *articulation* of the real. It distinguishes itself from other forms of order such as the ascending dialectic, the syllogism, the order of reasons, the various 'transcendental analytics' (Kant, Husserl), Hegelian dialectic, structure, etc. Philosophical decision always has a syntactical side that may be provisionally isolated and fixed even if it itself does not constitute a concrete moment of this decision.

b. What is the specific experience of the real – the *experiences* – animating this syntax and rendering it concrete? What type of real does it articulate that specifies it in turn each time? Does it concern Being, Substance, Spirit, Power, etc.? the Other – and which Other?

A concrete philosophical decision is each time the totality, the unity of the co-belonging and co-penetration of a syntax and an experience of what it calls the 'real'. Syntax and experience reciprocally determine one another and thus individuate each other to the point of being rendered undecidable. Yet specific to philosophical decision, precisely in distinction from a thinking of the One that would be not a decision but a science, is to distinguish, no doubt locally and provisionally but necessarily, between opposites; it is to tolerate, even if only to suppress it, the distinction, for example, of a syntax and a reality – before the re-unification in this functional synthesis that is every philosophical system. Just as the scientific thinking of the One excludes its dismemberment into a syntactical side and a real side, so philosophy, which is a functional rather than theoretical activity, demands it and, like every practice stripped of genuine scientificity, founds itself upon the practical moment of scission.

The analytic of Difference thus comprises two descriptions. The one, syntax, which could serve as an introduction to a particular sector of the science of philosophy that one might call the *problems of philosophical syntax*. The other, the experiences of the real presuming the idea of a syntax destined to articulate it, such as Difference, which could introduce the *problems of philosophical materiality and reality*.

HOW DIFFERENCE HAS REQUISITIONED THE ONE

1. Difference (in general, with all its modes even beyond Nietzsche) is at the same time a repetition of the oldest Greco-Occidental question – that of duality-as-unity: how to think the unity or the passage from one contrary to the other – and a solution to this question. What has changed with contemporary thinkers? The response has been modulated, but the question has remained the same: always the Greco-unconscious problem of the *passage from one contrary (to) the other*. Here is the oldest point of interrogation, never resolved, of Occidental memory, the 'dialectic' in a broad sense. And how has one usually responded? By requiring . . . the One: how should the One be *used* in order to insure the passage, the unity of contraries? To what *use* should the One be put *in view* of this unity? As contemporary solution to this archaic and originary problem, Difference comes after many others and in particular after that of the Dialectic. Yet as a solution that claims finally to be able to hold everything entirely within the simple

limits of the repetition of this question, it is perhaps the last possible, the last Turning, that which no longer ceases to 'turn', that in which thought takes, no doubt once more, but also once and for all, its re-departure. Yet as to the question of the unity of contraries, Difference cannot help but respond, like everyone else, through recourse to the One as to the Without-division, to the Indivisible par excellence. Difference inscribes itself regularly in what is still more profound, more extensive and more necessary than a 'problematic', in *this deep habitus that wants the One to be thought as a function of the problem of the unity of contraries, as requisitioned in a dialectical mode and ordered to the governance of an economy, of economy in general.* Would there be nothing more evident in the contemporary practices, however modest, of questionings and clarifications, of vigilant and deconstructive critiques, of productive and differential unconsciousnesses, than this so little elucidated evidence according to which the One not only is what 'binds' diversity in contradiction – in Difference also where it makes diversity exist as diversity, but exhausts itself in this function of the unification of a diversity more or less exterior to itself and transcendent? From where do the Greco-contemporaries take this evidence which has never appeared before their eyes? From the One itself; this is indeed more obvious than it is for the philosophers themselves. *But have they exhausted the One, its essence and its proper 'evidence', when they reduce it thus to founding the Dialectic or Difference, a task which, despite its 'height' and its abstraction, may perhaps be subaltern?*

2. *Polis, Physis* and *Kosmos* are the names of the Same, and the Same serves to order and conjoin beings in the One. Here is the most originary crossroads of Occidental thinking: to know whether we ought to meditate upon the Same, *Physis* or *Kosmos*, the All that presents beings to the One so that it will adjoin them through its unity, to take up once again the path of metaphysics and of its contemporary critics who, all together, assign to thought a mixture that puts the One and beings in relation, assuming the essence of the One to be well known and thus in fact to remain indeterminate; *or rather if we will endeavour to elucidate the essence of the One and its truth independently of its requisition in the service of Physis and Kosmos.* Greco-Occidental thinkers put their care, their concern in the All of being, while the 'somnolent' are pre-occupied by particularity and give themselves over to the adventures

of its 'idiocy'. But from another mode of thinking which thinks not only the All as One, but the One as All, the One under the species of *Physis, Logos, Kosmos*, etc., is somnolent with a sleep hardly less profound: philosophical sleep. To wake oneself to the One as such, to its essence as distinct from that of the Same and of cosmic tautology, this is at any rate the condition for understanding the magnificent absurdity that is the emergence of *Kosmos* or of *Physis*, in order to understand this otherwise than as a Greco-Occidental fact, even as taken into history as what opens its space and overflows it, in order to undo the philosophizing forgetting of philosophical decision.

3. Difference is a theory and a practice of *mixtures, but mixtures as such, in their very essence as mixed*. But mixtures are par excellence what give rise to the fundamental aporias of Greco-Occidental thought. Difference is the thought of aporia *as such*, in its aporetic essence, the Greek aporia become positive. Difference repeats the primitive couples of philosophy with the difference that it repeats them and wants them in their essence as couple. What it affirms is no longer the terms themselves, with their determinate cultural and historical content, suffering their contradiction or their combat as a necessary evil or a strange fatality. To the contrary, Difference affirms the superiority of their combat, of their coupling and hierarchy over the content of the embattled terms; it is sober with respect to the metaphysics attached to the position and the claims of each of the opposites, but it is drunk with metaphysics in its essence: the mélange at worst, the coupling at best, of opposites; it raises aporia to the truth of essence. 'Aporia' must be thought with the same rigor as *a-letheia*: as the tautology of an 'aporia aporiating', whose 'positive' trait of progress, like the 'negative' trait of failure and impasse, must be repeated or turned in and as the immanence of the One, each trait alone as well as in their reversible unity. As an impasse that makes things pass and turn, philosophy is the superior form of passing . . . The aporetic power of Difference comes from what in it is *ontico-ontological*, of what in it is neither a transcendent difference between two beings, as between human being and God, nor purely intra-ontological difference, but what definitively enchains Being to beings, the ideal to the real. It ratifies an amphibology which it raises to the status of an *a priori* fact and then to that of the essence of metaphysics, as the most dignified and worthy of being questioned.

But why, under what conditions, is Occidental thought or metaphysics born as essentially aporiating? Will we ever be cured of it? This means at the very most: what relation to the One does the essence of the One cause metaphysics to lack and thereby constrain it to the aporetic form as to its own essence?

HOW A THEORY OF DIFFERENCE IS POSSIBLE

1. It might be objected that it is impossible to find an invariant common to Heidegger, Nietzsche, Deleuze and Derrida. How in particular may Heidegger and Derrida be interpreted as sub-sets of Difference as formulated by Nietzsche and Deleuze, since the former thinkers claim, each in his own way, to 'deconstruct' the latter? If there is a real genesis, is it not the reverse, from the deconstruction of metaphysics to metaphysics? Does the claim of an invariant not annul their specificity, their attempt to delimit metaphysics, that is to say precisely their Difference? The historico-systematic modes of Difference, in effect, are not the species of a genus – such a generality does not exist; they are concrete and irreducible types.

Take the case of Heidegger, both in himself and in his relations to others: is there a logic, a general argumentation of his thought, an invariant that would unite the before and after of the 'Turning' (*Kehre*)? *If* such an invariant exists, it is detectable neither before nor after the 'Turn', it is the Turning itself as the in-between of the before and the after. There would not be two Heideggers any more than there would be one, in the sense that this unicity would *oppose itself* to a duality. There is an 'in-between-Heidegger', Heidegger as the in-between of his own thinking of the in-between. If the Turning can signify something for us, it is that thinking is always-already in the Turning, constrained to let itself be carried and carried away by its swerving. And the experience of the Turning must be undergone; it is the specific movement, the moving proper to Difference, only Difference can 'turn' in this absolute sense. The problem is still more delicate for the relation – if it exists – of Heidegger to the 'other' experiences of Difference: is there a 'specific difference' for Heidegger, or for anyone else, at the interior of the formation of 'The-Difference'? One cannot respond by invoking Difference here where certain of its themes precisely 'turn' it: there is something 'of' the Turning, of a thinking that does not cease 'to turn' continuously, that is, to differ from and towards itself, that does not cease to move from and towards Difference as its ownness and that must devote itself to turning in an ultimate and absolute sense; there is this, there is nothing but this in Nietzsche on the one hand and in contemporaries such as Derrida and Deleuze on the other. What then distinguishes Heidegger at the interior of a dubious 'general logic' of Difference, if it is not the syntactical aspect of Difference, its mode of the articulation of contraries? *It is perhaps its other side, no longer its syntax but its reality, the conception of Difference as finite.* More exactly: not as finite, since there is always finitude in no matter what thinker, but as *ontically finite*, finite because of beings or the real in the last instance. Difference is always and in every way as much finite as infinite, but this can mean – for example – that it *makes itself* finite, in the sense that Heidegger will speak still of Kantian Reason; or else that, in a more authentically Heideggerean manner, Difference *lets-be* its finitude. If the concept of (ontic) finitude signifies something that distinguishes Heidegger from Hegel, Husserl or Nietzsche and allows him to de-limit their enterprises, it is not what there is of beings or the real as illuminated by Being: even the idealists think the real in this way. It is 'to the contrary' – even if this does not suffice, here is precisely the essence of finitude as irreducible – what there is of beings as *not* illuminated by Being, a kind of ontic or real transcendence completely distinct from what is understood ontologically by 'transcendence'.

Yet real Difference works just like its syntax: its experiences are completely distinct and vary in their turn the general syntax of Difference, which thus seems to escape our grasp and vanish in its own always singular effectivity. Would we never have the right to speak of *the* Difference and would we therefore be condemned to speak of it only by submitting ourselves in turn expressly to one or another of these particular systems, not to speak of Nietzsche for example except in the Heideggerean idiom, or of Heidegger except in the Derridean idiom, etc., without being able to extract a universal of Difference? Or is perhaps this aporia none other than that of *the* philosophy? In our desperate search for what may resemble at first a meta-philosophy or meta-language, it is rather towards THE philosophy as such that we are thrown back. These types (even this word is now perhaps too much) still have in common their being modes of *philosophical* thinking, and is there perhaps finally, this time, an ultimate philosophical invariant, more concrete than a generality but not without universality? This invariant that would shelter the types of Difference would be the reciprocal correlation, more or less tightened or delayed, of two terms – the oldest Occidental matrix, the contrary or contrasted coupling. The heterogeneity of these singular types does not contradict their belonging to a unique invariant, whatever in turn the relations may be, more or less tightened or delayed, of this singularity and this universality.

But THE philosophy, in turn, does not exist any more than THE Difference, if what is meant are abstract generalities with their various species. What exists is only the game, the games of 'more or less', the philosophical language games. Certainly the types of Difference have a 'family resemblance', an objective appearance, indeed a certain univocity, but this property must be particularized each time in its turn. We are decidedly spinning in place, that is, still and always *within* philosophy.

2. In effect. Perhaps in all this we have straightaway posed the problem badly, *by posing in a still philosophical way* the question of THE philosophy or THE Difference. We have given the impression of looking for a 'meta-differential' thinking, an absurd project if ever there was one: there are 'effects' of meta-difference, there is not a point of view sure and certain of itself upon Difference in general. In reality, it is now time to say it, we have only proceeded thus in order to make apparent the vanity of Difference and of philosophy, their incapacity to acquire a scientific, non-aporetic knowledge of themselves, of THE Difference. On the other hand, this aporia of a Difference *at once* multiple-and-unique, unique-as-soon-as-multiple, but newly-multiple-as-soon-as-unique should awaken and introduce us to another thinking – scientific – that is straightaway indifferent to this aporia that puts philosophy in motion. A thinking whose 'introduction' would be unnecessary, if not perhaps still for the philosophers standing at a complete loss before the interminable pitfalls they have set for themselves, of which Difference is perhaps the most rigorous. A critique of Difference – and through this of philosophical decision in general – addresses itself by definition to philosophers

and must provisionally, at least in order to suggest to them their lot, enter into their favourite games, sacrifice to their customs, honour their rites of fascination and initiation. But in reality such a project has no chance of acquiring a rigorous and grounded experience of Difference and of not sinking immediately into the comedy and tragedy of philosophy, were it not to hold itself straightaway, not in another place, but in another manner of thinking, *in an experience of the real that would no longer be co-determined by philosophical decision, despite what philosophy will always claim, a claim that prohibits it from being a science of the real and of itself.*

3. From where, in effect, do we take this point of view allowing for the description of *the* field of philosophy without being in its turn *a* philosophy included in this field, yet without in consequence wanting to be an impossible metalanguage? If this 'invariant', in a new sense, of Difference is unthinkable and improbable from the standpoint of the 'semi-systems' of Nietzsche–Deleuze, Heidegger and Derrida, it is because it is acquired from entirely other 'positions', rather from a mode of thought other than philosophical which, alone, is capable of perceiving in these three systems the distinct regions of the same domain of reality rather than the modes of a common essence. This experience is what here and there we have called the One, endeavouring – we will come back to this – to describe its essence as indifference to the Unity of which all the philosophers speak – in particular those of Difference – which is always the unity-of-contraries, or scission-as-unity. Without yet entering into this description, we may ground ourselves upon *the indifference of the One to philosophical decision and its modes of 'Difference'* in order to establish in what sense we have the right to speak in all rigor of THE Difference or in order to dissolve an equivocity, and how the One finally founds this rigorous description:

a. Inasmuch as one remains in the 'positions' of one of the types of Difference, it is impossible to unify these in view of rejecting them globally. From a philosophical point of view, Difference cannot be an invariant except in its Greco-Nietzschean mode; Nietzschean difference alone is able to ground a typology of Difference; it is Nietzsche who varies and extracts the principal invariant of metaphysics: it is here we find one of the established conventions of the Heideggerean interpretation that, itself, delimits this operation. In this case, *Differenz* (Heidegger) and *Différance* (Derrida) cannot be considered as modes of this essence, since they are rather attempts to 'deconstruct' both Difference and 'invariance' in general. More precisely, each type has its own singular manner of conceiving (itself as) the universal and reducing the others to a deficient modality of itself. There is *the* Difference of Heidegger, and that of Deleuze, and that of Derrida.

b. If therefore we rather put on an equal footing these three types of what, at one moment or other, collectively call themselves 'Difference', and if we silence their conflict by means of a certain indifference, it is because the 'invariant' at which we aim is no longer completely and simply one or another kind of Difference (the Greco-Nietzschean for example), but a still more 'universal' entity – *universal in a new sense still to be determined* – than every universality of which metaphysics would be capable. This can no longer be a simple invariant of the Greco-ideal type, but what determines the belonging of types of Difference to one and the same way of thinking which denies the One: philosophical decision. This is what allows us, beyond the last homages that Heidegger and Derrida are constrained to render to 'the' metaphysics and to its regularities, to consider globally these three systems as effects of this more universal invariant whose law includes them all.

Let us assume then the experience of the One – yet we do not have to assume it just to please the philosophers; we are in it as in the real in itself, *in the way however in which science immediately knows itself, and in a non-positional way, as science (of) the real –:* under what form henceforth may appear to us, we who do not philosophize, philosophical decision and its mode, Difference?

The One is such that it distinguishes absolutely from itself – in the form of a unilateral duality without reciprocity or reversibility – a domain of reality that we call *effectivity* containing all the entities, philosophical or not, that are obtained through the unitary combination of the two parameters of immanence and transcendence; that are thus the mixtures whose excellent model is the philosophical Unity-of-contraries. The One is not what distinguishes itself from these mixtures – this is the old gesture of philosophical transcendence in which we no longer think; it is what is sufficiently finite or 'autonomous' to constrain the mixtures themselves to be distinguished from it. The power of distinction is that of the One, but it affects the philosophical mixtures and not the One itself. Here therefore is the 'reason' that authorizes us to speak of THE Difference: not a universal type of Difference, a general and invariant syntax, but its nature of mixture or combination *inasmuch as this is an object of the unilateralization to which the One constrains all that presents itself in experience as not being it and, for example, as protesting against or resisting this experience of the One*. This is the One's power of 'real distinction' under the form of the unilateralization with which it affects all that refuses it; that is the true transcendental foundation of a rigorous description of Difference. This science of Difference will no longer be the simple auto-application or affection of Difference to and by itself, one of those philosophical games to which, interminably, it would give rise and which would seem to prohibit us from acquiring from it a rigorous concept founded in a 'scientific' manner.

On this foundation, nothing prevents us then from considering *indifferently* one or another type of difference, then extracting no doubt the local invariances, but *we no longer take this to be the rigorous knowledge of Difference*. These studies in effect do not still have as goal to develop – save for the last chapter – the transcendental and scientific description of Difference and philosophical decision in general – we have outlined it elsewhere – but only to mount a scientific or real critique of Difference. This is a project for the use of philosophers: to denounce the transcendental illusion that Difference entertains with respect to the real which it believes itself capable of determining. These studies assume the One – the condition of a *real* critique – but limit its effects to a simple *critique* preparatory to the positive and scientific description of philosophical decision.

THE GRECO-OCCIDENTAL INVARIANT

1. These limits of contemporary research thus made precise, we may, on the foundation thus acquired, but always from the interior of philosophy, partially re-commence philosophizing and summarily characterizing philosophical decision and its dominant mode, Difference. We remain within the aporias of Unity and Multiplicity,

the Universal and the Singular: the descriptions which follow thus possess an ambiguous status which the present work, let us repeat, will not clear up, its object being to awaken philosophers to a problem, to an experience rather, that is non-philosophical but that is capable of founding a rigorous science of philosophy.

With these reservations, one may say that the types of Difference are *reciprocally* heterogeneous, but that this *reciprocity*, that of their heterogeneity, is their unitary essence of mixture, which can no longer be perceived from themselves, but only from this new mode of thought. In what does Difference consist in this broader sense that denounces the scientific-transcendental mode of thought? In the combination, each time, of an immanence and a transcendence, of an ideality and a supposed real. A combination that, usually and with great rigor, has been called 'difference'. Despite their variations in defining alterity and the real, the three types of Difference still honour the foundational model of Occidental thought, that which Heraclitus and the Parmenides of the 'third way' have revealed to the Occident. That the definitions of identity and disparity, unity and scission, ideal and real, immanence and transcendence, etc., vary from one system to another and would be more or less incompatible, *this no longer matters to us and is no longer pertinent to our project*. In every case, it has to do with a coupling or an arrangement of two terms that is dual, or rather *duel* yet continuous, reciprocal or symmetrical (in the last instance, and despite all efforts to introduce asymmetry and unilaterality into their relation). It is to this unitary way of thinking that we intend globally to 'oppose' a certain *duality* that is yet irreversible and ensues from the One: on the condition that this duality is extracted from the wrappings of poorly founded religious 'dualisms', dualisms which are to be sure every bit as well founded as the 'dialectical' unity-duality of Difference. Duality here is no longer as philosophy understands it: two heterogeneous terms finally equal or reciprocal in their exclusion or else in their unitary hierarchy. It is the unilateralization and contingency of a 'second' term by the One which however *does not posit* this second term and, consequently, is not determined in turn by it. What duality, thus grounded transcendentally in a thought of the One, allows us to tear out at the roots is the oldest model of Occidental thought, that of which Difference is none other than the purest mode, the model of Unity-in-tension or the One-Multiple.

2. To perceive the sheer expanse of this model, one must go back to the canonical enunciation: *Everything is (Water, Earth, Fire, etc.)*. What is the internal structure of such an enunciation, a 'differential enunciation' as much as 'speculative' whose law the Occident has only very rarely and in a flash escaped? The predicative judgment is a logical model that may also receive a transcendental sense, but the Milesian enunciation, itself, makes apparent the oldest concrete philosophical matrix, a matrix of the empirico-transcendental parallelism and/or circle (with all its variants: logico-, physico-, psychologico-transcendental). It even grounds, in a generality that must be cleared of the Kantian or Husserlian modes to which it would be wrongly reduced, the empirico-transcendental Circle that is the essence not only of metaphysics, but of the attempts to 'surpass', 'overcome', 'turn' or 'deconstruct' metaphysics as well and that altogether surpasses, as circle, any attempts to distend it, split it, break it, etc.

What then does the empirico-transcendental circle define through this enunciation? It is to think the real as all (*the* all: not only the universal, but an absolute or unifying universal) and thus, inversely, the *all* of the real as still an element of the real, indeed as Other: *it is ontico-ontological 'difference' in its broadest sense*, in the sense that Being is here definitively affected by the beings that it conditions. Of this paradigm that like all philosophy they continue to honour, the Nietzschean, Heideggerean and Derridean 'differences' are only the most recent and most positive concrete types. Unity remains transcendent here, that is to say, still affected by what it unifies. It is this matrix of *duel* Unity, of circle or of parallelism, more or less deformed and distended, but in which each term is indeed the essence of the other, *but on the condition of being affected in return by it*, that unilateral duality, founded upon a 'unary' and no longer *duel* conception of the transcendental itself, freed finally from every affection of the empirical in return, must, if not break, at least reject as a domain of experience immediately reputed not to be the One; as a reality affected by the (*non-*)*One*.

3. The systems of Difference thus reconcile themselves in the reciprocity or unity of their heterogeneity, in this empirico-transcendental matrix – but upon the foundation of their common affection by

this *(non-)One*. Because in order to see this more intimate necessity in which the differences among *Difference, Differenz* and *Différance* would here lose all pertinence, one must of course cease, but this is still not sufficient, conceiving this empirico-transcendental parallelism in the conventional, crude and 'recent' manner, that is, as rationalist and subjective, in a Kantian or Husserlian mode; or even in the Nietzschean, Heideggerean and Derridean modes which 'work' this matrix in which they have their common infancy and where their fate is already programmed. This 'detachment' however is not *possible* unless it is *real*, that is to say, already 'effectuated'; unless thinking has already replaced itself in the immediate givens of the One as transcendental non-reflexive experience (of) the Absolute and something like a (non-)One, or an irreversible dualization, a uni-lateralization globally affects philosophical decision and its modes.

Let us repeat: we do not pursue here the absurd project of confounding all of the above, of showing that Derrida 'amounts to the same thing' as Nietzsche or even Heidegger, and reciprocally: in a sense, and we will insist upon this point, the three types of *the* Difference are incommensurable. But empirico-transcendental parallelism is the Greco-Occidental itself, and it is in this that the heterogeneous usages of Difference reconcile themselves as in a common heritage and at any rate in the common domain of mixtures and effectivity that the One unilateralizes. It is not thinkable except from a mode of thinking that is not *duel* but *dual* or dualist (we will make the necessary nuances later), *a duality of the One and of Being that metaphysics and the current attempts towards its 'deconstruction' have always tried to suture, to re-inscribe in a unity that is 'torn', 'in tension', 'differentiated', etc.*

FROM THE SCIENCE TO THE CRITIQUE OF DIFFERENCE

1. We develop here, across Nietzsche, Heidegger, Derrida and Deleuze, across Difference in general and its contemporary modes of effectuation (power, desire, textuality, perception, etc.), a description and above all a critique whose foundation is both scientific and transcendental. 'Transcendental' here no longer designates an ultimately circular syntax, but an experience which must be reduced to its essence, to

the *veritas transcendentalis* experienced as such and distinguished from its rationalist and subjective usages (Kant, Husserl), more generally from the underlying notions which carry, restrain, capture or pervert its scientific essence in the circularity of philosophical decision: metaphysical *a priori*s (intuition, categories, formal and material essences); the I think, subject, or *ego*; reflexivity and constitution; synthesis and its contemporary modes of connection, etc. *Difference, and not only in Heidegger, disposes with a variety of means to destroy, deconstruct, defer the transcendental as circular epistemology of the objective conditions of knowledge. But it remains transcendental in a more profound and irreducible sense: inasmuch as it makes of the One, of that whose very essence excludes the empirico-transcendental circle, a requisite, a condition of possibility for its own functioning, while leaving its essence absolutely indeterminate.*

If in effect there is an irreducible transcendental kernel of ultimate givens without which there is no longer anything to philosophize, it is this: all division between objects, between genera and categories leaves intact a higher indivision which serves as its unsurpassable limit. An analytic, for example, is transcendental because it has for a horizon – both end and means – not synthesis itself, but the unifying unity within synthesis. Thus the One is perhaps not only one among the transcendentals, alongside Being, Diversity, Contingence and Necessity, Truth and Falsity. It is the necessary condition such that there be *any* transcendental in the World and in History, and above all *for* the World and History. The One is that indivision which forms the essence of all the transcendentals. *Except that this formula is itself ambiguous*: since the transcendental such as we must now understand it is no longer the higher or eminent form of the *a priori* (transcendental designates in Kant the higher usage of a faculty which becomes capable of legislating *a priori* with respect to experience, and the One in turn *from this point of view* is the higher form of the transcendental itself); it is still something other than a 'form', a meaning or ideality, other than a limit-unity. And in the same way the very expression 'One in the transcendental sense' is here defective or in withdrawal from what is here intended. It has to do with *the One as non-reflexive transcendental experience or absolutely immediate and non-thetic givenness (of) itself.* Absolutely immediate: the One or Indivision is given (to) itself without passing through the mediation of a universal horizon, a nothingness, extasis or scission, a 'distance'. It is strictly non-reflexive, that is to say absolutely singular and autonomous as such before any universal (form, meaning, relation, syntax, difference, etc.). It is this 'unarity' inasmuch as it is distinguished from 'unity': unarity is inherently immanent (to) itself, and non-thetic (of) itself, while unity is always *both* immanent *and* transcendent, nearly identical to Difference.

2. It is therefore the One and its denial (its position, its restrictive philosophical usage, its 'unitary' limitation) that will be at issue in Being and Difference: with the suspicion that in always wanting to think the One in terms of 'superior form', that is, with the means of transcendence and as one of the modes of transcendence, philosophy prohibits itself access to the truth and continues imperturbably to relate this Non-relation to what is sublated of Relation. Difference purifies the One (for example in Heidegger's *Ereignis* where it appears masked however as and by division or nothingness), while at the same time relating it to Being, without being able to detach it entirely. It is this which must now become problematic: this intrication of the One and Being, this amphibology which is the greatest Occidental errancy. What exactly is the 'power' of the One? Is it a power of 'placing between parentheses' or 'suspending' Difference? Is the One sufficiently vast and universal – yet is this not still a bad posing of the question? – for inserting Being or Difference between parentheses? Is it a matter here of mounting a reductive scenario, a slowly broadside attack rather than a frontal one? Of tracing a 'line' or of assembling a more complicated machine? Of dredging up from the depths of Heidegger some hidden presupposition which, from being repressed, would breathe poorly? The One, while it would be required by Difference at the same time that Difference would deny and misrecognize it by leaving its essence indeterminate or determining it in a unitary mode, is perhaps no longer only and from the beginning an ultimate presupposition that philosophy, taking up an interminable effort, would undertake to wake and reactivate once more, arranging a supplementary version of the crossing of philosophy and psychoanalysis. That there would be presuppositions, the unthought, the unsaid, the sedimented – here is precisely the philosophical argument *par excellence* that Difference has used to the point of abuse when it has put its essence not only in the search for and critique of presuppositions, but

in their very *positing*, in the form of this principal and constitutive presupposition that philosophy names *Place* or *End*, *Thing* or *Concern*, *Body* as well, when it is not *Continent* or *Epoch*, and which philosophy needs as an unmoved mover. It is not certain that the One, itself, would be capable of parenthesis or suspension; its weakness allows it to go only as far as the *(non-)One*, which is not an operation, however modest and discreet. By speaking of parentheses or quotation marks, one would only wish to bracket or bait thinking in a finally rather philosophical mode. This would already be significant if it could only be made apparent that there is no 'critique' of Heidegger or any real 'exit' outside of Difference in general that would not be borrowed once again from the schemas Difference already mobilizes and, in particular, the schema of a philosophical-style 'critique'. The true power of the One is to affect us with this knowledge: the knowledge that we do not have to 'exit' from Difference or come back to it in a better and 'more thoughtful' manner because we have never entered it in the first place and we have never adhered to such a philosophical decision except through an illusion and perhaps even a hallucination proper to philosophy itself. What is Difference, what is its mechanism, and how, in what mode, does it intervene in the Absolute, that is, the One? Of what is its 'finitude' itself the symptom, and what is the relation of this more profound cause of finitude to the Absolute or One? By these questions, which we will try to answer, we make no claim to discover, finally hidden in Difference, rendering it real and not only possible, yet denied by it, some Archimedean point of the One. We already possess this and we can take support from it to see that to 'exit' from Heidegger and from Difference in general is just as much a hallucination as to enter it. The One is a real absolute and not only a transcendental principle, and it is capable of grounding Difference itself without letting itself be exhausted, in its essence, by the use that Difference at any rate makes of it.

If there is a power of the One, it is here: in this unilateralization of philosophy, its rejection to the abyss or to indifference which accompanies each person who comes into this World as into a strange land. The unilateralization or the duality, given their transcendental foundation in the One, cannot pass for an 'exit' beyond the World, beyond philosophy and its mixtures, but are rather what give us this indifferent and non-alienating access to the World as to philosophies.

On this prior foundation that we give ourselves in a non-thetic manner, we can disengage the presuppositions of Difference, those on which it founds itself all the better to deny them, but of which we are henceforth certain for intrinsic reasons, *a priori*, that they form its absolute and irreducible overflow, and which, being absolutely given, are still other than presuppositions (at least if Difference and the very notion of the presupposition, the unsaid, the unthought, etc., form a system from their side). *Real* critique is a type of thinking that, without denying Difference, is content to deny what there is in it of restraint, limit or non-autonomy, its lack of the One and its hallucination with respect to the One which it believes itself to have the power to determine.

CHAPTER TWO
Syntax of Difference

DIFFERENCE AS FORM OF ORDER

1. The One, insofar as its essence saves it from philosophical decision, is not Difference and has no need of it. But Difference, itself, is a philosophical interpretation of the One and has need of *it*. How does one pass from the One, from the concrete or absolute without-division, that which founds science, to the syntax of Difference as articulation of philosophical decision, as the syntactical minimum or residue of any possible philosophy?

The One becomes Difference in its most 'metaphysical' form (Nietzsche for example) when it unites itself with what – in this very operation and here alone – must thus appear as its contrary: division and all the modes of transcendence, cut, analysis, decision, nothingness, withdrawal, etc. What our contemporaries call 'Difference', at least its absolute or metaphysical type, but this would hardly have been overturned, is indeed the unity of contraries, but under two conditions assuring it a surplus-value of 'positivity' relative to the Dialectic: (1) that this unity would be rigorously or immediately one with the disjunction or division of contraries, that it would neither precede nor dominate nor interiorize these; (2) that inversely the disjunction of contraries is still understood as a mode of Indivision (Nothingness, for instance, 'as' Being). This is the objective point of hesitation where the *neither . . . nor* of contraries, with which we are familiar from its compulsive usage in Heidegger, Merleau-Ponty, Derrida and others, far from being abandoned to its representational decay in exclusion, is re-included, repeated not *in* or *under* the One, but *as* One. Difference marks out a way in representation with claims of 'neither . . . nor', but this is a technique that is only its transcendent aspect. Difference is an *inclusive dis-junction* in which each 'neither . . . nor . . . ' or 'not' is so little simply negative that it immediately returns or produces Indivision. When this effect frees itself from Difference, from its immanent play, it thus becomes a philosophical technology, one which founds the *via negationis*, and distinguishes a certain Neo-Platonism from the specific usage that Difference makes of this on its own account: no longer 'in view of' the One but immediately 'as' One – here is all the difference of Difference with respect to Neo-Platonism in general. However, that the One may be attained by means of a technique, albeit one immanent to the essence of what is attained, would doubtless indicate only how much Difference had delivered over the One and the true, according to a traditional gesture, to the adventures of transcendence and decision.

For the moment at least, Difference does not wish to dominate the contraries and their distance; it does not bring to them an exterior and already accomplished unity. To the contrary, Difference immediately divides any transcendent unity of this kind; it destroys what it calls Presence, Identity, Representation, Logo-phono-centrism. But it does not divide without, always immediately as well, retying the thread which ensures that the contraries would never cease to be 'all of a piece'. Without retying rather than tying, because the thread would never be broken. The One with which it is concerned is no longer unified unity and thus divisible, but unifying unity, the One in a transcendental rather than empirico-ideal sense, the One no longer only inasmuch as it is invested in a form of ideality always susceptible in effect of being divided, but inasmuch as it is Indivision itself par excellence and something else entirely than a transcendental signified. Difference, inasmuch as it contains the One, is not a category under which one orders a variety of contraries, nor is it an Idea sublating this variety. Its operation is neither a sub-sumption nor a super-sumption (*Aufhebung*); it is something like a co-sumption, a mutual 'intertwining' of contraries, which defeats both subsumption and supersumption, overcoming both. The passage from one contrary to the other is possible because there is, to be sure, not only a division of contraries rendering the passage or transition necessary and thus possible, but, more profoundly, because there is no exterior passage or transcendent leap providing a way from one contrary to the other. There is a point, but it is no longer a point, a place, but it is no longer a place, through which contraries have always already been intimately knitted. Not knitted: individed *a priori*, without link or thread, because it is neither a link nor a thread since the contraries are *immanent* and consequently not susceptible to being affected exteriorly by division, by scission, by nothingness. Difference is Scission-immediately-as-Unity; Becoming-as-Being; immobile transit; transcendental hesitation, etc.

2. The One thus ceases in this way to be a transcendent Unity, the prior domain of some neutral reality, neither ontic nor ontological, that would share out or distribute, for example, Being and beings. Both of these, to take this contrasted pair, 'participate' in the One, their sharing out is their very unity. The One is not an anterior and neutral unity, it is 'to the contrary' the *sharing out* of Being and beings, their *and*. It is this which distinguishes their 'sameness' (*das Selbe*), from their state of representation, from their similitude, resemblance, equality (*das Gleiche*) *under* an exterior unity already given by itself, which sub-sumes or super-sumes them. The sharing out does not affect the One, does not divide it; it affects only what there is in it of idealized unity or presence. It conserves the One in each of the differends, and this is immediately the One itself. The One reigns in and through division and the divided, it at once constitutes and does not constitute itself at each division. The differends are themselves always-already identified with the One which is unconstitutable and which preserves the relation as indivisible: each division 'produces' or rather 'reproduces' the Indivision of contraries. Their 'difference' as such is precisely the genealogical or destinal element of every meta-physical distinction as such, that of Being and beings for example. Inversely, cut and withdrawal (these, moreover, are not at all the same thing; we will distinguish them later) are constitutive of this unity. This unity does not stand above division: even when it transcends beyond representational forms of division

or transcendence, presence, identity, etc., it continues to be joined with a division which is in any case specific to the One, positive or indivisible, and which it uses against such forms.

To be sure, this is but one concrete type of Difference, even if it is its most invariant syntax. With this reservation, let us take the case of Heidegger: in all rigour the Clearing is not founded on Forgetting nor is Withdrawal founded on Clearing. The ground/form relation cannot exhaust the essence or immanence of a Clearing which is immediately its 'own' Withdrawal, of a Withdrawal which is immediately its Clearing. In metaphysical Difference or Difference in general – with *Finitude* set aside for now – the ground/form relation is at least generalized and extends beyond its perceptive constraints: every ground acts also as form, every form 'gives rise' immediately to the ground as such. The chiasmus of ground and form (every form represents a ground for another form, every ground represents a form for another ground) is a means of thinking the intertwining for example of Dionysus and Apollo, and also, but this is still insufficient, the Heideggerean intertwining of Reserve and Clearing.

3. Thus the syntax which would be lacking in 'metaphysics' or 'representation', etc., in order to be able to speak its essence and its truth, is that which leaves itself, through positivity, deprived of logico-grammatical or even onto-logical articulations (philosophical logics) that continue to submit this essence to transcendent models of causality. This is transcendental tautology or hesitation as the very opening of the relations of subject and predicate as having become differends – or of any other relation. If we measure it against the criteria of logic and grammar, it is a syntactical aporia, but an aporia that is rather the becoming-positive of the essence of any possible syntax. That the syntax would be partially 'voided' of its transcendent determinations only better serves to carry it to its essence of *syntaxis*, of originary order or of primitive and grounding synthesis. This transcendental syntax is the essence of logico-grammatical syntax or is what possibilizes it. It is the superior form of logical tautology and substitutes itself for all relations of an empirical and transcendent kind, whether scientific or metaphysical. No phenomenon may be considered any longer as separated and transcendent; all are ordered to the primacy of their 'indivisible relation' or their

syntax *as such* – finite or otherwise – which prevails over them and makes them enter into the sphere of its immanence. Syntactical interiorization this side of the linguistic opposition of semantics and syntax – here, then, is the work, occasionally idealist, everywhere and in every way idealizing, of Difference. It is a simple mechanism, even 'technically' simple. But it is such that it produces, in metaphysical discourse, in vulgar and philosophical discursivity, effects of seemingly complex turbulence. Seized as invariant, which is perhaps possible only from the One in its truth, it allows for the resolution of all aporias, Heideggerean for example, since it is none other than the system of affirmation of aporias *as such* and no longer as logical or metaphysical aporias. Yet is this perhaps at the price of the essence of the One as placed at the service of this universal syntax, and of what its tautological usage still leaves undetermined?

4. That Difference is grounded – without knowing it – in the authentic One is not a tautology, but rather the condition for Difference to acquire its superior or 'tautological' form. The One is never, by its essence which is non-thetic (of) itself, a tautology; it is solely tautology's necessary and not sufficient condition. Paradoxically, it is Difference that introduces a 'tautological' usage of the One. Tautology begins when thought escapes or believes itself to have the power to escape from the One and when it introduces separation and division *with* the One and *as* One, critical decision *with* and *as* the Undecidable. It is quite rigorously that Heidegger characterizes 'his' thought as tautological. Par excellence, one might say, it is the superior (transcendental) form of tautology: no longer that of logical identity, but that of the Same-as-Difference. The One is not the Same, but it becomes this once it is united to its contrary and itself becomes partially a contrary.

In effect, Difference uses the One but without thinking its proper essence, in order to insert it in a complex where division and its avatars will enter, among these Nothingness. Difference assumes an absolute Undecidability, but this is not other than that of the contraries, and it attaches to this in order to make a communal work with division. It aims at a final immanence, yet as associated with a transcendence or scission. It thinks the One, but by putting it at the service of the Greco-Occidental problem of the unity of contraries. The circle of philosophical decision accomplishes itself as tautological thought: that which holds, in the about-face of one contrary into the other, the held presence or clearing of the Same. This is what philosophy has made of the One: at worst, the formal identity of non-contradiction; at best, the sublime tautology of the Same. Philosophical decision moves between these two extremes: for the One itself they are perhaps indifferent or equivalent, but not for the thinking that would claim to replace metaphysics and yet enchains itself to metaphysics . . .

PASSAGE FROM THE META-PHYSICAL TO THE TRANSCENDENTAL FORM OF DIFFERENCE

1. Difference is no simple 'fact', not even an *a priori* or universal one. In contemporary philosophy, with Nietzsche and Deleuze, it has become explicitly a principle. The mechanism of Difference as principle comprises two phases that form its process or its becoming and that are characteristics of philosophical decision in general. This latter is always in effect a discourse of double articulation. It is therefore necessary that the mechanism previously described, despite its formal simplicity, develop itself according to a continuous movement and pass through two levels, one interpreting Difference *rather* as a function of disparity and multiplicity, the other *rather* as a function of unity. The movement of Difference is the unity of these two articulations, the unity of itself in progress and which is itself at stake. A philosophical syntax is always real in the sense that it must realize itself in a process; it is never just a formal mechanism. Difference accedes to its most positive essence when the division with which it is concerned not only ceases to be empirical but is no longer even *a priori*, in order to become transcendental or real. This is the authentic sense of the requirement, even if it no longer wishes here to make of Difference a principle: to think Withdrawal *as* Clearing and Clearing *as* Withdrawal. This task does not imply any passage of the differends *in* one another since they are already 'One' or 'Undecidable' each through its own essence or distinctive trait. On the other hand this does imply the surpassing of the formal aspect of the syntax, its becoming-concrete or becoming-as-One. Thinking attains its highest, tautological form when it renounces the explicit use of contraries and

contents itself with speaking in a voice at once clear and faint, at the very limit of In-articulation or the non-syntactical: language speaks, or better, *die Sprache spricht, das Sein west, das Nichts nichtet, das Ereignis ereignet, die Welt weltet* (Heidegger), etc., formulae constraining us to think, on the hither side of the opposition of subject and verb, the Same or the opening that differentiates them as differends.

2. What we must now redescribe is the first level: *the meta-physical articulation of Difference*. The One, as we know, does not precede, here at least, division; it is an immediate that is at one with mediation. There is Difference when division immediately gives or re-gives Indivision, but after having purified it of its idealized and transcendent forms: this is its first operation. Metaphysics or representation is thus not understood through Difference in an empirical way, in its doctrinal and historical diversity, but as already reduced (with respect to finitude or not) to its metaphysical essence extracted as an *a priori fact*: already no longer an empirical fact and not yet the real possibility or the possibilization of a fact, but fact itself as 'possible', a possibility-of-being. However one must distinguish the *a priori* as understood in an ahistorical and rational manner, Kantian and Husserlian, from what Difference introduces, on its side, but always at the interior of metaphysics: a plastic concept of the *a priori*, not only as 'possible', but as historical 'possibility' or possibility in becoming. The spirit of Difference thus pierces through already in its definition of the 'metaphysical' *a priori*: one will speak less of *form* than of *power-to-be* (the 'active forces' in Nietzsche, 'desiring machines' in Deleuze, 'possibilities-of-being' in Heidegger, 'textual forces' in Derrida, etc.). The 'power-to-be' for example is the original type of *a priori factum* that the differential analytic of Being provides for itself; it is an *a priori* or a universal that is always said finally of beings in general. These plural *a priori* are relations, but already, though implicitly, non-relations or Indivisibles. Their syntax is, to be sure, that of Difference: their division or analysis cannot be other than the affirmation of their inseparability, the repetition of their indivision; the powers-to-be cannot be otherwise than continued through their division, their rupture or multiplicity: immediately projected or thrown as *themselves*, as what they are in their essence, more exactly pro-(jected) or continued as soon as they are thrown or separated. This syntax of multiple

powers-to-be is therefore already that of Difference, of the 'connecting leap', of the 'continuing rupture' or of the 'relay': such a being does not become itself except through its own rupture, the division of its identity to self or to others, but conversely to divide is immediately to project and continue (*endlos* or 'interminably').

This then is the first, meta-physical level of the articulation of Difference. Yet this *a priori* is always abstract because it is still too close to what it intends to leave behind: the sensible, beings, representation, reified metaphysical differences between Being and beings, etc., and their very multiplicity which is itself introduced here back into the *a priori*. It is threatened with falling back into what it proposes to leave behind, precisely because its principle remains transcendence, and transcendence, characteristically of meta-physics, is always insufficient and fragile, and risks becoming again empirical, foundering upon the facticity of the 'given'. *A second transcending is thus necessary which is still more than a simple transcendence, what Heidegger calls an 'absolute transcending' because it is henceforth Unity that must be charged with transcendence, cut or withdrawal,* and it is the inessential (relative to the metaphysical type of reified essence) that must henceforth co-belong to the very 'essence' of Being. This would be the transcendental level of philosophical articulation in general.

3. Why must one pass in effect to the transcendental stage of Difference? What distinguishes the first level, that of the meta-physical as *a priori* fact of metaphysics, already 'essentialized' and partially reduced, from the properly transcendental level, that of the abandonment to the Essence, the Ownness of metaphysics? It is that Being at the first level is determined despite everything still from the point of view of scission and multiplicity, which is always of ontic-objective origin, and not yet from the point of view of its essence or its ownness as One (or here, Unity), as immanence that will repeat in a transcendent mode its ontic origin and destination (at the same time that these will penetrate into essence). Difference does not become principle or Same except when division and its modes, one of which is 'withdrawal', are at last repeated or 'included' as the One itself. It is thus necessary to 'overturn' Difference, to surpass the reversibility for example of the ground *and* the form, in order to affirm this reversibility (this *and*) as such, their very chiasmus inasmuch as this would be the immanence

of the One or co-belonging. To think 'in' Difference is to affirm that the undecidable relation of opposites is worth more than any decision in favour of one or the other, a decision which is however not absolutely alien to Indecision, but which condemns indecision to be not merely affirmed, but re-affirmed. We know the immense and over-worn effort of Heidegger to 'return' 'ontological Difference' into the essence of metaphysics, to assign to Being *rather* than to beings, to Being itself *rather* than to Being-present, to the essence and truth of Being *rather* than to metaphysical Being and to man – each time to assign to one term of these couples Difference as the birthplace of contraries. Yet this mechanism is none other than the re-inscription of division, in particular the division of the meta-physical, *in* or rather *as* the Immanence of the One or the Absolute.

This second movement thus affects – this is capital – transcendence, but because it is itself more than a simple transcendence. Nothing transcends towards the One without the One 'transcending' towards itself, in reality without transcendence inscribing itself in turn within an immanence. From this follow all these ultimate operations of Difference: Re-affirmation (Nietzsche), Re-version (Deleuze), interiorizing Turning (Heidegger), the 'Yes' to the Same or to Difference (Derrida). These over-come the meta-physical in general and lead it back to its essence, to its 'ownness', that is, to the Unity or unicity of the Unique. The One itself is here affected with transcendence: far from excluding division – namely the withdrawal characteristic of Being or the meta-physical *a priori* as distinguishing these from beings and from empiricity in general – the One rather includes division in its immanence. Withdrawal, forgetting, difference (to which, let us repeat, we still do not give their 'finite' essence; we are concerned here with simple phenomena of syntax) change sense in certain ways, or more exactly, change truth and place: they cease to be merely traits of the *a priori* (of Being or the universal) in order to be thought in their co-belonging with the One itself and as forming the essence of Being. Nothingness or its modes are what produce transcending: but when thinking undergoes the experience that is the One itself which transcends absolutely in 'turning', in reversing upon itself, or more profoundly, when the One inscribes in its immanence the scissions that produce its transcending and as whose absolute Limit it serves, then one may say that nothingness in its turn transcends itself as One and is no longer solely what produces transcending: it is then this tautological Nothingness that 'nihilates' and that merits the care of thinking.

There is here a general logic of Difference that holds for all its types: whatever their material; whatever the technical modalities of the transcendental that effectuates them; whatever the degree of deconstruction of their epistemo-logical forms. The passage from the metaphysical to the transcendental is an invariant that is displaced and worked, yet conserved, from Kant or even Plato to Heidegger and contemporary thought: the becoming-active of forces in Nietzsche, the Heideggerean passage from the Difference between Being and beings (= metaphysical *a priori*) to the One-as-withdrawal or the One (of) withdrawal, the becoming-dispensational or 'destinal' element of the metaphysical relation of Being to beings; the Derridean passage from 'differance' to the Yes-to-Difference, etc.

Difference is at times an 'overcoming' (Nietzsche), at times only an interiorization of the meta-physical to the Unity (of) withdrawal (Heidegger). This interiorization is evidently no longer psychological nor even metaphysical or logico-ideal; it is transcendental. However, that the One would still be thought as capable of *sur-mounting or amounting to a return, that is, of operating an immanence in the mode of transcendence*, is the most certain sign of the failure of philosophy, whether contemporary or otherwise, to think the essence of what the One's immanence really is.

THE IMPOSSIBLE SURPASSING OF METAPHYSICS

1. Difference is both interior and exterior to metaphysics and representation. Interior, because metaphysics and representation move within it, and their 'surpassing' does not pass into some completely other experience of thinking. Exterior, because a supplement of difference or alterity is always necessary in order to actualize what resides in the very representation that denies it. This double relation constrains Difference to 'turn' representation and to 'turn' absolutely – to turn and interiorize representation into and as the mode of transcendence. It is in this fashion that the task of thinking becomes a 'return' into the essence of metaphysics as much as

an 'exit' beyond its reified forms. Because Difference is not only an empirical generality or a universal *a priori* but also a transcendental decision, metaphysics has never fallen completely outside of its law. Its essence is inalienable; it must thus both become and be, together, its own. Therefore metaphysics is not properly speaking surpassable – except in its most reified forms – since it holds itself already in the opening of Difference. The passing step of the passage – of 'sur-passing' – goes from Difference to metaphysics, and the very deconstruction of representation re-engenders representation as one of its 'effects'.

'To surpass metaphysics' is still a very metaphysical formula, and it *indicates* a problem to which Difference is the solution. 'To surpass' is the very operation of metaphysical transcendence: as applied to the *whole* of metaphysics, it implies that the surpassing would be inhibited . . . by itself, that transcendence would be hindered . . . by its own means (self-paralysed). The surpassing of metaphysics is limited because it is turned back against itself. But this is not possible in the manner of a revolving door or an unlimited nihilism: one must disengage, from the transcendence relative to beings or the empirical, a kernel of scission that acquires from the One its irreducible consistency and the very possibility of being *turned-*(back) against its empirical or representational forms. Transcending or withdrawing do not become absolute except as Turning. To make the surpassing and the non-surpassing of metaphysics coincide, to inhibit the metaphysical surpassing of metaphysics even while affirming this inhibition, this Unsurpassable as the truly 'finite' surpassing of metaphysics, this would be 'the summit of contemplation' or the 'serenity' of thought.

2. Difference is thus rather what looks after metaphysics as such and renders it unsurpassable since the *neither . . . nor*, which repels the reified exclusion of contraries all while offering them guarantees, is not only an operation of thinking towards the One, but, in its essence, the movement of the One 'in' itself. To transcend towards the One (Unity, not the authentic One) is to surpass; but to transcend as One is no longer to surpass. The One surpasses but is not itself surpassed; every surpassing is made within its limits: one does not overcome metaphysics except by interiorizing it, not to a subject or self, but to

the One. Interiorization means inclusion of the onto-logical fact within the immanence proper to Difference, within the One at least inasmuch as it is here finally organized with transcendence and forms the 'Same'. Each 'Turning' re-affirms a bit more the Same as such, or Difference as capable of giving rise to metaphysics.

3. From this, two solutions are possible: either the Turning is still an autonomous principle forming a system with transcending (Nietzsche: the Eternal Return of the Same; Deleuze: Repetition); or it is a transcending that is immediately One or Turning (Heidegger). Either it is the-One-that-is-scission-of-opposites, or it is scission-that-is-One, Withdrawal-as-Turning. Yet in both cases Difference, in keeping to itself, keeps also to what is essential in metaphysics, the transcending proper to philosophical decision.

THE THREE STAGES OF DIFFERENCE

1. Thus understood as what is itself at stake, as what it itself has to become, Difference, or becoming-difference passes through three continuously linked levels of which the last two define *the double articulation of philosophical decision in general*:

a. Difference as present in object-being, ontic difference, and corresponding to this, the category of 'difference': this is the empirical level of Difference, which tends always towards the reciprocal exclusion of contraries under the law of a representational and transcendent unity.

b. Difference as 'ontological difference', the metaphysics *as such* of metaphysics, the transcendence of presence relative to present being. This is no longer the empirical but instead *a priori* level of Difference. It is metaphysics in the sense understood by Heidegger when he thematizes in this mode the difference of Being and beings. Yet this operation still leaves transcendence in its relation of origin, in its relativity to the object-being or the present.

c. Difference no longer as metaphysical or ontological, but as transcendental (in the rigorous sense of a thinking of the One, which is to say, immanence inasmuch as it *at least* 'surpasses' every empirical, generic and even ontological division). This is the point of view of

Heidegger's search for the essence of Difference, but also of those who make a principle out of Difference and who, after a certain fashion, thus accomplish metaphysics. At this level metaphysical or *a priori* transcendence is torn away (entirely, as the Nietzscheans believe; or partly, only partly because of Finitude, as Heidegger would have it) from its relativity to the object or to present being and affirmed in its co-belonging with the Absolute. It is 'absolute transcendence', alone capable of the genesis of ontological Difference or of the 'gift/giving' of the relation of Being and beings and of any relation of two contraries in general. This is why the Same is characterized finally as the unity of the differentiating or topological manifestation of contraries, for example of Being's upsurge in beings and of beings as the dissimulation of the advent that unveils them. Thus understood, Difference makes possible the deployment of the relation of metaphysical transcendence, itself steeped in reified negation and unity. It is *das wesende des Seins selbst*, Being *as* Being in its essence of being shared-out. On the one hand essence is the 'already accomplished' (*schon vollendet*) of the dispensation of presence to beings, in the sense that the All it is concerned with is indivisible or transcendental because of the One (which it *is*) that transcends – still . . . – beyond the metaphysical relation being/beings or that *surpasses absolutely* as only the One can. On the other hand, it gives rise topologically to this other difference, 'fallen' or reified in a flat identity and a flat exclusion, of Being and beings, such as metaphysics has thought it: unmoored from its transcendental support, the *neither . . . nor* falls back onto the empirical plane where it remains relative to what it excludes and gives rise to more 'positive' if not positivist interpretations.

2. The contribution of the contemporary thinkers of Difference to the problem of philosophical decision is to have found in this syntax a means – the most positive – for the delimitation (at once internal and external) of earlier forms of decision, while still renewing the essentials of philosophical decision. Then, on this restricted base of a still philosophical critique of philosophy, to have made of the age-old category of Difference what all philosophers have always made of their principal procedure (dialectic, syllogistic, order of reasons, analysis, etc.): to have assured the passage

from its *a priori* to its transcendental concept. Here is the real content of slogans of 'overcoming/surpassing' and even of the 'critique' of representation. As the analysis of its phases (empirical, *a priori*, transcendental) has shown, Difference, even non-'finite', is an instrument that repeats, sometimes in displacing, aggravating, intensifying it, an ancient problem which is not that of the 'overcoming of metaphysics' (which is only an actualized historical form of it), but that of the passage from the categorial or metaphysical to the transcendental. These thinkers have conceived the problem of philosophical decision in restricted, intra-philosophical modes of a new, differential form of critique (ontological destruction; deconstruction; affirmative surmounting, etc.) no doubt positive or on the way to becoming so, *but which place transcendental truth, the essence of truth once more in the service of the carousel of metaphysics.* They have repeated, but this time upon metaphysics in totality since Kant is included here, then Nietzsche himself, then Heidegger, etc., an operation that can be found already in Plato and Kant, but in a restricted form since this latter, for example, would exercise it only upon metaphysics understood as dogmatism and scepticism, an operation that finds with them a new extension and new means: the philosophical critique of philosophy, a project rendered possible only through the denial of the essence of the One and its Greco-philosophical requisition. To be sure, the fact that the Heideggerean and post-Heideggerean usages of Difference, and even the problem-beacon of the interiorizing surmounting of metaphysics or the metaphysical, would be only masks for this older problem as inscribed necessarily in the theoretical matrix of Difference in general does not prevent, but rather to the contrary, that they have renewed its forms and extended it further.

Difference has become a powerful factor of turbulence in the margins of metaphysics and the historico-systematic formations that develop in its element (Text, Power, Desire, the Political). However it has turned in Heidegger and beyond him into an obsession and a fanatical ideology of surveillance, without its internal reason and still less the limits of these 'effects' being elaborated for themselves. From this results a sterile repetition and an auto-inhibition confirming at an unprecedented scale the vocation of philosophical decision to get bogged down in itself.

GENERALIZATION OF THE PASSAGE FROM THE CATEGORIAL TO THE TRANSCENDENTAL

1. This passage from the categorial to the transcendental may be extended, beyond Nothingness, Being, Difference itself, etc., to all the categories of thought. Accomplished Difference is more powerful than the categories, more univocal than they; it is their essence and procures for them the *veritas transcendentalis*, but it also sublates, as we have seen, philosophical decision's mechanism of double articulation.

The passage of such and such a category from its metaphysical usage to its transcendental truth has always and everywhere the same type of effects: the category ceases to entertain relations of meta-physical transcendence or causality, whether ontic or ontico-ontological (relations of substance/accident, subject/object, ground/form, causality and processes of transformation in general). These are in effect relations in which the terms, identical or present to themselves, but also exclusive of one another *under* representations, always end up prevailing over the relations themselves. Included in concrete Difference, on the other hand, Nothingness, beings and Being, for example, cease to entertain relations of reciprocal technical causality, of 'ontic' negation or production. Being, Nothingness, Language in its essence, etc., cease to be ontically determinable through relations that assume not beings or the real in general, but a being determined as object (idealist Difference) or instead an object determined as being (finite Difference). Suspended are not only the ontically transcendent multiplicities or cut-outs given immediately in experience, since these empirical cut-outs would be considered – according to the status given to 'finitude' – irreducible or of simple appearance without reality and empirically dissolved; but also the space of ontological diversity, of the ontic plurality of the ontological which is, at any rate, that of the *a priori factum* or of the *meta-physical fact* obtained as the point of departure for thinking. It suffices that such an ontic multiplicity of Being could give rise – which it effectively does – to the appearances of representation, to the well-founded illusions of Presence, of Identity, of Logocentrism in order that its suspension would be required and its ontic origin surmounted through becoming-One (specifically, in a differential mode). For example, Nothingness or the Nothing (*das Nichts*), from the point of view of its transcendental truth, is not only the meta-physical *a priori* of the negation that 'precedes' empirical facts of negation or destruction. It transcends through and beyond negation, but with a transcendence impeded or inhibited in a way in the immanence of the One that 'turns' it thus 'in' its 'ownness' or its essence, that appropriates it to its essence which is no longer that of 'denying' or 'annihilating', but of 'nihilating'. Thus, ap-propriated, Nothingness ceases to act either ontically or ontologically (ground, sublation or supersumption, production of beings through the self-negation of Nothingness) upon beings, upon Being or upon whatever else. It becomes from this point of view indeterminable.

2. What is more, the categories thus 'appropriated' to their essence detach themselves from one another in order no longer to possess anything other than the form of the Same or of superior tautology. They share no equivalence, they are not identical or similar under an identity. To be deprived of their former ontic operations does not deprive them entirely of all 'operation'. Rather, operation has become immanent to their essence: Nothingness nihilates, Essence essentializes, Language speaks, Desire desires, the World worlds, etc. This becoming-immanent in the form of tautology is fundamental. The sur-mounting of any metaphysical category, its appropriation to its essence or ownness, its unary 'turning', absolves it of its metaphysical relativity and frees it from its contrary. To assign Nothingness to Being rather than to beings or to the relation of Being and beings is above all not to identify Being with Nothingness, which would not lead to the exit from this relation. It is primarily to autonomize Nothing as *Selbst*, as *das Selbige*; as capable of nihilating. It is also to show its (co)-belonging *with* Being, or *to* the essence of Being: precisely the difference of Being and Nothingness, their (co)-belonging rather than their identity. Each of the contraries (co)-belongs not to the other, but, more profoundly, to their difference, and, at the same time, may be thought as autonomous: this does not mean absolutely separated, since autonomy will be thought in turn as Difference. *Language speaks*: this is not a thesis about language, it is a way of making language speak that itself takes the form of a transcendental tautology, the unity of a Same on the hither side of the disjunction

of noun and verb. The logico-grammatical correlation of subject and verb is the reified form of a unity-of-the-Same or a Difference that joins all in one piece *Die Sprache* and *spricht*. The question of the unity of the multiple significations of Being – what does 'Being' signify? – thus receives a solution that does not annihilate its essence as a question, that reveals it as Difference 'to be thought'. At the limit, each signification of Being would have to be able to be thought under the 'tautological' mode of Difference.

3. What finally is the effect of accomplished Difference? On the hither side of the logico-grammatical subject and attribute, categories become supra-universal attributes, equipped with the One as with their differential essence; machines that divide themselves only to restart themselves immediately and continue. Not that their internal cut (Nothingness and its negating) would be subsumed under the Same as under an identity: the cut is immediately an indivision; not only a synthesis but the transcendental Unity of a synthesis. We will interpret in this way the negating of Nothingness, which is no longer – or nearly so . . . – a transcendent operation, but the immanent play and the indivision of a Nothingness-that-negates. Such a universal or *a priori* is supra-universalized as One or immanent (to) itself, related to itself as without-relation = absolute. This explains how Nothingness or Withdrawal thus enjoys an absolute autonomy, if not, as Heidegger would have it, relative to Being itself (the idealist usage of Difference – Nietzsche and Deleuze – is opposed to this), at least and in every way relative to the ontic and particular forms of negation. When Difference passes from the meta-physical, more exactly from the *a priori*, to the transcendental, not only is it it itself that it receives for its essence, rather than Being or Nothingness, but it becomes essence for Being, Nothingness, Desire, Power, Text, etc. No longer having one of these contraries for essence but rather Difference-itself-as-their-coupling, Difference includes them in its play and snatches them from themselves: Difference as the essence of Being is not ontological; as the essence of Language is not linguistic, etc. These formulae of indetermination apply beyond Heidegger, to Nietzsche as well (although with less radicality).

CHAPTER THREE
Reality of Difference

1. Difference thinks or reflects itself in itself. It thus entails the disjunction and belonging – precisely Difference – of syntax and reality, of the real's articulation and the experience of the articulated real. We would now like, in the case of the distinction of Nietzsche and Heidegger, to make evident the necessity of passing from problems of syntax to perhaps more fundamental problems of reality.

'Metaphysics', in the sense given to the term by Heidegger then Derrida, does not ignore Difference, it is even the fundamental 'category', whether explicitly or not, of thinkers such as Nietzsche and then Deleuze and Foucault. But this 'metaphysical' experience of Difference has its place in a more originarily experienced Difference. According to Heidegger, Nietzsche like the rest of the tradition fails to interrogate the dimension of (co-)*belonging* that is the essence of Difference, the essential provenance of this correlation, the truth of Being as such. Thinking should not forsake 'ontological Difference', but it will allow it to come into what it is in its essence-of-Difference, into its 'own'. What metaphysics, according to Heidegger, leaves indeterminate is this essence (of Being), even if it in its own way has to determine Being: simply at the interior of Difference as the correlation of Being and beings and in function of this relation alone.

This is what Nietzsche does, for example, in determining the very essence of Being as self-determining (Will to Power).

Yet in order to understand the possibility of such a critical delimitation of metaphysics, it is necessary to 'exit' mere syntax and to examine what these thinkers understand by the real, that is, specifically, by 'beings' rather than 'Being'. Beings are not only named at the interior of syntax: all the weight of the real rests upon them from the beginning. In effect, Difference does not 'lift itself' from empirical cases towards generalities; Being is not a generality, determined always locally and regionally. Instead Being is *a priori*; it is a formal rather than general notion. Beings are thus not treated in their particular properties, but straightaway *as* beings, and Being from its side is not acquired at the end of a process of abstraction; it is the horizon that we must deploy from the start, that we must have in prior view in order that we may accede to beings. Metaphysics sets itself up in the relation of beings and the *a priori*, a relation that is in turn *a priori*, a prior place of thought. It is this *factum a priori*, as extracted through a prior reduction, that distinguishes metaphysics for example from science. Thus Being refers necessarily to beings, like reality to the real; it intends them in the broadest possible way.

2. *Yet perhaps there is an ambiguity in the very notion of beings.* Metaphysics understands beings straightaway as objects or within the horizon of Being: metaphysics determines Being at the interior of this *factum* of the being already *as* being, of the speculative and circular mixture of ideal real and real ideality. But is there not another experience of beings that would straightaway open and delimit this circle that Difference has become?

In effect, what is specific to Heidegger's relation to metaphysics has been given once and for all and despite the inevitable subsequent re-interpretations and objections to this word, by 'Finitude'. *In quasi-Kantian terms, Finitude is the irreducible distinction of the being in itself in relation to objectivized or present being, the ob-ject.* To this radical hypothesis touching upon the essence and origin of Finitude, we will return systematically. Heidegger does not reject the Kantian thesis of the 'thing in itself', but only its dogmatic and idealist interpretation. He gives to it on the contrary a transcendental sense beyond Reason and strives to think its (real) unity and distinction with the phenomenon or Being: it is thus one of the necessary ingredients of the *essence* of Being. Here we have a 'maximalist' hypothesis concerning the sense of Finitude, but it is the only one that allows us to understand how Heidegger is able to claim to de-limit all of metaphysics and in particular the powerful systems of Hegel, Nietzsche and Husserl.

What is specific to Nietzsche's 'metaphysics' relative to Heidegger is, on the contrary, the lifting of this Finitude (exteriority, alterity or withdrawal even outside of Being) through the auto-position of Being that becomes essence. The Nietzschean experience of Difference (*Pathos der Distanz*) is in effect inseparable from a quasi-'auto-position', of idealist and classically metaphysical spirit, of Difference's syntax and of the moment that, at its interior, represents already the insertion of the real: the diversity of this 'distance' (forces, perspectives, etc.) *This diversity is straightaway ideal or ob-jective, a diversity of objectivity; this is supposed as autonomous relative to a being or a thing in itself that is suspended in a preliminary manner.* This metaphysical lifting of Finitude is not possible except through the means – and the compensation – of a super-position of the One (or the Unity) of Difference. This super-position is what becomes auto-position in the context of Difference.

From Heidegger's point of view, this auto-determination of essence is none other than a still objectivizing or idealist determination that is made as a function of the particular being, that is, the 'present' object and its mode of presence. A more originary determination of essence would instead have to *include in itself an irreducible dimension of withdrawal in relation to the object-being: precisely what Heidegger calls Finitude, which is the distinction of the being in itself in relation to the objectivized or present being.* The notion of 'beings', as well as the correlation of Being and beings, is fundamentally ambiguous in its generality. *Inasmuch as it is finite, the essence (of Being) is un-objectivizable in a real mode, and not only in the merely ideal mode that metaphysics and the idealist-Nietzschean usage of Difference tolerate.* It is a real that is indeterminable ideally, that is, in the being-objectivized or being-present mode of the object-being. This is not an indetermination of essence that would be merely ideal, in the idealist manner of the Will to Power (or the 'desiring machines' and desire as 'immanent principle' in Deleuze), an indetermination which thus would not have the last word and which would be re-included in the 'auto'-determination of Being as one of its means.

3. The 'metaphysical' version of Difference, Nietzsche's, determines Being, its essence, by abstracting from the point of view of Finitude and confiding itself to the sole necessity of the syntax or the chiasmus of Difference. It cedes to absolute idealism the syntax's positing of itself as the sole real. In effect, Being is still the essence that determines beings, but the determination is circular or iterative; beings affect or determine Being in turn: *even when Being determines itself as (a) being.* Being or essence does not content itself with determining beings in *how* . . . and *what* . . . they are. Being – and we have seen through what transcendental necessity – is *also* the yoke, arc or dimension that holds together Being and beings as disjoint = contrary; it is the Difference or Indivision of the two, all while also being, as Dimension of the two contraries, an indivision mediated through their disjunction. It becomes, in this absolute-idealist context of 'auto'-position, what determines *both* beings *and* itself as Difference; it is the determining of beings and of its own coupling with them, that is, of the manner in which it determines them. There is here a phenomenon that we have examined systematically, a passage from *a priori* to transcendental determination. This passage is a law essential to philosophy; it signifies that the first determination is included in the second, but conversely that the latter is thought more (Nietzsche) or less (Heidegger) according to the mode and the prolongation of the former, that the passage of the first to the second is only, particularly in Nietzsche, the passage from the ontic *diversity* of the ontological to the uni-fied and uni-fying *totality* of the ontological. The syntax of Difference appears as though liberated by the 'auto'-position of the One. In its metaphysical form, if it is conceived precisely as a difference or a chiasmus and not as an exclusion of self-posited contraries, if it is articulated as the *essence* of metaphysics, it becomes a mechanism containing the immanent necessity of its passage to its transcendental sense, to its autonomy of the absolute or 'One' process. The determining determines Being or the meta-physical to determine beings, and it is itself determined to this in two ways simultaneously that laminate Finitude: by another object-being and/or by itself (*causa sui*). *The full essence of metaphysics, essence in the transcendental and no longer only meta-physical sense, is Difference that auto-determines itself or is absolute.* Or, more exactly, relative-absolute: this passage to the Absolute is precisely a continuous passage and does not abolish the relativity of Being to beings. Difference, even as

absolute, remains the distinction of the determining and the determined, and is so in both its modes (essence/Being, Being/beings). Inasmuch as it is determined in turn by beings, Being is a being and does not really become Being or essence except when it auto-determines itself. But it is still determined or relative and posits itself as the Difference of essence and metaphysically determined Being. The chiasmus renders definitively the contraries of Being and beings strictly reversible and functional and does so as far as into the Absolute. Being is taken there in the circle of the determination determining-determined and is still not really the Other (of) beings in the sense in which Finitude experiences this Other.

This is clearly what Heidegger means when he attempts to de-limit the 'absolute' Nietzschean Difference by Finitude. The development of the chiasmus, of the supposedly isolated syntax, holds above all for Nietzsche (and for Deleuze) and corresponds to the absolute-idealist usage of Difference. In 'absolute' Difference reigns the reciprocity – the reversibility – of Being and beings, or of Being and Nothingness, that *co*-determine one another. *The functional and reversible character of the differends at the interior of Difference is not delimited or impeded, as Heidegger's account would have it.* There is a continuity or an invariant of structure – the chiasmus – that comes up from metaphysics into Difference itself. Difference is the sense, the truth, the locus of Being, Difference that wants itself finally as such and no longer ontological Difference in the sense of the meta-physical. The syntax potentializes itself; the metaphysical Difference associating Being and beings is finally supposed to be capable of reflecting itself in itself and of auto-determining itself, in reflecting consequently its chiasmic structure that ensures that Being is forever mediated by already objective beings themselves. This potentialization of ontological Difference cannot therefore correspond to the *Differenz als Differenz* sought by Heidegger, in which the *als*, the *as*, signifies that it is Finitude, and not Difference itself, that is the essence . . . of Difference.

However this chiasmus of Being and beings is a law holding also, even if only partially so and its signification is thereby limited, for finite Difference: Being is here never abstracted from its relation to beings; even in its essence it continues to entertain a necessary reference to beings – here is what will remain at any rate of the chiasmus and what defines the empirico-transcendental parallelism in general. The debate between Nietzsche and

Heidegger is one of knowing: which notion of beings? Not: *which* particular beings? but: of beings as real in themselves, or rather of 'particular', that is, objectivized = present beings? The point of view of Finitude, that is, of the autonomy of the real, introduces itself into the chiasmus, while modifying the 'ontological' import (its pertinence in exhausting the-real-essence-of-the-real). Yet Finitude does not entirely destroy Difference; finite essence remains the correlation of Being *and* beings (in themselves, as non-ob-jectivizable), the One as this very correlation. *Heidegger just as much as Nietzsche continues to honour this paradigm of Difference and 'forgets' to determine the essence of the One, for his need of which no doubt its function of 'One' suffices.*

HEIDEGGER'S DIFFERENCE WITH RESPECT TO IDEALISM

1. Difference, and particularly its Heideggerean mode, 'destroys' or 'deconstructs' the rationalized forms of the transcendental, but it remains transcendental in a broad sense where it is still a thinking of the One, though in the mode of Being. Yet in general transcendental thinking, even with anti-idealist aims, normally delimits all the operations of analysis and description that it can arrange, all the possible 'turnings' to which it can abandon itself, through a preliminary reduction defining the particular space of the real or of experience of which it then looks for the essence and condition of possibility. Whether this residual ground is called *'factum a priori'* or 'fact of reason' as in Kant who designates by this the rational fact of the existence of the Sciences or of the Moral Law, or called 'the History of metaphysics' or the history of the epochs of *parousia* (*Anwesen*) as in Heidegger who himself does not escape this necessity, transcendental philosophy always will have begun by disengaging an *a priori* relation to the 'real', a relation that is itself the authentic real, philosophically elaborated, with which it deals and which it distinguishes, as primitive *factum*, from a *datum* or an experience, either vulgar or dogmatic, that it reduces: the judgment of perception in one, the natural attitude in another, the autonomy of beings in still a third. In general one opposes Husserl and Heidegger too quickly: Heidegger too plays with a reduction even if he does not content himself with it; he posits a *factum a priori* that is not that of

beings but of the *presence-of-beings* in their Greco-historical modes, that is, 'ontological Difference' as the idealized content of metaphysics. Far from being a point of arrival, if there is one, ontological Difference, in its metaphysical experience, is at the point of departure and is there already an elaborated *factum*. To designate, even before denouncing it, 'inauthenticity' as a veritable *a priori* of experience, is already a first reduction, one which undoubtedly has the particularity of appearing to deny itself as reduction, but which remains one all the same. There is no philosophical decision, even of the deconstruction of philosophy, without a prior reduction, of an idealizing sort, that isolates the object to be deconstructed and constructs it as *factum*.

2. However, the function and nature of this *factum* are complicated by the original dimension of 'Finitude'. What is it in general that leads us to believe that Heidegger ignores the reduction? Precisely Finitude. Finitude is an already philosophical thesis of the real, even if it is not exactly a reduction of the idealizing sort. In reality, there are two ways of reducing the real in the immediate and vulgar sense, and one ordinarily confounds any possible reduction with the most radical of these two forms. At once Finitude is a 'reduction' of vulgar presuppositions or of inauthenticity, *and* there is a kind of idealizing reduction that weighs on Finitude itself.

'Idealizing' reduction: this radically suspends, at least in principle, the thesis at once vulgar, dogmatic and sceptical, of the transcendence of the in-itself, according to which the real (as object or not) exists *in itself* and in an autonomous manner outside of all constitution or its being or its sense. This transcendence of the in-itself or of its auto-position is thus thought to be mere illusion or appearance. But its suspension never goes all the way to its complete destruction since this suspension always takes as its aim to operate its genesis or genealogy and, at any rate, to suppress only the in-itself of Transcendence and to conserve it in immanence. One will have recognized Husserl, no doubt, but many others as well, about whom we will not argue here, practising this radical epoche: Nietzsche first of all; partially contemporaries such as Derrida who suspend the transcendence of the referent, but in order to substitute for a finitude through ontic exteriority a finitude through 'differance' that is at once internal and external; or Deleuze above all who relates to an immanent

transcendental principle, straightaway infinite, auto-affirmative and auto-productive, the arrangements and functionings of desire; or finally Michel Henry, with aims quite different from those preceding, who declares the conditioning of Being by beings and the notion of ontic finitude sophistical and absurd. This (idealizing) reduction of all finitude is the pillar of idealism, its effect and its act of faith.

'*Finitizing' reduction*: this is still a reduction, a philosophical decision about the real, but attenuated, so much so that one no longer discerns it as soon as the radical, idealist form of the reduction of the referent and its transcendence is confounded with any and every possible reduction. Relative and no longer absolute reduction of the in-itself: the vulgar or dogmatic transcendence of experience (object-in-itself) is still denounced; the auto-position of the object-being as autonomous and not constituted becomes the expression of the inauthenticity that must be reduced. Yet, from another side, finitude, the affection of Being by beings that it does not create and that must be given as non-objectivizable, conserves a certain transcendence of beings. *No finitude, here 'ontic', without beings determining Being in return, even if finitude, one might say, is itself reduced.* The notion of finitude allows at once: (1) to pose as *a priori* real that of which thinking makes its object, no longer the vulgar concept of the in-itself (object = in-itself), but the relation of objectivity itself between Being and beings, otherwise put a *factum a priori*, that of the presence of beings rather than beings in their pure and simple affection, and to proceed thus to a first reduction of the 'real'; (2) to conserve however and to include in Being, under the name of finitude, a relation to the real in its ontic transcendence, and to avoid the illusory radicality of idealist reduction. This solution, such as is found in the avatars of finitude in thinking after Heidegger, where it will never be sublated but only transformed, is evidently drawn away from the Kantian reduction of the dogmatic and sceptical in-itself and towards the 'thing-in-itself'. The thing-in-itself is the same being as the phenomenon, as Heidegger says; it is therefore reduced, but at the same time it answers to another point of view than the phenomenon, that of the non-creation or transcendence of beings in relation to Being, the milieu in which Being must open and clear itself.

3. There are thus at least two usages of Difference: an absolute-idealist usage that entirely reduces its real moment to its ideal moment and its

a priori of objectivity and presence; and a more realist usage that refuses to sublate definitively, in Being or presence, and through these, the ontic inauthenticity which can only be thought without being sublated. The finitude of Being is not such that it would be affected by nothingness; it is that this nothingness, itself thought as relative to beings, would thus be irreducible to its being thought through, for and as Being, signing by its real transcendence the definitive failure of the 'Turning' to constitute an immanence and an autonomy of thinking that would no longer be in any way metaphysical – if not to believe itself so through a supreme metaphysical illusion.

In the first case, inauthenticity is supposed as definitively surmountable; in the second case as definitively insurmountable, with thinking held in a posture of failure, of a constitutive failure that will vow the 'forgetting of Being' to return always to its own auto-dissimulation despite the 'Turning' that makes it return *as forgotten*. What is proper to Heidegger is that he does not content himself, like the idealists who themselves also wish to think the real, with conceiving an already idealized real, a merely *a priori* real proper only to Being, *an only ontological finitude*, that is, he does not content himself with tying Being and beings in a cross or chiasmus, *but that this ontic real is supposed to conserve a transcendence that is still something other than the simple and general necessity that Being and beings co-belong to one another, that they form an ontico-ontological coupling; which is rather a sort of irreducible withdrawal, ontic withdrawal opposed this time to the ontological, and that founds this coupling, the necessity for Being not to clear itself or open itself as clearing except in and from beings.* Beings are thus still something other than their sense of Being, they are also a sort of index of the exteriority that plays the role of supplement, at once internal and external, to the presence-of-beings. *Finitude is not only a thesis of syntax; it is a thesis of reality.* The force of Heidegger in relation to Husserl, Nietzsche or Deleuze is that in maintaining a properly ontic finitude and refusing to sublate it in an idealist way in Being as ideal division, diversity or cut, as ontological finitude, he recognizes that the effort of Difference to autonomize itself and become immanent is condemned to fail because it cannot entirely sublate the autoposition of beings and their absolute transcendence which are the heart of common sense and of dogmatism *but also* the index of an insurmountable finitude that must be recognized as such. Heidegger's weakness on the other hand, a weakness from the standpoint of Nietzsche's absolute idealism, is that his finitude *risks* remaining partially realist and dogmatic, that the facticity of Being, for no longer being that of the present fact, for being transcendental, still contents itself with interiorizing empirical factuality in the *a priori factum* without daring to suspend it radically. However, one will respond that Heidegger has the merit of denouncing, in his own way, what there is of deception or illusion in the idealist reduction: since finally *even if the transcendence of the in-itself is an appearance or an illusion, this is not nothing; it must have, as illusion, a kernel of truth and positive reality that idealism denies once and for all. Heidegger is the thinker who, with Kant, denounces the illusory or deceptive unilaterality of idealism that denies the real in believing itself able solely to suspend it*. The *factum* is not entirely separable from the *datum*; it is relative to a given and not only relative to itself, and Presence, for example, is not only a foundational event of history: it is also intra-historical. But idealism will respond: Finitude is a last concession, disguised and shameful, to mere common sense.

What are we to think of this war? It is a war – it is unthinkable; we can only watch it, watch the combatants who tear each other inevitably to pieces and who know not what they do. For the moment, let us simply enjoy this inevitability and content ourselves with describing this *Kampfplatz* and this *agon* . . .

A MAXIMALIST HYPOTHESIS OF THE SENSE OF FINITUDE

1. Would Hegel's objection to Kant be valid against Heidegger as well? Heidegger continues to tie finitude to the reception of beings and therefore, in a certain manner, to the empirical. But he essentializes finitude, withdraws its empirical sense or origin from it and gives it a transcendental sense. On the one hand, he generalizes it beyond finite understanding; this is the condition for making of it an intrinsic structure of reason traversing all of reason. Above all, Heidegger is able to render finitude aprioric and essential, before raising it to the status of a principle, only because he 'de-empiricizes' it or removes from it its *ontologico-*(ontic) character of affection by an ob-ject. A cognition is finite when its apriority is receptive of beings: yet *beings 'in totality' are*

distinguished from 'particular' and 'fragmentary beings', that is, given empirically, not as a generality is distinguished, according to empiricism and the theory of abstraction, from particularity, but on the basis of the distinction of the 'thing in itself' from an empirical object. The thesis of the finitude of Being bears upon the status of beings or the real and their relation to Being; it is thus ontico-ontological, but it is not purely ontological nor yet purely ontic, that is, 'empirical' and therefore still ontological. Heidegger does not form for himself an empiricist idea of finitude but a 'realist' although transcendental one. This remains incomprehensible inasmuch as 'beings' (which Being as 'beings in totality' must surpass in order to expose itself to them and receive them) are understood as *particular* beings, that is, given objectively through Being. Not only would there then be a particularly obvious vicious circle, but this would be a confusion of the same kind as that of the 'thing in itself' with the known object. Beings that are received and not created or constituted by and in Being and that enjoy a real transcendence are to be sure not the objects themselves, that is, such and such particular beings. This is however something real, a real condition = X that affects Being. The thesis of finitude remains incomprehensible if one does not perceive in it a reprisal of the Kantian 'thing in itself', that is, a distinction that is not empiricist but realist and transcendental between 'particular beings' and beings 'in themselves'. Being and 'beings in totality' cease to be metaphysical formulae when this 'totality' no longer designates a summation or totalization of objects that is *itself objective and rational*, but a transcendental totalization of beings *in themselves*, that is, pre-objectivized.

It is necessary to distinguish with respect to *beings*:

a. the being 'in itself', the criterion of Finitude, a concept that therefore does not hold except for Heidegger and for 'ontic' rather than 'ontological' finitude;
b. the object-being, the being or presence of beings, which therefore excludes, if the transcendence proper to beings is reduced, ontic Finitude (Hegel, Nietzsche, Deleuze);
c. in the object-being (1) the *particular* or *determined* object-being; (2) its idealization or categorization: object-being *in general*, which thus must not be confounded with the being in itself.

We will take these distinctions as assumed in what follows.

2. Understood as *a priori* constituent of 'ontological Difference', as the already reduced essence of metaphysics, Finitude unites all in one piece the opposites of Being and the being = X or the being as 'thing in itself'. In this state, which is however only *a priori* and not yet transcendental, its true face already appears, namely that it is not one character of Difference among others, but the very essence of Difference. It is not the diversity of an *intra-ideal* real, as seems to be the case in Nietzsche (or Hegel) where the Will to Power signifies that an (ideal) *a priori* represents a (real) diversity for another *a priori*, where the real and its transcendence are determined integrally not only *in* but *by* ideal immanence. Difference no longer designates in Heidegger a diversity or a transcendence *by* immanence. The reduction does not suspend the transcendent (or in itself) real in the idealist manner, but only its objective particularity: it is therefore a transcendence of the real with respect to immanence in its totality or as such, a remainder irreducible to its constitution, even if it is also, or still in a certain manner – but one notes the ambiguity of the formula – a transcendence *in* immanence (the 'Turning').

Finite Difference signifies that Being is definitively bound to beings, not to 'particular' beings no doubt, but to beings considered in their real transcendence; Being is finite in an ontic but not objective manner. Being is unable to 'liberate' itself as Idea indivisibly producing its own diversity. If there is a diversity specific to Difference, it would not be an ideal and therefore real diversity, but a diversity *both* real *and* ideal which does not deny Finitude but contents itself with affirming it. Finite Difference introduces another experience of essence (whether that of Being, Nothingness, Language, Technology matters little here) already as regards its syntax (it would be not only a tension, an immediately unifying scission, but a 'withdrawal', the One as gap or tear and not as resolution), but above all as regards its reality. Real transcendence, in the attenuated form of 'Finitude', destroys, within restrained limits, Difference as reversible immanence of opposites (Nietzsche), but also especially the metaphysical conception of essence as identity 'in itself', given to a more or less originary view or intellectual intuition.

3. The hypothesis of ontic Finitude as essence rather than as a psycho-epistemological property of the understanding marks an effort not to liquidate the 'Thing in itself' but on the contrary to save it

from what still remains dogmatic and rationalist of it in Kant and in order to assign it a transcendental function. Transcendental yet not ideal: this is what distinguishes the Heideggerean usage of the thing in itself from its neo-Kantian identification with the noumenon and then the Idea, since it is the withdrawal of beings and then of the One beyond the noumenon and the rational Idea. *This hypothesis radically illuminates the difference between the 'systems' of Heidegger on the one hand and of Hegel, Husserl and Nietzsche on the other.* It suffices to give the full sense to this thesis:

> What is the significance of the struggle initiated in German idealism against the 'thing in itself' except a growing forgetfulness of what Kant had won, namely, the knowledge that the intrinsic possibility and necessity of metaphysics, i.e., its essence, are, at bottom, sustained and maintained by the original development and searching study of the problem of finitude? (*Kant and the Problem of Metaphysics*, trans. J. Churchill, Indiana University Press 1962, p. 252–3)

The majority of Heidegger's interpreters *shrink back* before this thesis, however clear it may be, according to which the essence of Being is finite if it is deployed by the withdrawal of the 'thing in itself'. This shrinking back proceeds always through an excessive idealization of Finitude, which is made into *an ontological trait*, that is, intra-ontological, while it is in fact *an ontic trait* of Being, and even a 'thesis' about beings at least as much as Being. The 'originary scission', the 'intimate connection and originary discession' must in effect be accounted for on the side of beings rather than Being and has nothing to do with the metaphysical and idealist isolation of Being that is rather the suppression of Finitude. It is on this condition that it will be finally the essence of the essence of Being. To assign finite Difference to Being and to its initiative is to idealize and to lose Finitude without meeting any opposition and to program the passage to Absolute-Logic as to what exhausts the essence of truth. The '*Es gibt*' as such, which gives Being, is not thinkable starting from Being, but from the withdrawal of beings before their illumination – which the withdrawal renders possible – by Being, a withdrawal that carries in turn the essence (of Being). This withdrawal or this absolute transcending are not theological since it is not the divine being or objectivity as divine, that recedes. Above all it is not God that recedes, but beings and then the One as non-objectivizable, and they give its dimension of question to the essence of Being.

The strength and the challenge of Heidegger are to have thought a Kantianism without physical restriction; to have universalized this in an analytic of being-there (*Dasein*); to have pushed the transcendental distinction of the thing in itself and the object or Being beyond its idealist and epistemological restrictions; to have universalized Being or the object past every limitation in the sciences, all the while guarding under the name 'Finitude' the thesis of the thing in itself; and to have thought under the name of essence the imbricated unity of Being thus universalized and of Finitude – their unity and their distinction, precisely their transcendental difference.

4. Heidegger has thus freed himself from certain objections of absolute idealism against Finitude, indeed turning the latter back against the former, saving Finitude from its psychological and empirical forms and raising it to the status of *a priori* or ontological structure (supra-general universality of Finitude or of everyday banality inasmuch as it is made *a priori*), then of transcendental essence. The distinction, identically 'real' and 'rational', intra-ontic as well as intra-ontological, between finite understanding and Reason, between finitude and the positive-Rational, the foundational distinction of Hegelianism because it allows for the preliminary idealizing reduction, loses not only its critical validity against Finitude, but also its foundational function, since it reveals itself finally to be merely intra-ideal or intra-rational. Finitude obviously does not prohibit the usage of the Idea or of Reason as particular conditions of Being, as ingredients necessary for its manifestation, but only their constitution – in the Hegelian manner – in the ultimate element of reality. It has as its function to guard Difference, 'the intimate drift of uncovering and sheltering' (Heidegger), establishment of proximity or neighbourhood, and to guard it by way of the real transcendence of the One and of beings against what most surely destroys this, the logical machine of *Aufhebung* and the superlogical machine of *Überwindung*. This real transcendence is what alone still allows for the distinguishing of the syntax of Difference from the Synthetic Unity of the I think and the real that is the element of the Dialectic.

Finitude, interpreted as transcendence of the real, as ontic and not ontological-objective transcendence, will be able then to become a transcendental trait that will confirm, as we shall see, the relay of beings by the One in this function of 'withdrawal' – indeed the very essence of Being. Understood in this way, Finitude appears as the unique means for uprooting the primacy of the Idea over the real and for relaunching in a transcendental mode, that is to say, as internal, autonomous and absolute rather than ontico-ontological (psychological, religious, political, practical and by this fact already condemned by Hegelianism), the most powerful assault against the walls of the System.

FROM THE METAPHYSICAL TO THE TRANSCENDENTAL SENSE OF FINITUDE

1. The passage from 'ontological Difference' to finite Difference as such expresses a certain 'potentialization', but includes a technical de-potentialization, its 'destruction' as meta-physical. How does Difference as such conserve Finitude?

Let us repeat. Being clears itself always *in the midst of* beings. Insofar as it has to do with any being whatsoever or, more profoundly, with the being that is not indifferent to its being, *Da(sein)*, beings (in the double sense of the objective and of the real that belongs to it) are the locale where the deployment of Being and its transcendence is rooted. Not only is it beings that Being illuminates, but Being cannot illuminate itself as forgotten except because its Forgetting still is decided in relation to objectivized or present beings. However, this still remains 'metaphysical'. We pass to the transcendental dimension of Finitude with *Dasein* when this is recognized as what projects or deploys Being as transcendence. There is not in effect any throw of Being or pro-ject except by a decision or a cut that must be said to be real and also ontic. To be sure, when we pass from the metaphysical to the transcendental plane properly speaking, it is Being or rather the essence of Being which throws itself as *Da*. However, there is here above all no simply and abstractly 'ontological', that is, ideal, primacy over the 'ontic' or the real: if

Being throws itself and illuminates the *Da* of *Dasein* which subtracts its own opening, *it is by means of a nihilating Nothingness that relays the ontic element and that is therefore the transcendental form of the 'negativity' belonging to Dasein and its de-cision* (*Dasein* is the being that, par excellence, introduces nothingness into Being). This nothingness acquires a transcendental dimension when it ceases to be assigned to some being, indeed to *Dasein* itself, in order to be assigned to the One or as One. Ontic diversity is truly 'included' as uni-que Nothingness, *but the ontic determination of Being subsists inasmuch as it is the non-objectivizable par excellence: this non-objectivizable simply becomes now the transcendental condition of the possibilization of Being.*

Thus Being is not and acts not without the beings in which it is inserted (*eingenommen*) and by which it is transfixed (*durchstimmt*); beings are the 'real' pole of Being from which it cannot be separated. Being is a transcendental for beings; it does not transcend them in the absolute manner in which one being transcends another. If an 'absolute transcending' is needed to render possible an illumination of the truth of Being itself, this would now no longer be that of some being but that of the One as indivision of this constitutive reference to the being 'in itself': a reference constitutive of Being or withdrawal-as-One. Simple 'ontological Difference' would already be a unifying scission *(Schied)* of Being and beings; it is now this correlation that is to be thought otherwise: no longer as a function of particular, objectivized or intra-worldly beings, nor as a function of the being-in-itself, but as a function of Being inasmuch as by its essence it is not only meta-physical transcendence, but immanence or indivision-(of)-withdrawal (of the 'in-itself').

2. Thinking is then a repetition of this correlation of ontological Difference by and from the One, a repetition that does not eliminate the ontic reference of Being. What becomes manifest in this repetition is in effect the difference of Being from beings: in the sense of its distinction or its ideal transcendence, but still more in the sense of this difference as such inasmuch as it contains this time a real scission. What absolutely transcends the object-being is not Being, but Being *as such*, its essence, *this correlation as such to the being-in-itself.* There is nothing here of negative ontology in this becoming-absolute of transcendence or separation; to the contrary, there is a re-affirmation of

the indivisibility of Being and beings. The essence of Being is in this indivision of its correlation to the being 'in-itself', and it is this latter that transcends absolutely and not Being in the meta-physical sense that is nothing but an abstraction from this and of which the mode of separation is here precisely what is at issue. The 'differential' character of Being ceases to be ontological so as to become genuinely 'differential': its 'difference' changes both state and function; it interiorizes itself – in becoming immanent – not to Being but to Being's essence and *as* its essence. And the essence (of Being) puts into play a moment that is real in general, ontic in particular and from which the ontological remains inseparable, if only through meta-physical 'illusion'. It is thus that Difference is the essence of the relations of the *Da* and the *Sein*. One could say in a still quite meta-physical way that it is Being that manifests itself in the locale, the *Da*, but it is rather Difference as finite (real) essence of Being. Difference as essence of nihilating Nothingness is the locale of Being's manifestation, the Same of the opening of the *Da* and the *Sein* prior to their difference reifying itself, as meta-physical, into its terms which thereby proclaim themselves to be autonomous and alternately dominate one another.

To summarize thus far, Heidegger's thinking is a transcendental analytic, itself finite, of Finitude. It sets out from Finitude as *factum a priori* after having distinguished this from the 'same' finitude as everyday self-forgetting. As *factum a priori*, it is none other than the metaphysical 'ontological Difference', not in its metaphysical self-interpretation, but for the first time as reduced to its *a priori* essence as precisely 'metaphysical'. It then seeks the 'grounds for its possibility' in Finitude *as such*, here insofar as it has become if not a principle, at least a quasi-principle that would be itself finite and have the 'form' of Turning. This tempered reduction, far from idealist, that would respect or disengage Finitude, turns out to be itself finite in its essence or its possibility. Thus the thinking that engages itself in its highest task, the determination of essence, remains throughout in this dimension of Finitude that is the making use of Difference for this very task. The essence of Finitude is itself finite in the sense that it is finitude alone that is able to become essence, and is thus capable of subtracting essence (of Being, of Nothingness, of *Ereignis*, etc.) from the empire of Logic and the closure of the Concept.

3. Finitude is thus the essence of Difference. But it is not such an essence without being in a certain manner taken up again into and structured by Difference.

Finitude has two faces: a technical and metaphysical errancy, but also a thinking that 'knows itself' to be finite and for which finitude is a means of thinking the Other of object-being. The two traits communicate: errancy and salvation adjoin one another. If Heidegger seeks the essence of the World or of Being upon the real basis of everyday banality and its instrumentality (rather than upon the idealist basis of the sciences), it is because it is there that the continuity of Finitude is experienced in its two aspects as at once distinct and 'identical': on the one hand the preoccupation, errancy and banality that are themselves self-forgetting; on the other hand *the a priori fact* of banality the condition of which is Finitude as transcendence of the real or of the being = X. Salvation is not found in the infinite dialectical suppression of inauthenticity, in its ideal reduction, but in the taking into account – something quite other than a sublating self-consciousness – of what precisely defies the calculations, whether dialectical or not, that it elsewhere renders possible: beings or the real. This taking into account signifies that the Turning 'outside of' inauthenticity is still finite. What assures the continuity of these two aspects of Finitude? *Beings*, first as particular or objectivized, secondly as real transcendence = X (thing in itself): the two senses of the word 'object' which Critique, as Kant would say, teaches us to distinguish and whose confusion marks inauthenticity as the inexpugnable residue of every objective illusion.

More exactly, the inaugural cut of finite philosophizing has the form of Difference as the in-between. It thus does not pass 'between' inauthenticity and authenticity, but in a point that is *at once* authentic and inauthentic and which is the necessary reference to the being = X as 'thing in itself': the indivision-(of)-withdrawal. This reference, this relation to beings 'in general' that is not a relation may be said to be as much the condition of inauthenticity as of authenticity. Finitude possesses two aspects between which it hesitates, of which it is the objective hesitation or in-between, only because it is already in itself Difference . . . and not only the essence of Difference. This line of demarcation is thus not neutral; there is no point or zone that would be neither authentic nor inauthentic, but all are both one and the other. This demarcation articulates the opposites of authenticity and inauthenticity in a chiasmus; it passes into and at the same time exceeds the interior of each of them. The point of application of the finitizing reduction is not a point; it is a moving frontier of displacement, a frontier of-the-empirical-and-the-transcendental – Difference itself, in its essence at least – and it is this that 'applies itself' to beings, or rather to *the relation of transcendence to beings*, redividing this always, each time, into an empirical and inauthentic version (Forgetting making itself forget) and a transcendental and authentic version (Forgetting as Forgetting).

From one (to) the other there is no neutral untroubled field, no reality to be distributed, but already the very Sharing-out itself, unruled, Difference or Di-mension without rule of sharing-out, the tension of the 'Turning'. This is why errancy, or forgetting buried in itself is an always present possibility of the Sharing-out that pivots upon this non ? pivot that it itself is or that Difference is. It is the Sharing-out itself that pivots on itself; there is no undistributed movement that would produce Di-mension *ex nihilo*. But if the Sharing-out, the Di-mension of Being *and* beings precedes these differends themselves, it is doubtful that the inaugural gesture, at once already begun and interminable, would serve to make a line of demarcation pass between Being and beings – such would be precisely a metaphysical and idealist operation – but rather between the being as ('particular') object and as thing in itself. This would be a transcendental rather than metaphysical distinction the transcendental nature of which would be experienced all the more in its being valid for what is already and in every way an indivisible relation – of Being *to* beings – a relation that *is* Finitude itself, *the* Greco-Occidental as the *a priori* of history, a relation that by definition would be able to receive this distinction and divide itself (inauthenticity and authenticity as distinct), but which is also indivisible (. . . as 'the Same').

THE IMBRICATION OF FINITUDE AND DIFFERENCE[1]

1. 'Ontological Difference', as soon as it is thought, is not an ontological thesis; it is a thesis of Finitude, of the relation of Being to beings

and consequently of the *essence* of Being. But the essence of Being is not itself 'ontological'; its essence is the imbrication of Finitude and Being or Difference. It is this imbrication that we must now think: the impact of the real on the syntax.

Heidegger wishes no doubt to think Being as Being, but such a formula is still too limiting: he thinks rather Difference as Difference. But the tautological *As* has here in turn the structure not only of Difference – it is no longer the 'as' that is applied to beings and designates the being of beings – but of real Finitude. There is a universal syntax of Difference, but *ontic Finitude is already an interpretation of this syntax and not only of the real*. Withdrawal is not merely a moment of Difference; it is itself *the* Difference as finite. Its repetition as Turning only unveils its intimate indivisibility, which it does not create, but which is necessary for it to assure its proper positivity.

Let us call Finitude, this transcendence in the form of withdrawal, the 'Other': the Other is as much syntactical as real. No doubt an absolute or metaphysical idealism would be capable of asserting this enunciation. But the Other as real is irreducible to the syntax of Difference, and if it cashes out in syntactical effects, it remains true nonetheless that Finitude signifies the anti-idealist irreducibility of the real to syntactical immanence, the primacy or hierarchy of the former over and above the latter. The Other or the cut of Difference in its idealist usage *remain intra-ontological; it is the real as cut-object, not a cut by the real in the objectivity of the object*. In Finitude, the real is not a supplement or surpassing programmed by the syntax itself, even if it manifests itself symptomatically by such a supplementarity at the interior of syntactical effects. There is a hierarchy that is non-invertible once and for all, *irreversible*, between the real and the syntax, an ultimate submission of Difference to the experience of the Other. Finite Difference is not composed solely of the principal Greco-Occidental invariant, the unity-of-scission (or inclusive disjunction in general), and the syntactical contraries of scission and unity are no longer developed only (as in Hegel and Nietzsche) in the unique element of ideality. Another couple, absolutely irreducible, comes to determine the first and is overdetermined by it in turn: Finitude is determination 'in the last instance', that is, the essence of Difference that from its side òverdetermines Finitude or gives to it its ideal and ontological conditions of existence.

2. How are Difference and Finitude imbricated? So far as scission as much as unity, difference as much as identity possess both a real side and an ideal side, this is the effect of Finitude upon the syntax of Difference. It is not possible to identify the couples term by term, scission as only ideal, unity as only real. The situation is much more complex than the simple chiasmus of Difference (to which we held in the preceding chapter) would allow it to be thought; there are many types of identity and distinction. There is a principal identity and a principal difference. They would appear when we summarize the situation in the following general enunciation: Being (being as object) is identical to beings (the unity of the conditions of experience and the objects of experience), but the being *in-itself* is distinguished from this. Or again: the being as object is identical to the being in itself, but the latter is not identical to the former. Finite Difference thus comprises two sides: a principal unilateral identity, a principal unilateral distinction. But the existence of two terms means that the unilateral distinction is also an indivision, the unilateral identity also a distinction, Being distinguishing itself at least ideally from beings. There is not a sole distinction and a sole identity, capable of being superimposed upon the couple real/ideal, but this latter, the base couple, is overdetermined by the former (identity/distinction) which is fully present *both* in the real *and* in the ideal. Finite Difference is a real distinction, operated by a term which is the real par excellence (the being, and then the One, 'in itself'); it is also an identity, that of Being or of objectivization as the intentional and ideal relation to beings. Yet conversely there is also just as much an ideal distinction, that which Being operates on its account with respect to the being in itself and which forms a system with its intentional identity to the being in itself; and a real identity, that of the distinction of the being in itself with respect to Being or to the object-being, a distinction that is immediately indivisible or that is not a relation.

Finite, that is, complete Difference combines identity and difference not only in each of the two sides as we have just established, but first of all between them if the principal identity is represented by the side of Being (ideally identical to beings) and the principal difference represented by the side of beings. As principle, in effect, as unity of Being (or the relation to beings) *and* beings (as what is distinguished in an absolute way from Being), Difference has two sides that are as much real as ideal, indivisible as divisible and that are such only through the first coupling, that which produces the essence (of Being). The unity of determination and overdetermination will not annul the primacy of the real side as difference or absolute transcending, but will reflect it in this unity that is the *essence* (of Being). Just as it will reflect in this essence the power of principal identification which is that of Being. The essence – of Being, of Truth, of Language, essence in general – thus shapes up as a double identity and as a double distinction, each both ideal and real. On the one hand essence is ideal, ontological immanence, 'Turning', but it is the One that turns 'towards' and as itself: this immanence is also an indivision untouchable by analysis. On the other hand it is ideal transcendence, scission or division that is still relative, still a relation of deployment; but it is also absolute or real transcendence, Withdrawal or One-(of)-the-Withdrawal. The unification of all these moments in essence conserves the primacy of Finitude over Difference and prevents the syntax of Difference from going all the way in its idealizing tendency and annulling this determining function of Finitude.

Let us go back over each of these two sides systematically:

a. *The side of Being.* – As 'objectivity' of beings, it is identical or continuous with the being-in-itself; the object-being and the being-in-itself are 'the same' being, but they are not said to be 'the same' except by and for Being or the object, not from the point of view of the being-in-itself. Now this very identity is ideal and divisible; it is the element of the analytic of Being. This analytic is precisely 'metaphysical' rather than 'transcendental' properly speaking; it consists in establishing distinctions in Being or the objectivity of the object, but distinctions which are still relations. But this ideal identity, fully relative to 'Being' in the metaphysical sense, will find its genuine usage, its truth and locus once it is reduced merely to overdetermining the difference of Finitude, once thinking, in passing from metaphysical Being to the essence (of Being), will find in ideality the element or continuum of 'Turning', all while it will order this element to the real One and to its Withdrawal that will 'turn' upon the use of the properties of this element. The transcendence of these properties with respect to the real 'in itself' will at once inhibit or defer Being and give to it the form-without-form of Indivision that individuates the infinite element of ideality, a real but no longer 'ontic' individuation.

b. *The side of the being 'in itself'.* – Beings are neither created nor constituted by Being, which neither constitutes nor produces anything other than their manifestation-as-*objects*; beings must be received by Being even 'before' being objectivized or manifested. This priority is no longer ideal; it is rather the anteriority of the real relative to the *a priori* itself or to Being in the meta-physical sense. We must repeat that Heidegger does not meditate upon Being, but solely upon Being's *essence* inasmuch as it gives rise to questioning. Yet in essence, and in order precisely to distinguish this from Being, it is necessary to include the structure of Finitude; this is at least the only means that Heidegger will have found in order no longer simply to have repeated the errings of metaphysics and of logic. And Finitude is a distinction that, because it is real, because it is not once again a relation or a relative, because it is absolute as a non-relation, remains forever irrecuperable, indomitable without remainder by Being, its ideality and its interiority. Finitude becomes an originary and transcendental concept once it forms a distinction, a remainder, a withdrawal that inhibits ideality itself, every ideality, even the entirely relative cuts, distinctions or withdrawals that it is still capable of tolerating.

3. Only the real 'in-itself', as beings but above all as One, is able thus to resist the power of idealization and interiorization, of identitarian presence, of Being. The distinction, forever in-distinguished, un-operated, of Finitude is no longer an intra-ideal and logical scission, nor even that of Being to beings such as metaphysics has understood it; it is not produced by the analytic of the sense or the conditions of Being. It is the difference without name, because *as such*, of the real and the ideal that limits metaphysics absolutely. So absolute is it that what it separates, the real, is no longer of the order of a category, a genus, a region or quality. It is transcendental in the sense that it transcends beyond the still relative distinction of the meta-physical, that is, of the real *and* the ideal as two exclusive regions. Heidegger took up the 'thing in itself' as the transcendental (indivisible) distinction par excellence, he took up the meta-physical distinction of Being and beings, and he made the former transcend beyond the

latter, displacing the doctrine of the transcendental, requiring that the essence (of Being) be a real distinction that really transcends – it is thus indivisible – beyond the variants of the relation Being/beings that itself would 'generalize' the problem of distinctions between genera or between categories. The 'Withdrawal' or the 'Forgetting' are characteristics of the essence of Being rather than of Being itself, from the standpoint of which it is necessary no longer, *no longer principally*, to understand them. It is surely a transcendence, but Finitude signifies that every transcendence is real in the last instance and transcends beyond Being or ontological transcending, although still within the element or the medium of Being with respect to which this finite essence, this *Un-Wesen* remains incapable of being estranged except at the risk of being 'transcendent' rather than 'transcendental'. One interprets Heidegger always in a too idealist-and-metaphysical manner; one makes of 'the thinking of Being' a continuous prolonging of metaphysics, apart from certain ideal (intra-ontological) nuances, variants or distinctions. But the thinking of the essence (of Being) must include the completely other of Finitude in essence in order to distinguish essence from Being. Being is not the genuine Other of beings; this Other must be sought as Finitude, that is, the taking into account of the being 'in itself' which alone may distinguish the really finite essence and Being or object-being; distinguish, as Heidegger says in a simplifying and misleading way, Being and 'particular' beings – that is to say the essence (of Being) and Being as object. To seek 'the Other of beings' is an ambiguous imperative both in Heidegger and beyond him and defines a direction rather than a grounded thesis. In effect: on the one hand Being is the Other of beings, but it is rather the essence of Being that is this Other; on the other hand it is the Other of particular or objectivized beings rather than of the being 'in itself' that is at stake, the confusion of Being with beings signifying here: with *particular* beings; finally this Other designates the element of the One's real transcendence, correlative to the more primitive transcendence of beings, which affects ideality and logical interiority, namely logocentrism and all its modes, dialectics, systematics, etc.

4. Finally one last paradox must be dissipated. Finitude has to do with a distinction and a 'withdrawal' that are yet at the same time 'one' or

indivisible. These are no longer relations; their essence is unary, and no longer ontologico-ideal. It is a 'scission' that is immediately the One, it is the One that is immediately 'withdrawal' and does not receive withdrawal as an accident or even as an essential property or attribute. The One cannot act except *as* Withdrawal – here is the sense of the tautology: 'Withdrawal withdraws', which signifies that it is the highest essence, not an affect belonging to Being, but Being's essence that affects Being itself. This is the resistance of a transcendence that is no longer integrally determinable by ideal immanence and that imprints upon this latter a new form of immanence, the real = indivisible immanence of the One (the 'Turning'). Essence is no longer a transcendent ideality, in the metaphysical fashion. It is rather a real or absolute transcending, obviously not a particular = objectivized being that would be transcendent in a theological fashion, but the transcending of the real *in itself* that no longer has any object-term, but that is an absolute scission. Under the name of Finitude, Heidegger thinks the absolute, real opposition, the 'Other' of every relation of objectivization, the real Non-objectivizable that is the essence of Being.

The circularity of Difference, Being preceding beings but on the condition of succeeding them as well, manifesting them but only if they are 'given' to it in a pre-objective or pre-manifest mode – as thing in itself –, is thus not a pure ideal immanence taking itself up in totality and without remainder in each of its divisions. The way in which beings precede Being is not simply identical to that in which Being precedes or surpasses them. The scission or real origin of transcendence does not exhaust itself in deployed transcendence – *these are no longer reversible* – but holds itself in or as withdrawal with respect to the latter. What distinguishes finite Difference from the idealist usage of Difference is that this gap, the scission from which transcendence deploys itself, is no longer *relative* to transcendence as it is in Idealism, is not in its turn a relation or an Idea. It is a non-relation or an absolute 'relation', in itself perhaps unthinkable since one of its 'terms' – the being in itself – is real, by definition non-objectivizable and non-manifest; and it is thinkable only through its other side, that of Being as relation (of transcendence) *to* beings, a relation which itself is ideal. Difference is indeed an indivision or a unity of Being *and* beings, and a real indivision: it is not an ideal and infinitely divisible *continuum*. Finitude is what gives its reality and consequently its indivisibility to Difference, its repulsion from every division and every integration in itself of new immanent relations. But from its other side, no longer the real or ontic origin of transcendence, but transcendence as deployment, as intentional continuity, it is divisible and able to insert new relations into itself; it is the locus where the analytic of Being or of the objectivization of beings is deployed, the divisions and new relations that philosophizing thinking operates in view of raising itself to the essence of Being.

5. The general form of chiasmus is not annulled but rather complicated, impeded, inhibited by Finitude. Its aspect was especially simple in its idealist usage, for example in Nietzsche: one of the opposites represents for itself the other opposite. The reversibility of the opposites was not merely one of their properties; it was their essence, because scission or division was in turn a relation – it was relative to another scission, etc. But the introduction of an absolute, not a relative but a real factor, of a scission that is no longer in itself a relation, that is One – but inasmuch as the One no longer exhausts its essence in unifying ideally, holding itself rather in the reserve (of) its absolute transcendence – perturbs this syntactical schema.

Finitude is thus the essence in the strict sense of what *determines*, of what contains not the empirico-metaphysical but the transcendental determination of Being. It is Finitude that gives its reality to the *real* possibility, the *possibilization* of Being and prevents its essence, its condition of possibility, from being in turn purely ideal and logical: Finitude is the real determination that at the same time inhibits the purely logical interpretation of the essence of Being. But correlatively Difference, that is, the totality of syntactical relations inasmuch as they are precisely relations, ideal and divisible, of modes of Being, represents the conditions of existence for Finitude in Being and Thought, in metaphysics and history as the history of Being. Yet it is because the ideal relations of Difference are determined by Finitude as real essence that they are able to serve as the condition of existence for Finitude, which has need of them in order to exit from its state of essence and to exist concretely in thought and history. Finally the unity of essence and existence forms a process that is the staking of itself, where this is not simply Difference, but finite Difference – that of which Finitude is not a property or attribute, but the essence – which anticipates and retrospects itself, which must become what it is. This process, full and complete Difference, may still be called *essence* (of Being), but in a richer sense than formerly. In this essence in the originary and prin-cipial sense, in the sense where essence is no doubt that of Being, but also of Nothingness, Language, Technology, etc. – there is necessarily a conciliation of the essence and the existence (of Being) which we had begun by distinguishing on a basis of metaphysical origin, but that is now partially destroyed by this imbrication of the opposites of Finitude and Difference.

Finitude, more so than Difference, renders this imbrication neces-sary and *it is this complex combination, this essential complexity of the full and complete essence* that inhibits the games of scission and identifica-tion – namely of chiasmus – that the Idea traditionally plays with itself in view of conquering a transparency and an 'at homeness', a proximity to self clothed in the colours of the oldest Occidental hopes. In this combination of two heterogeneous couples, the second destroys or deconstructs the Idealism that grounds itself upon the absolute autonomy of syntax (of Difference) with respect to the real (of Finitude), upon the radical idealization and abstraction of syn-tactical relations. So much so that the primacy or absolute (non-rel-ative) autonomy of syntax is still in itself an – idealist – thesis about reality, such a thesis being inevitable at least Finitude if is the tran-scendental essence of Being, if consequently Finitude is inalienable even in the very metaphysics and logic that would deny and yet still express it, that would be in fact its symptoms.

REVERSIBILITY AND IRREVERSIBILITY

1. The finitude of Difference corresponds to a primacy of the real over and against syntax, to which it remains irreducible. Yet the primacy of the real with respect to syntax signifies the primacy of irreversibility over and against reversibility.

In its Nietzschean form, Difference is a non-static equilibrium that proceeds through reversibility or 'passage' from one contrary to the other (rather than as one contrary *into* the other) such that neither of them definitively carries the movement or stops it at itself. Irrevers-ibility (always one side rather than the other) or disequilibrium, preserved at the very heart of equilibrium, always remain ordered to reversibility. But then everything is inverted since without ever being able to say that one of the contraries prevails over the other, it is finally this very equilibrium, the superior form of identity, that prevails over the other side – reversibility over irreversibility: proof that, by definition, *in reality* it is irreversibility that prevails . . .

Even as finite, Difference contains from the beginning an essential reversibility. It is the type of distinction that is meant to overcome the alternative: *either* the ontic *or* the ontological. It thinks the unity of contraries as indivision that escapes the division to which every idealized unity supposed as given is susceptible. And as distinction, it itself escapes as well, at least in principle, the alternative of being either ontic or ontological: when Heidegger assigns it to Being rather than to beings, it is necessary to understand these latter as *particular* beings, everyday or objectivized, since it holds also for the being 'in itself' or puts this latter into play. Its merit is even in the stubbornness and rigor with which it affirms its primacy over and against Being and beings, its irreducibility to its 'terms': it is the essence no doubt of Being, but equally of Nothingness, of Language, of Desire, etc., and its univocity triumphs little by little over the metaphysical temptation, always active in Heidegger, to say nothing of his interpreters, to localize it once again as essence of *Being*. If Being must be 'barred', it is because its essence is still more uni-vocal indeed than it. What raises itself up to the way of Heideggerian Turning or Pathmarking, from Nietzschean Re-affirmation or Reversion is not Being so much as Difference or, in all rigor, Being-included-in-Difference. Like the One itself of which it is a certain usage (in the mode of scission or transcendence), it no doubt finds itself again rather on the side of Being than of 'particular' beings, but it finds itself as well on the side of beings as pole or necessary reference. Conversely it is always a *one*-side, an indivision-of-twos, that operates the distinction; this latter is never *ex machina* but transcendental or the fact of the One. Yet this does not signify that its irreversibility would be absolute. To the contrary, that Difference would finally be reversible and capable of passing 'from one' contrary to the other, from Being (to) Nothingness for example, or (to) Language, (to) Desire, etc., belongs structurally to the iterability of the chiasmus of contraries through all of which it conserves and raises itself up as Difference. What is irreversible is not Being rather than beings; it is

Difference itself, but Difference is *at the same time* reversible. There is here a fact of structure proper to the chiasmus, and it is distinct from the dependence of the chiasmus relative to particular beings.

However we still have here a unilateral formulation which holds principally for Nietzsche rather than Heidegger. It dissimulates this: that reversibility as equilibrium of contraries is still, in its essence, a form of irreversibility and that irreversibility always prevails, but it prevails only in appearing to deny itself, *the reversibility of contraries being not a third term, but only the primacy, or irreversibility, of the positive side, of Being or of Presence over Nothingness.* The formulation above (reversibility prevails over irreversibility) betrays the fragility of metaphysical Difference, its claylike consistency, its latent finitude (its irreversibility) that it cannot deny except by re-affirming it.

2. Metaphysical Difference may always be interpreted as a symptom due to the repression of a finitude of Difference: so much so that Heidegger intends, against Hegel, against Nietzsche and all metaphysics, to reinstate irreversibility as such, *or the form of irreversibility that does not finally deny itself.* For this, he must, making use of this same schema of Difference, give primacy to nothingness as 'finite' or to the withdrawal that inhibits the side of Being, that prevents it not from manifesting itself but from constituting finally and despite everything the supreme point of view or from reinstating the primacy of reversibility over irreversibility. It is thus advisable to distinguish carefully the irreversibility or unilaterality that is no more than a moment of Difference in which it forms a system with the reversibility that is proper to the chiasmus – *and a potential irreversibility of the one side that would be grounded in Finitude, for example the Heideggerean and Derridean primacy of the cut, the withdrawal, inhibition over continuation and immanence*: here is the way, the first step, still uncertain and purely indicative, towards a radically irreversible transcendental condition that implies a meditation upon the essence of the One as such.

Heidegger has rendered thinking sensible to these full absences that remain nonetheless absences, to these presences lived in the mode of loss, to these essences that manifest themselves in the clearing of their withdrawing or in the breaking of the presence which conceals them; to the definitively *un-wesend* character of withdrawal, of nothingness, of death; to the pain (*Schmerz*) of the tearing that conjoins and that is no longer dialectical pain or the final triumph of Being, of Parousia, of Reversibility. He raises for example the concept of limit to the state of essence, he thinks limit *as* limit, no doubt, thus as immanent, as 'turning', but such that this *as* and its immanence do not finally prevail over limitation itself, that this to the contrary would still be limitation that projects 'itself' as unlimited.

There is thus Turning, but *it is finite*. Reversibility does not exhaust the real; there is a remainder that dedicates the Turning no longer to dominating Forgetting and appropriating it to itself, but to being 'operated' in the last instance by Forgetting itself. The Withdrawal 'turns' as such or comes into its appropriating essence not in the idealizing mode of a dialectical lifting or as the other of Forgetting forgotten, but in the mode, itself finite, of a Forgetting that 'turns' rather than a Turning that suppresses Forgetting. It is the real transcendence (of) the One that moves the by itself unmoved mover of Being or that gives its transcendental energy to the Turning. This explains the extreme Restraint (as essence of Being, and essence in general), that is, the Restraint that turns, neighbour to the Restraint that loses itself in itself or dissimulates itself. Through its transcendental essence, Withdrawal or Forgetting are inalienable up to the point of their foundational forgetting of errancy. Forgetting *as* forgetting is thus an ambiguous formula that may also receive an idealist sense, for example in Nietzsche. It signifies here rather that forgetting holds itself in a reserve and a transcendence still more irreducible than thinking is able currently to experience, because these are irreducible to the becoming-immanent of forgetting *as* forgetting. The same nuance holds for all the tautologies (Nothingness as nothingness, Language as language, etc.) that are unary tautologies and yet ontically finite and, more generally, *really* finite. If Difference remains 'to be thought' and holds thinking spellbound, this *to be* is no longer solely the irreversibility internal to a process or to the becoming of an immanence, but the index of a real, two-faced transcendence (unary and ontic), of an irreversibility that never lets itself be taken hold of in an ideal immanence.

3. The moment has come for us to examine the exact sense of this irreversibility. It is clear that it is the very instance of the real and that the real is conceived as Other. Difference is devoted to thinking

the real as Difference or, better, as the *differance* or *differancing* of Difference, as Other in general. Is this the ultimate experience that we have of the real? Or indeed is this an experience that is still historico-metaphysical (namely religious) and contingent? And is this perhaps, as measured against the One in its essence, a philosophical hallucination of the real? Finite Difference remains incapable of conceiving irreversibility in its positive transcendental essence, as an effect of the One's unilaterality; it conceives it only in a negative manner: (1) through correlation with a certain empirical facticity that it attempts to sublate but relative to which it still thinks the 'facticity' of the essence of Being or of Difference and consequently the essence of Nothingness or of withdrawal; (2) through the recourse precisely to (essential) Nothingness rather than to Being, to withdrawal rather than to unveiling, that is, still to one of the two contraries and to the one that appears to carry the chance of irreversibility. Thus the essence of irreversibility, instead of being thought in itself, as effect of essence, remains finally still a mode of negativity that cannot, by definition, become radically positive or of which the positivity would remain permeated by facticity.

FROM NOTHINGNESS SLAVE OF BEING TO FINITE NOTHINGNESS

Finitude does not confound itself with Nothingness, and Nothingness is not finitized unless it is itself already finite from elsewhere. This thesis needs to be tested. *Under what conditions does Nothingness acquire its transcendental truth inasmuch as this latter is finite?* How are we to pass from Forgetfulness as categorial or metaphysical to Forgetfulness as essence, that is, as the 'condition of possibility' of metaphysics and the History of Being?

1. Let us begin by assuming Difference in its metaphysical state, and provisionally suspend Finitude. What would result from this for Nothingness, how, on what grounds may Nothingness enter into Difference and receive it as essence? What is there of Nothingness in the idealist usage, 'Nietzschean' and Deleuzean for example, of Difference?

As affected by non-being, Being will remain undetermined in opposition to any 'metaphysical' type of determination. This latter concerns itself with the particularity of beings. The transcendental or unifying (-unified) All will thus be 'ontically' indeterminable, that is, more rigorously, indeterminable in the mode of ontic multiplicity. This indetermination – a point of chief importance – is not decided in relation to beings in general, but only in relation to beings inasmuch as in general they are multiple and particular: to think the intrinsic variety of Being itself is thus not to wish to break its (necessary) relation to beings. Being as such may be distinguished from the Being of beings only to the extent that its essence remains unexhausted by, not the necessary circle of the reciprocal determination of Being and beings or the chiasmus, but the functions that the chiasmus makes it fulfil from the very beginning, that is, ontically; that is, to the extent that its essence remains irreducible to the functions of foundation or origin of/for particular beings. It is solely from this point of view that it is undetermined and indeterminable or that it 'contains' a nothingness of Being-beings. It does not escape determination save through the *intra-ontic* form of determination: not that in which the determining is in turn relative to the determined, but that in which this relativity would be the sole form of determination. It is thus still determined otherwise, all while being intra-ontically indeterminable. The essence of Being has *nothing* of the ontological nor of the ontic, but it cannot remain thus surreptitiously determined as simply 'indeterminable', as *all of beings* that is *not* any particular being. To assert only the indetermination or the dissimulation/obsession of Being as the All of beings is still to think these as a function of intra-ontic determination. *To the contrary, to save indetermination, or dissimulation as such, that of the All of beings or of Being-One which is no longer solely linked to ontic plurality, is to assign nothingness to Being-One itself, or, still better, to assign nothingness to itself or to give Being-One to it.* This would mean: to guard-preserve this indetermination of Being with respect to particular beings, to prevent it from being, if not taken into the circle of Being and beings, at least opposed simply to particular beings.

Difference in general is a chiasmus and, in its superior or transcendental phase, we know that the chiasmus conserves itself, that it remains an invariant in the passage from ontic diversity to transcendental unity, that the One appears and affirms itself, certainly not in 'itself' but in the form of unifying Difference, of the indivision of Nothingness and Being, in the transcendental and no longer metaphysical sense of these words. This correlation of Being *and* beings conserves itself as such; it is not destroyed. What is destroyed is the version of this correlation as a function of ontic multiplicity, but the correlation itself is rather extracted and re-affirmed as such. In this primacy of Difference ('and') over above its terms, we may include a 'destruction' of beings in their objectivity and their transcendent and metaphysical particularity, but we must not confuse this destruction with that of beings in general. Much rather it is as Nothingness-One, unique Nothingness that this reference to beings appears in essence. Beings weigh down Being in a metaphysical manner, imposing on it their particularity and, in this way, denying or dissimulating it. This would not still be Being dissimulating itself; it would be first of all, in metaphysics, beings that would deny, divide or dissimulate Being-One; Nothingness would first of all affect Being with bad 'finitude' – this signifies that it would put division, particularization, exclusion, 'nihilism' in Being. Yet this nothingness, which is one with particular object beings, is conserved, but supra-idealized or supra-universalized in Being as the unique All of beings in general. This is why Being as essence or as 'Other than beings', to take up this ambiguous formula, would appear not only as beings in general = nothingness in general, universal nothingness (= general-empirical), but as transcendental = One. This is no longer a determined nothingness in the sense of the 'particular'; Being is not only universal (= general-empirical), but transcendental = One, and with it Nothingness which co-belongs to it indivisibly.

Being remains in every way determined, that is, relative to beings and 'beings' themselves in turn (this is the reversibility of ontological Difference). But it is, still more, absolutely determined by itself, self-determining to the extent that it is no longer only relative to beings, but relative to itself = absolute = One. Yet the other contrary, beings or Nothingness, is itself also absolutized through its passage under the law of the One and its transcendental immanence; it acquires the form of the Same: *das Nichts nichtet*. Nothingness is relative to itself or absolute; it is no longer relative only to particular beings: this formula holds *also* for Nietzsche.

2. However if the Idealism of Difference is thus capable of retaining a certain function for Nothingness and for indetermination, it is a matter of a Nothingness that is functional and determined finally by Being-One, by the One understood as Being or Idea. To this idealist usage of Nothingness, it will perhaps be necessary to oppose the notion of a finitude of Nothingness that is alone capable of saving it from metaphysical Being.

Nothingness may be attributed to Being in the sense that it is the nothingness-of-beings. But this nothingness of beings may be that of beings in general, in the sense that this generality is obtained through the destruction of particularity. Nothingness thus obtained is an empty and metaphysical generality, hardly a formal and universal *a priori*. Consequently when Heidegger 'opposes' the ensemble of beings or Being to the particularity of beings, such particularity cannot be any generality, but only an *a priori*, and this *a priori* cannot designate any empirical particularity, but only the very objectivity of the object. The Nothingness that veils Being is not the generality of Being, Being as beings in general or as any being whatsoever, but an *a priori* that is already *related to its transcendental essence, that which opposes Being to the object-being, that is, more rigorously, the finite and non-objectivizable essence of Being to the object-being. Nothingness cannot enter into the essence of Being unless it nihilates not mere empirical particularity, but Being itself as objectivity or presence.*

Thus Difference – in Heidegger at least – is the prodigious attempt to uproot Nothingness and Forgetting from their state of meta-physical subjugation, from their subjection to Being – without simply reversing the relation. It is a matter not only of giving them Difference as essence and a 'tautological' positivity: this project knows necessarily a double realization and is as such ambiguous. One may first of all correlate Nothingness once more with Being – at any rate this is what Difference always does – but in such a way that Nothingness would save itself only in its Other, in the Being of which it would become the instrument, nothing but an instrument, losing all its transcendence with respect to Being; this is Nietzsche's solution and his usage of Difference. This latter no longer plays itself out from this point on except in the Idea and in Being since the *ontico*-ontological Difference is straightaway suspended at the same time as Finitude. To the contrary, when Heidegger revives Difference as that of Being and beings, it is with the goal – among other things – of assuring, against metaphysics and Idealism, the autonomy of Nothingness and of attributing to it a positivity that it would take neither from Being nor from the Idea to which it would otherwise be the absolute slave. Nietzsche subjugates Being to Difference as transcendental principle, but he begins by subjugating the ontico-ontological form of Difference to Being or to the Idea by means of a radical reduction of every being 'in-itself'. Heidegger, to the contrary, begins by recognizing the positivity of this banalized, everyday and inauthentic form of Difference in order to posit the irreducibility of Finitude, and, in consequence, that of Nothingness to Being. Being, as 'the ensemble of beings', 'shrinks back' in relation to particular, that is, objective beings, a dis-junction or 'decision' (*Abschied*) that is given again immediately as In?decision. This latter and its transcendence hold just as well for Disjunction or Nothingness as for Being and for their co-belonging. Nothingness, the concealment of *a-letheia*, the predicament of *a-poria* – these become 'essence' and cease, at least partially, because of this real withdrawal (of) the One, being mere means relative to what they allow to be abandoned. Not only Being, but Nothingness too is spared, is not technologically exploitable, once both are finite.

Difference always associates Being and Nothingness; it may thus put itself in the service either of Being (Nietzsche) or of Nothingness (Heidegger). In the former case it claims to save Nothingness, but it only amplifies, through Difference itself, its metaphysical forgetting. Heidegger, on the other hand, registers *all* the senses and all the experiences of Nothingness even before thinking it in its indivision with Being. Nietzsche is thus able to say: *das Nichts nichtet, Nothingness or Negation* (as quality of the Will to Power) *denies*, which is perhaps still something other than the 'negation of the negation' that is developed in the ideal milieu of *Gedanke*. 'Nothingness denies' because it receives in any case its positivity from Being, from the One and perhaps from its immanence. Yet the formula would no longer have the same sense as in Heidegger where Being, which is certainly always the side taken in the debate with Nothingness or with the One, does not begin by reducing or absorbing Nothingness and its difference. The inauthentic forms of Nothingness, as tied to the transcendence of the object-being, are not reduced by Being, that is, by Nothingness-as-instrument-of Being and of the self-affirmation of the Will to Power. Not only is Being finite because of Nothingness – a banal thought, no doubt, formulated like this – but because Nothingness itself carries a finitude that does not come from Being. *Nothingness itself is finite*; it never passes to the rank of instrument of Being or the Idea, it will never be entirely destroyed in the self-affirmation of these latter. Heidegger reactivates a tautological thinking of Nothingness in order to guard it *as* nothingness (*Nichts nichtet*), not to reduce or sublate it. Nietzsche establishes the difference only of a Nothingness (already reduced by/in Being) to Being, in the infinite element of Being and its attributes, rather than 'between' the infinite and the finite, at least the irreducible finite as withdrawal-(of)-the-real.

3. In the evaluation of the function of Nothingness in Heidegger, we will thus distinguish first of all, before putting them in relation, Nothingness itself and its Finitude. It is perhaps Nothingness that introduces Finitude in a privileged way, but Finitude, imbricated with Difference, is the transcendental element of Nothingness itself. Nothingness and Finitude are always interlinked in one another, but without confusion. The reduction of Finitude, that is, of the withdrawal-(of)-the-real and, consequently, of the essence (of Being) to Nothingness has immediately an idealist sense. Heidegger's project is just the reverse and just otherwise than reversed: it is Finitude that is the non-objectivizable, non-idealizable essence of Nothingness. The confusion of the withdrawal-(of)-the-real, of Difference as scission (of) the One or as One-scission with Nothingness is the project rather of metaphysics which has always thought Being and Nothingness together. Together, but to the profit of Being, *therefore* of Nothingness (nihilism) rather than to the profit of the *and*, of their Difference but as Finitude. It is thus completely insufficient to remain content with general declarations of the passage of the nothingness of *Dasein* to the nothingness of the Being in which *Dasein* holds itself, of the indivisible co-belonging of Being and Nothingness, of Being as no-thing or nihilation of beings. That thesis is always metaphysical which says that it is Being that nihilates rather than *Dasein* as 'subject'; or that Nothingness is assigned to Being rather than to a for-itself, etc. The formula 'Being nihilates inasmuch as it is Being'

signifies that nihilating Nothingness belongs to the essence of Being, but it remains ambiguous insofar as that essence is not thought as Difference and Difference as Finitude.

Nothingness is not given indivisibly with the All of beings except as due to, in this game of One-as-Difference, its holding the place of non-objectivizable being. Beings as non-objectivizable are the nothingness of Being; this is the true sense of Finitude: Being is finite, less because of nothingness than because of beings. The inverse formula: Being is the nothingness of beings or is nothing of beings, is a metaphysical formula (among other things, Kantian: Being is nothing of the real in the sense of *res*) that presents an ambiguity since Nothingness here repulses not only particular beings, but the being in itself, which can only increase confusion and make it appear in a nihilist way that nothingness is opposed to beings, thus rendering it impossible that beings would be 'saved', that is, thought not as identical to Being (nihilist conception of Being as nothingness of beings), but *as co-belonging to Being or to the essence of Being*, in the One-as-Difference that holds them indivisibly adjoined. Nihilism is founded upon the identity of Being and Nothingness and upon the opposition of Nothingness to particular beings rather than to their very objectivity or presence. The thinking that overcomes nihilism gives back to Nothingness a positivity that it is able to find only in the One: no doubt partially in the power of the Same to hold Being and beings, Being and Nothingness, in their 'reciprocal' opening; but fully only in the One inasmuch as it is the means of Finitude and is itself finite, that is, not immediately identical to Being or to the Idea, identical rather to a certain real transcendence or withdrawal 'beyond' or 'in the margins of' Being.

NOTE

[1] Given their technicality, the following three sections may be skipped on a first reading that would only want to follow the essential line of demonstration.

CHAPTER FOUR
Hegel and Heidegger

INSUFFICIENCY OF THE SYNTAX AND
THE PASSAGE TO FINITUDE

1. In order to treat the problem of Finitude to its fullest extent, it is necessary to pose not only the question of Finitude as essence of Difference, but – this is another aspect of the same question – what distinguishes 'Difference' and the dialectical 'Concept'. To what extent is Finite Difference 'dialectical' in the Hegelian sense or interpretable from this standpoint? We know that there is an inexhaustible problem here clarified little by Heidegger himself. In any case, the ways of conserving and suppressing, of arranging the given are not the same in Difference and in the concrete Idea precisely because this latter is meant to be all reality . . .

Difference is circularity, even if its circle is open and unlimited; it is the passage from one contrary to the other in both directions, reversibility: Being manifests beings which have need of it, but Being itself has need of beings in order to surpass them. Continuous surpassing and 'situation', comprehension and fluency co-belong to one another originarily; there is no third term, but only this co-belonging, this reciprocal natality which is their essence. Such circularity is the weakness of thought, its 'finitude' understood in a vague and general sense, but also its force, its autonomy. Such syntax says nothing yet of the nature of facticity, of this insurmountable portion of shadow or reality that affects thought even in its effort – thus finite – to overcome it. The in-between of beings and Being, of the manifest and manifestation is indeed essence itself as 'difference', but such circularity is so general a constraint that it has been recognized by all unitary philosophies. Even in the form of the subject–object relation which is itself never simple, which is always the supreme transcendental unity or indivisible immanence of subject *and* object. And above all by absolute Idealism which has made this law of thinking explicit and has placed it at the centre of its interest.

Thus *solely from the point of view of syntax*, Difference appears to offer certain guarantees to *Aufhebung*. It is a reversible immanence of contraries, each opposite being *one* with its other and with itself, and therefore also the contrary of itself. All the more so given that 'Finitude' and 'Absolute' are not, contrary to what is usually said, always and necessarily strangers to one another. Finitude must become absolute all while remaining finite, and the Absolute is not without a scission signifying its finitude. Through its syntax or internal articulation, as synthetic or unifying Unity that is immediately a scission, as tension or non-tearing of the tear, Difference responds at any rate to the sole invariant in which Occidental thought will have been able to hope to close itself through its own forces, since here is the very essence of the invariant, that which contains the immediate identity of the invariant and its variations, the superior equilibrium where the disjunction of contraries ensnares itself – *enlyses* itself perhaps – where it raises itself up as Unity-of-disjunction par excellence, where primitive duelistic thinking plunges back into itself, confirms and intensifies itself, elevating the triumph of Duality-as-One above its ruined terms. Difference does not exceed, *in its general conception of the mechanism or syntax of essence*, the Greek horizon; and as for the Hegelian horizon, perhaps it does not exceed this either save for this immediateness in the indivision of contraries.

Its efforts to distinguish itself from any dialectical identity in which the opposites pass *into* one another, and to affirm the simultaneity, the hesitation of their indivisibility *and* their alterity, do not cause Difference in any case to exit from the ideal of the *coincidentia oppositorum*, but rather to carry this to its most positive essence, that is, outside its dialectical Hegelian form. Scission does not oppose itself here to anything other than the dialectical-ideal form of coincidence, not to the irreducible form to which it would rather carry it. The *coincidentia oppositorum* is able to lead to an ideal and remainderless identification of opposites, but just as well to indivision in the mode of a discord which, far from sinking into a dialectical resolution, re-affirms itself as *a priori* hesitation or discord. Even as post-dialectical adventure, Difference does not reach Being as 'pure Other' (Heidegger) of every 'being' except in confiding the Other to alterity or to transcendence even *before* confiding it to the sole immanence of the One. In its desire everywhere to substitute alliance and affinity for oppositions, inclusion for exclusion, supplementarity for complementarity, the One that claims mediation without being itself mediated for the mediated One, but also Combat for dialectical Resolution and the Conciliating for Reconciliation, Difference does not really change the question – the Greek question – but is content merely to recast this in a play of mirrors.

No doubt in order to save Difference and to distinguish it from Dialectic, we may go so far as to say that the contraries are not mutually enveloped and finally identified by Difference. No more than either one of them may appear simply as an imperfect immediacy or an accident of the other: withdrawal is not an accident of disoccultation; it is its essence. But to the extent that the exact range of 'withdrawal' is not elucidated and distinguished from the reversible and metaphysical form of Difference, Difference always risks being submitted to the *Hegelian logic* of 'Essence', without its positivity and immediateness, its 'affirmative' character being sufficient to resist this re-appropriation, or at least to resist it in an indisputable way without any chance of return.

'The true is the becoming of itself, the circle which presupposes at the beginning its own end as its aim and which is effectively real only for its developed actualization and in consideration of its end' (Hegel). What is the content each time of originary Difference, which moves in a circle and which in one case founds a finite circularity and in another an infinite circularity? We should say: *rather* finite in one case, *rather* infinite in the other, since a circularity is always precisely both a finite and an infinite syntax. A supplementary determination is needed to decide whether it will remain rather 'finite' even while not ceasing to be an interminable movement, or rather infinite, that is, freed in the last instance from the finitude which was however not alien to it. A certain invariant syntactical process of thought was recognized and identified as much by Hegel as by Nietzsche and Heidegger by means of a return to the at once duel and unifying Greek experience of thinking – a return to Heraclitus. Each of these thinkers has tried to give weight and reality to this syntax of the identity of difference and identity, from which none moreover has claimed to exit, but which each to the contrary has wished to lead back to its accomplished essence. This is why it is insufficient merely to take inventory of the structures and syntaxes of thought, which quickly proves undecidable among these authors. The exclusively syntactical point of view might indeed be already a certain conception of reality, a conception that is precisely idealist and that would level the reality of the differends: this will be the criterion that distinguishes Heidegger from the tradition.

2. The insertion of Finitude into Difference – and of Finitude understood as real (ontic and then unary) – allows for the liquidation of the appearances of the identity or even the simple opposition of Heidegger and Hegel on the one hand, and Heidegger and Nietzsche on the other, appearances which we know have been able greatly to mislead or even render mute certain interpreters. Such levelling of Finitude in its strong and precise sense has alone permitted the belief that Heidegger merely repeated the schemes of thought already mastered and exhausted by Hegel's Logic or by Nietzsche, of whom nothing, no 'specific difference' would distinguish him finally from Hegel. It is not in effect any *specific difference* that distinguishes Finitude from the System; it is a *real difference* – (of) the real: real – *and transcendental*. From a certain point of view Heidegger cannot claim to have outflanked the closure of the Hegelian *Concept* except by giving the appearance, like all those who have searched for the 'real' that Hegel misses, of a 'stepping-back', of a pre-Hegelian regression: like Feuerbach, Kierkegaard and others. It would be a matter here of a Kantian regression. Yet on the one hand the Kantian apparatus is purified in Heidegger of its epistemological determinations and constantly generalized in view of the conquest of a horizon of Being that would be really universal and no longer simply rational = general = regional; this implies a radically non-rational concept of Difference. On the other hand, the real, in the name of which thinking tries

once more to circumvent the high walls of the System, is in Heidegger no longer an empirical and given form of the real, a mode of the object (the sensible Object, the Thou, the I, Practice, etc.), but the real inasmuch as it 'holds itself' precisely in withdrawal, more exactly as it (is) withdrawal, the non-objectivizable par excellence or the transcendental form of the non-objectivizable. In rescuing the 'thing in itself' from its theological origins or uses, in elevating it to the status of essence or in requiring that the thinking *of* Finitude be still in turn a finite thinking, Heidegger seems not to regress in relation to Hegel except insofar as he initiates (let us here withhold a last reservation) the only 'hither-side step' still possible, the only 'withdrawal' that would no longer be relative (*in relation* to Hegel *and in view* of another term), absolute withdrawal, without term, and without term because the One – the real – is no longer a term in a relation.

3. It is thus that Difference, which Heidegger says has been effaced by the subject–object relation and also by Idealism, through the very usage that Idealism has made of this relation which it has transformed and generalized, is not reducible, in its essence, to this circularity in general, for example to its Kantian, Hegelian, Nietzschean or hermeneutic versions. The nature of Difference is not only a certain anticipating-retrospective articulation of Being and beings: its concrete mode of articulation must and can be specified only as a function of the reality in general of its terms, a reality that may, for example, consist of a certain ideality, *ens imaginarium*, of Being as active no-thingness. The syntactical couple is also in general a real couple; its terms have a determined content of reality. It is only on this basis, that of reality and its modes, that finite Difference may be distinguished from its idealist-objective form. Heidegger cannot save the Difference as such of the differends from the idealism of Hegel and Nietzsche except by saving in point of fact the differends' reality from its idealizing reduction or its interiorization by relations and syntaxes, by preserving it from the latent idealism of Difference and its bacchic delirium. The finitude of Difference signifies that the 'terms', the differends rather, are not content to arise and to perish in the continuum of a movement that itself would neither arise nor perish and which would thus constitute their effectivity, their in

itself, but that they resist their birth and death in and as this effectivity and that essence – this would be so difficult to think precisely because this still remains 'to be thought' – is the unity of this movement, but only when it loses its effectivity and when its infinite reversibility becomes poor and simple 'Turning' (Kehre) rather than Circle of circles. Finitude is this withdrawal of differends that refuses to accept interiorization and idealization in a supreme Idea that would exhaust the real without remainder. The primacy of the side of nothingness, withdrawal, dissimulation, the primacy of inhibition, delay, difference, no doubt changes almost nothing, from the syntactical point of view, of the quasi-'dialectical' character of Difference. But the syntactical point of view is abstracted outside of the real that it articulates, and this primacy expresses in its own way the most profound distinction of Difference from Hegelian Dialectic: Finitude, of which such primacy is the symptom. Perhaps one cannot isolate a supposedly pure and abstract syntactical point of view, with Finitude being thus suspended. In fact, Finitude is not suspended by Idealism; it is denied. It is thus in general from the point of view of its point of application, from the type of real to which it applies itself, that Difference distinguishes itself, possibly even syntactically, from the dialectic of the pure Idea. However things stand with regard to its point of application, finite Difference separates the Idea from the One or beings, which are the two possible indices of the real, through a transcendence that is the index of their reality and irreducibility. Relative to the dialectical-idealist usage of the Unity of contraries, Difference is precisely difference as such in the strict measure that it refuses to reduce the two poles of beings and the One to ideal immanence and affirms a moment of real, ir-reducible transcendence, even if this co-belongs to ideal immanence. It is this which inhibits the attempt of the idealizing reduction of the real 'in itself' of which we have seen that it was the preliminary condition of the idealist usage of Difference.

4. What then distinguishes in the last instance, under the name of Finitude, the Absolute as parousia of the supreme Idea and the Absolute of finite Difference, if this very distinction refers to the constitution of the reality of Difference and of the differends themselves? Hegel thinks Difference as the self-sameness of consciousness or of

the Idea. So that differends will be purely ideal or *a priori*, these are organized through the ideal structures of the objectivization of beings or of Being (Hegel is in a sense even more and even more radically than Heidegger a philosopher of Being; he inscribes Difference in the pure *ontological* element), purely ideal divisions and identities – and real only inasmuch as ideal. Beings do not appear in self-consciousness or in the Idea except under the form of its objective-*a priori* structures, except as object or correlate of objectivization, except as a diversity the transcendence of which is integrally determined not only *in* but *by* the immanence of the Idea which remains itself in objectivizing and alienating itself, of which the alienation is not sufficiently radical to be without return or without accomplished (remainderless) reversibility, since *it is merely an alienation in the objectivity of the object, and not in its reality inasmuch as this latter would be something still other than its objectivization: the absolute de-limitation of objectivization.*

In having substituted Will to Power for Self-consciousness or the pure Idea, Nietzsche has not fundamentally exited from this if not Hegelian than at least absolute-idealist terrain. Hegel already surpassed the phenomenology of self-consciousness, but this was in order to retain, like Nietzsche after him, the reduction of all the reality of beings to their object-form or to the ideal structures of their objectivization. What is a *differential* 'relation of forces' for Nietzsche? It is the *a priori* structure of experience, the *a priori* or ideal constituent of the Will to Power that would be from its side its transcendental essence, its supreme principle of unification. Now such a relation is truly a 'difference', but this difference is integrally relative and ideal as a relation, each of the differends exhausts itself in its relativity to the other. Real beings are only a moment of the ideal field of presence, a field of presence that is never really present. It is not the Will to Power itself that would be able to escape this idealization and this reversibility without remainder of opposites. As the essence or possibility of relations of force, it is the transcendental and therefore real = indivisible factor, which communicates its reality to the otherwise divisible relations. But this is a 'mere-bit-of-reality' that it communicates to them: the One of the Will to Power is immediately closed upon the Idea and effectuated in the relations. There is an immediation of the Idea and the One, of ideal and real immanence.

It must be called precisely 'difference' (cf. the reinterpretation of Nietzsche by Deleuze, and Deleuze's entire oeuvre), but it remains at once *either* strictly unthinkable and merely postulated *and/or* immediately thinkable as simple Idea or purely ideal and divisible structure. This difference is simply itself infinitely, unlimitedly at stake; it is *integrally reversible*. The final triumph of the Will to Power over reactive forces and gregariousness is programmed straightaway as possible without remainder; gregarious inauthenticity and evil are only the appearances and phenomena of a supposed mimesis having no reality other than that of their objectivization-without-being, reality-without-the-real. Every idealist usage of Difference, from Hegel to Nietzsche, conceives the *division* or *distinction* internal to Difference as having no more 'reality' than that of a relation, as being merely (according to the precise formula of Deleuze with respect to 'desiring machines', that is, 'relations of force', the *a priori* of Will to Power or of Desire desiring) *'object-cuts'*. This formula is to be taken precisely in the sense that the real, the only real diversity tolerating the Idealism of Difference, would be the diversity of objectivity or the *a priori* itself, and not an ontic-real diversity independent of the ideality of the *a priori*.

ABSOLUTE FINITUDE: AGAINST ALIENATION

1. Thus any too quick identification of Heidegger and Hegel, of finite Difference and the Concept, cannot but deny what distinguishes *in the last transcendental instance* the former from the latter, namely Finitude as the anti-idealist thesis of a withdrawal-(of)-the-real (either ontic or unary) 'in relation to' the ideal element of the relations: the 'thing in itself' beyond the object that Heidegger tears away – need we even say this? – from its epistemological context, both idealist and empiricist, in order to find in this 'absolute transcending' of beings and the One 'in relation to' Being, beyond the *a priori* (and beyond a transcendental essence that would be in turn nothing but a superior form of the *a priori*), the means of safeguarding Difference from its auto-interment in its own ideality, its degeneration in itself, its accommodation to its own latent idealism.

This resistance does not exclude the Absolute; one cannot simply oppose Finitude to the Absolute. Finitude excludes or limits only a certain idealist interpretation of the Absolute, but remains itself unconditioned as Finitude. Instead of the Absolute prevailing over Finitude and being its essence, it is rather Finitude that is the essence of the Absolute. But of this finitizing essence, we may say that it is, in its own way, absolute, in the sense that Heidegger, far from abandoning Finitude itself – the transcendental source of everyday degeneration and banality, of the 'natural attitude' – to this banality and this empiricist degeneration, for example to the 'finite understanding', instead assigns to it a structure that is itself differential and an essential, transcendental function of Difference. Of finite Difference we thus will not be able to say that, because of its absoluteness, it is near to itself and to us as being at home with itself, a parousia of the Absolute, pure unveiling that finally would not know Finitude. This withdrawal or veiling resists the *parousia* of the Absolute, but becomes, in its own way, the Absolute.

Finitude is alone capable of saving Difference, not from the Absolute but from the ideal form of the Absolute, from its levelling by the logical machines of Hegel, Husserl and Nietzsche. The Absolute is no longer what *super-sumes* difference and retains itself beyond itself as near-to-itself, it is what overcomes difference in a Turning that never achieves nearness to itself, that is rather retained or withdrawn outside of its *self*-transparency or *self*-manifestation. Difference, as syntax in which scission is supposed never to be entirely recovered in the Absolute coming back to itself, ceases to be 'a moment of the supreme Idea', of the self-reconciliation of the Idea or of Self-consciousness, that is, of objectivizing-objectivized or self-reflecting structures. There is no alienation and reconciliation: *the finitude of Difference is not what alienates Difference outside of itself.* Difference is not an Idea, and above all the real of Finitude is not an alienation internal to the Idea. *It does not risk exiting from* itself, because its essence is precisely already and definitively real scission, a scission that is not internal to the Idea and its power. This secession is too essential, too structurating of Being still to be a surmountable moment: Difference is not itself or does not accede to its own essence except as di-fference, a scission so insurmountable that it is no longer the simple scission of a prior unity; an 'alienation' so positive that it is no longer alienation. We will not confuse the relation and the non-relation of *Ereignis* and *Enteignis* with any dialectic or 'sublation'. The primacy of di-fference over reconciliation signifies that this scission is such that it does not *reconcile*, that it is no longer a means for some reconciliation greater than itself, *but that it is the absolute emergence, once and for all, of conciliation (Versöhnung), of the One as such or as the Conciliating-without-synthesis. Conciliation, as One that emerges in the form of an originary scission without ever through itself giving rise to a Reconciliation that would be made at the expense of the scission, is rather the essence of absolute Reconciliation and the workings of the Concept. Conciliation* is not a self-differentiation or self-engendering like those of the Absolute Idea; the differentiation prevails over the *self-* or the *Selbst*, that is, finally over the Absolute understood in advance as All. The withdrawal (of) Finitude is what inhibits the self-re-affirmation of the Idea and the All.

2. The *Schritt zurück* thus can be neither the negativity of which the supreme Idea has need provisionally in order to reconcile itself with itself beyond the nothingness of the 'finite', of finite determination. Nor even the retrospective distanciation of Being, which is identical to the surpassing of beings. The *step(-in-)reverse*, or backwards step, is not programmable through the reversibility of the chiasmus, is not the moment of irreversibility that co-belongs to the circle of metaphysical Difference or hermeneutics: it is a dimension completely other with respect to the chiasmus and its purely syntactical withdrawal; it is the withdrawal-(of)-the-real to the margins of ideality, of its circularity and its games. The penetration into what is proper to metaphysics is not even the contrary of its sublation in the Absolute Knowledge in which Reason grounds itself and attempts to render itself autonomous with respect to this Dimension; the deconstruction of Being is not the contrary of its construction in Absolute Knowledge. It is the instauration of a *proximity* or *neighbourhood* that does not imply any identification or exclusion since it is neighbourhood as 'originary scission', the continuity of a topology founded upon a reserve and immediately identical (to) a withdrawal. Difference *inasmuch as* Difference: this *inasmuch as*, this *as such*, these are no longer merely ontological (Being or beings *as* beings), ideal and hermeneutical; they are, quite paradoxically, the sole tautology

that would dare say itself of an absolute scission (of) the real, of a secession (of) beings.

There is no opening that would be an asserting of one differend by another except as due, more profoundly, to the opening made through the unilateral withdrawal of beings before the force of Being, a withdrawal that is not opposed to Being but that renders it possible, as it renders possible the sheltering of beings in Being, their becoming-present (or, in a broad sense, 'object'). *The pure Idea ceases to be the essential element, self-moving; it is relegated at the very most to the status of essential condition of metaphysical or ontological existence or of Finitude.* 'Being opens in-the-midst-of beings' does not signify that beings are *the milieu* of Being; it is rather Being that is the milieu of ontological existence or of the manifestation of beings, yet beings as *il-luminable* (non-'luminable') belong in any case to the essence or the 'condition' of illumination, even if this does not suffice to define them completely.

THE ABSOLUTE AND ITS TEARING: PAIN AND PHENOMENOLOGY

1. The transcendence with which we are concerned is not that *of* the real or *of* the One, in a Platonizing manner. It is the real or the One that (*is*) this transcendence: thus Difference would have it. Moreover a transcendence (of) the One in relation to the Idea, the manner in which Difference combats Idealism 'from above', is necessarily of a piece with this other transcendence that is equally 'real' but in an ontic sense of the real which no longer holds for the One, that (of) beings in relation to the Idea. One must keep these two points in mind.

Heideggerean tautologies (of Being, Nothingness, Language, etc.) are of immediacies. Yet these are not secondary immediacies produced by the accomplished mediation of an abstract or primary immediacy. This Hegelian interpretation is not especially pertinent and it is always necessary to save the specificity of Difference. In Difference, immediacy is immediate in a transcendental sense, as the immediate given of the One (at least assumed as such, since at the same time, as we know, Difference does not rightly conceive this immediate donation which must rather be that of the One (to) itself), and this as against mediation as 'particular' ontico-ideal operation (Heidegger), that is, as objectivizing. This is an immediacy alien – *at least in principle or in its intention* – to the mediation of scission, of nothingness, of transcendence inasmuch as one would understand these as 'particular' and transcendent operations: it suffers these, rather, and is constrained to uniting itself to them. The only mediation of empirical immediacy – a mediation compromised by this as a result – will not suffice to produce a qualitatively different and 'essential' immediacy if it is not, by its essence, this other immediacy already, and if this latter is not already recognized as such for this very essence instead of being simply produced. The immediateness of essence should rather be, as far as its 'relation' to a mediation, *a remainder, a residue irreducible to the operation of mediation upon the empirical*. It could be that in the Dialectic such an immediacy would be *also*, despite everything, an irreducible and non-constituted remainder, or even, perhaps, that there would be a continuous identification between this transcendental residue of immediateness and the operation of mediation itself. But it is the specificity of thinking in a 'transcendental' rather than 'dialectical' mode to have to want the recognition of this immediacy *immediately* as what it is or *as such*, independently of mediation, at least of that which is the objectivization of empirical immediacy. It rejects this outside of the immediate essence that it does not accomplish positively, but of which it is the instrument, the negative but in no way positive condition, and through which essence extricates itself without having to integrate the determinations and effects of this 'particular' or objectivizing mediation upon the empirical.

2. In fact the real situation is a bit more complex. For if Difference is an immediacy that does not realize itself as the product or result of a work of mediation, it remains no less subjected to *the pure essence of mediation inasmuch as this latter is indeed Finitude or real transcendence.* Subjected not to its concrete work, but to it *as such* or as 'real' scission (of) Finitude, still susceptible, however, of becoming immanent to itself. *Difference, here as elsewhere, frees itself from 'particular' mediation, but not from the essence of mediation as such or Finitude.*

So much so that in a sense Difference seems to invert at its own expense the situation of the Dialectic. In the Dialectic mediation is finally itself suppressed in the Absolute and its parousia. The Absolute of the Concept is not unaware, perhaps even in its essence, although this remains uncertain, of scission, but what it is unaware of in every way and leaves outside itself is scission as Finitude or the transcendental distinction of the object-being and the being-in-itself. To the contrary, Difference is finally subjected to this at the very moment when it seems to free itself from its particular work, that is, its phenomenal and objectivizing work. It affirms mediation in its unobjectivizable essence without suppressing it dialectically, in suppressing only its particular forms. The Dialectic suffers from an excess of logical, ideal, metaphysical positivity and does not take mediation seriously enough, assigning it to the understanding, that is, reducing it to an ideal operation and thus losing its essence. Only 'Finitude' is capable of taking mediation seriously, but this implies its conservation *in* or *as* the essence of Difference.

Here, from the syntactical point of view, is its distinction from the Hegelian *Concept*: it remains fundamentally a chiasmus, a play of opposites that does not survey them 'dialectically' or, rather, does not survey them in a 'rational-positive' manner, and thereby avoids rejecting scission itself as an attribute of the understanding, thus 'of' the dialectic and its bad unilaterality. Difference finally does not oppose the unilateral work of the understanding and the unifying positivity of Reason. Nor no doubt did Hegel oppose these in the sense that he re-unified them. But the genuine problem is that their unity in the element of the Idea as 'real', of the ideality of the Concept, is still a form of identifying exclusion *from* the point of view of Difference itself which is not grounded, like the Concept, in ideality, but conserves of ideality only division as real 'in itself' or inasmuch as this is susceptible to being thought from here on as the real One. As soon as scission is no longer 'finite', non-objectivizable and non-objectivizing, as soon as it becomes that to which ideality is susceptible and in which the One is thus occluded and becomes objectivizing-objectivized scission, as soon as transcendence is no longer *to think* through and as Turning or as One, and the One from its side is no longer affirmed in its immediateness beyond ideal unity, as the attempt to make of it transcendental thinking – scission suffers this characteristic exclusion/

interiorization of *Aufhebung*, but not of Difference, which, from this very fact, annuls and interiorizes it finally in the Idea.

3. Finitude as transcendence (of) the One cannot but introduce a distortion into the dialectic of the pure Idea. Instead of the side of Being or presence prevailing once again over Nothingness, not only over the empirical forms of Nothingness, but essential Nothingness itself, with Reaffirmation triumphing over Nothingness as reduced to the level of 'surpassed' instrument, as interiorizable absolutely and without remainder in essence – this is the case in Nietzsche as well as Hegel –, it is rather the side that by essence testifies to *the relativity of Being to beings understood as 'things in themselves' or as real rather than as objects,* Nothingness, that prevails in essence precisely due to the primitive irreducibility of the real to Being.

Let us repeat this problem. The clearing has its essence deployed not in itself, but in withdrawal. The opening is a recurrence in and of dissimulation; it emerges as an absence more profound and more permanent than the absence of particular beings, also more immanent than they because it has the 'form' of the Same and because 'withdrawal withdraws', which signifies that it withdraws *itself* or that it is the essence of unveiling. This essence takes or transfixes withdrawal and does not content itself with being only its still transcendent 'condition of possibility': it is a transcendental and not merely *a priori* condition. Heidegger proceeds in his own way to a *Transcendental Deduction*, desubjectivized and deontologized, of Being and the clearing from withdrawal-withdrawing. Here as elsewhere, the withdrawal or the veil does not affect Being from the outside; no longer has (only) an anthropological nor even an ontological root: withdrawal must be thought as essence, that is, from itself and as 'essential' tautology. But tautology of dissimulation or Forgetting: it is thus an in-essentiality that ceases to be an accident or an 'adjunction' (Heidegger), and that conquers the space proper to positivity that returns to essence even when it is Nothingness that fulfils its functions. Heidegger attempts to liquidate the romanticism of Forgetting as obscure and unconscious ground; he raises withdrawal to the status of essence and experiences essence as a '*self*-withdrawal'. Being or rather the essence of Being is this withdrawal-self-withdrawing in the opening of beings as such. Appearance is immediately an essential Non-appearance, the essence of Non-appearance par excellence. If the passion of unveiling may be attributed in all rigor to human being, the passion (of) withdrawal, passion (of) the-veil-veiling-itself, of the Forgetting more profound than any forgetting, transcendental weakness more autonomous than any failure of Memory, may be attributed only to Being, that is, rather to the essence of Being. Here is the transcendental and no longer empirical concept of Finitude, which is another way of saying that if not Reason, if not even *Dasein*, if not even Being, at least Being's essence is the 'making itself finite' of finitude, the immanence of a 'finitude-that-finitizes'.

The final reason for this fact is that finite Difference postulates a transcendental experience of the One as immediation (of) a withdrawal or (of) an Other in the element of which it inscribes mediation *as such*, rendering secondary the ontological-ideal synthesis of contraries and the usage of negativity as instrument. Certainly Dialectic must also – like any other philosophy – 'postulate' the immediate experience of the One, but it does so in the mode of a synthesis or an Idea, of a purely ontological element that *a priori* reduces every 'thing in itself' or Finitude, that *a priori* dissolves ontological Difference *as such* in the closure of the Concept. Against this latter, Difference puts forward, with more or less anti-idealist rigor, the affirmation of the immediateness of Finitude as such and the irreducibility of the Other to the ideal identification of contraries. All the effort of the Dialectic is in order to suppress Finitude, while that of Difference, even Nietzschean or metaphysical, is in order to give to Finitude an immediateness that acts without ideality thereby – armed not with nothingness but with negativity – coming to sublate or suppress it.

Measured to the operation of the Concept, Difference reintroduces a transcendental rather than metaphysical or ontological style and, in this conception of the transcendental that it recovers from the tradition, it introduces with more (Heidegger) or less (Nietzsche) vigour a thinking of Finitude. It elaborates precisely a transcendental or unary concept of Finitude, which it saves from its empiricity through recourse to the immediateness of the One rather than through its suspension, reduction or prior rejection, its reduction to a moment to be mediated in the *purely ontological* manner of the Dialectic that is content to deny Finitude in order better to enjoy its own limitless self-intoxication.

4. All these differences are decisive for the interpretation of the central thesis: 'the Absolute is identically its own tearing', which is present in Heidegger as in Hegel. In the former case, the tearing of the Absolute is truly the mode, and the only mode, in which it is experienced. Nothingness is not that of the object-inasmuch-as-finite (Hegel), it affects even Being and it is when the *presence* (of beings) is broken and suspended by the withdrawal of the being in itself that it reveals itself and is caught hold of again in its absolute source. The break to which Heidegger exposes phenomenological experience is not that of the object-being at the interior of objectivity; it is that of objectivity globally, that of the presence of beings inasmuch as, to be sure, they tend from the very first to confound themselves with particular beings aimed at this interior, for example, in a relation of tool-hood. Once this mode of presence is broken, presence *itself* is able to manifest itself. Beings manifest themselves in their being, no doubt, but in the sense that it is the being of *these* beings – of *being(s)* rather, not of these particular beings themselves in their particularity – that manifests itself and attains to its proper essence. Nothingness intrinsically and definitively affects Being, that is, the *relation* of Being to beings: nothingness is not a term of the relation (beings = nothingness . . .), it *is* or affects the relation of opposites and in consequence the essence of Being still more profoundly than Being itself. It is this that we intend by saying: Difference saves mediation, or rather the essence of mediation, while the Concept annuls mediation in its idealization, its final suppression in a 'real' of 'result'. As if, paradoxically, there were to subsist a certain *indifference* (in the sense, to be sure, of in-Difference, of the idealist refusal of finite Difference), between the ontic sphere of the 'contingent', which Hegel abandons to its infra-rational idiocy, and the work of the Concept.

In the second case, in effect, the tearing of supreme Unity does not really belong to its most intrinsic and most positive essence. It lacks Finitude, or Finitude is for it no more than a means, an instrument qualitatively and essentially distinct from the Absolute and destined to be suppressed globally. The Absolute in its idealist form (Hegel, Nietzsche) programs *in the last instance* the destruction of Nothingness (that is, of the real transcendence that alone is able to assure the irreducibility, the resistance, the remaining of Nothingness with respect to the Idea), *the accomplished negation of the negation* (or again, all else being equal, the destruction *through itself* of the Class Struggle). The Absolute distinguishes – without distinguishing, since it is finally indifferent to this – between its realization and its effectivity accomplished in the work; it does not test itself and its essence in the unique mode of Finitude; it does not raise pain (*Schmerz*) to the status of essence, but is content to make of it an instrument. Nothingness is not in Finitude and *as* Finitude, as Absolute (as Nothingness-that-nihilates) or essence; it is rejected into finite or particular beings.

5. This is why a phenomenology that has pain not only as an instrument but as an affect of scission for every phenomenal content, is immediately – in Heidegger – a phenomenology of the Absolute or the sole content of the immediately di-ffering essence, whereas it is not this in Hegel except in a preparatory and limited way where phenomenology, that is, the type of immanence that is that of pain, still does not exhaust the essence of the Absolute and remains an instrument. Difference 'finitizes' the Absolute and, due to the real transcendence of beings that is the content of pain (non-dialectizable *Schmerz*, yet also finite essence of the Dialectic or the work of the 'negative') – it restores it within the limits of a phenomenology. Not in the anthropological limits of a consciousness of self – since Difference and its finite non-dialectical scission, exceeds the 'particular' human being and its idealist correlate, self-consciousness – but in the limits that are those of the *Da*, of *Da-sein*. The Absolute as Difference cannot experience itself and manifest itself as finite save for in the limits of the *Da*, that is, the pre-dialectical scission. The *Da* alone is the site not of nothingness, but of *finite* nothingness – in the sense that even nothingness is affected by the transcendence of the real and is irreducible to the Idea – in the limits (not finite, but of essential Finitude-as-Limit) to which Difference or the Absolute is constrained in order to be able to reach its proper essence: *Verwindung*. This latter is the over-coming that does not over-come without appropriating itself or accepting what is over-come, more exactly without letting be and without accepting not so much what is overcome, as its very essence. This is what it is 'to enter' *into* metaphysics. The appropriating to the proper makes itself into a partially non ? metaphysical 'proper', into the essence of the overcome inasmuch as

it is nothingness-*as*-One, dis-appropriation *as* Proper which appropriates or as *tautology of the proper.*

Ereignis is not impossible despite Finitude and the primacy of withdrawal, of suspension. Yet it is *Ereignis* of the withdrawal itself, the appropriating Turning of the Forgetting. Reversibility is not missing, but it is put at the service of Forgetting rather than Parousia, while Nietzsche, for example, would have put Forgetting at the service of Parousia.

SYSTEMATIC DISSOLUTION OF THE RESEMBLANCES OF HEGEL AND HEIDEGGER

1. The 'identity of identity and difference' is a syntax that appears to hold for Heidegger as for Hegel.

Even if Finitude is the essence of Difference, more primitively, on the plane of the *a priori* rather than that of the transcendental, it is first of all Difference that is the essence of Finitude: no doubt, but Difference . . . understood as Finitude. Whatever there is of reversibility in these phenomena and their precise significance, the first position of the 'ontological Difference' of Finitude is a declaration of war against the Transcendental Logic and the Absolute Logic, against the idealist postulate: 'the unique idea that has reality and genuine objectivity for the philosopher is Being as absolutely suppressed of opposition' (Hegel). The idealizing reduction does not in effect suspend the 'oppositions' founded upon the transcendence of the thing in itself, that is, upon Difference and its real rather than syntactical specificity, except on the condition of reestablishing the disjunction of the real and the ideal, this time under an intra-ideal form, for which opposition is identically its being-suppressed or its identity. The formula: 'the identity of identity and difference', that of the indivision of Being and Nothingness, does not at all have the same sense, nor the same functioning – even though these designate a syntactical invariant – no doubt abstract – in Dialectic and in Difference, in the element of ideality or the element of finite Being, that is, of real transcendence in relation to this ideality. Neither 'difference' as disjunction, nor the identity that stands opposed to it, nor the superior identity that unites them, 'one sole and same synthetic unity' (Hegel), are the same from the point of view of their constituents in transcendence and in immanence, in reality and in ideality, at least once Finitude is brought out in its specificity. The originary synthetic unity, that which gives itself always in the mode of disjunction or tearing and which is able, in this broad sense, to be an invariant, is immediately varied by the 'ontico-ontological Difference' such as Heidegger understands it. Finitude is the reason that, in the last instance, radically distinguishes the Dialectic and Difference; it is the essence of Difference.

The scission is no longer 'internal' to the Absolute, by and for the Absolute, it (is) the Absolute or the One itself – it is this that distinguishes Heidegger from Hegel. The cardinal form of the identity of difference and identity not only no longer has the same sense from the one to the other but perhaps it no longer has sense for Heidegger: difference (is) immediately identity, or rather the unity of the One. The reversibility of contraries is not entirely destroyed, but subordinated. It is no longer their essence; the essence is the irreversibility or the very withdrawal, and it is difficult to perceive still, in finite Difference, this rebound or this redoubling of identity, this 'synthesis' of opposites. If there is a rebound, a resurgence, it is rather that of withdrawal as Turning – a poor synthesis since it is that of real transcendence. The scission is no longer *internal to* the One, itself supposed covered over in ideal immanence and founded in the element of the Idea; scission or absolute transcending are no longer even those *of* the One: this would be to incline towards a negative thinking of essence. *Absolute transcending (is) the very One.* Finite Difference is not so much the transcending *of* the One in relation to the Idea – this would be to give here a Neo-Platonic version of Heidegger – as the very transcending as One. Not only is withdrawal no longer internal to ideality, by and for it, but it is not even any longer an in-between 'between' the Idea and the One; *withdrawal is the indivisible essence or even the One as the transcendental locus of Being and its relations.* The ultimate reason for the distinction of the two syntaxes resides thus in what is no longer only a fact of synthesis but is already a 'thesis' of the extra-ideal reality of the One: in a certain transcendence (of) the One (as immediate in the transcendental sense) that maintains Difference with respect to the Idea, while the Dialectic entirely lowers the One to the ideal type of immanence.

2. Being transcends beyond beings and, in this sense, it is no-thing. In the same way the Absolute according to Hegel is 'pure annihilating of finitude'.

Yet this nothingness of Being is itself finite and defines itself through the real in itself transcendence of the being = X, whereas the nothingness proper to the Absolute is decided in relation to a real that is already immanent or ideal. The first nothingness thus contains in itself a difference of the ideal and the real that the real itself transcends; an ontic transcendence affects the ontological transcendence and co-determines it. In the Absolute of the Logic, transcendence is solely ontological and 'pure'; it is immediately its own immanence or is infinitely 'at home'. In Difference, Finitude precludes that even Being, as Turning, could ever be 'at home'. An errancy, rooted in the last instance in an irreducible ontic transcendence, remains an always-present possibility to which authenticity entertains (as to technology) a relation of *neighbourhood*. Difference does not suppress beings that are non-objectivizable, but only objectivized beings; it does not interiorize them ideally as does the Concept that suppresses and interiorizes the finite precisely because it considers them before all else as *objects*. It is Being that is nothingness in relation to beings, while it is the finite that is nothingness in relation to the Absolute. Nothingness changes place; it passes from the real (Hegel) to the ideal (Heidegger). From Idealism to Finitude, it is inevitable that Being change sign and be cut into by the transcendence (of) the real, by its 'difference', and that its idealist identification with the Idea that, much more than Being at the beginning of the Logic, holds the place of 'Being' in the sense understood by Heidegger, be inhibited. Moreover, it is no longer nothingness that introduces finitude into Being, a formula that Hegel would be able to proclaim, but the nothingness (of Being) is itself – as Being – finite in a more essential sense. As said above: nothingness or ontological transcendence is affected by an ontic transcendence that 'finitizes' it, and the task of the subversion of the Dialectic, of the Logic and of Metaphysics begins not with the problem of Nothingness, *but only with nothingness inasmuch as it too expresses Finitude*. To revive the sense of Nothingness against the metaphysics that would have forgotten it, would be possible only if it were no longer altogether a matter of the same Nothingness as that of which metaphysics, nihilism and Hegelianism itself have always made use. Here still, the essence of nothingness must be such that it saves nothingness from the pure Idea that reduces it to the instrumental status of negativity and may thus claim to overcome it. What the absolute-idealist form of the dialectic annuls is not nothingness; it is its *finite essence* inasmuch as, through this latter, it is irreducible to a play internal to the Idea, to a scission by and for the Idea (and even by and for metaphysical Being that annuls nothingness in interiorizing it) *or inasmuch as it is itself ontically finite*. It is not nothingness as finitude that Hegel suspends; it is the ontic finitude of nothingness, its affection by a real transcendence, the only finitude that would be able to inhibit the becoming All-presence of the Idea or the absolute parousia as parousia of the Idea. The efforts of Heidegger to save nothingness from its metaphysical annulment by Being, is at one with a thinking more originary than Being, a thinking of its essence, which is also the essence of nothingness. Yet only the taking into account of a real finitude that is irreducible and doubly dimensioned (unary and ontic) allows for the inhibition of the interiorization of essence to meta-physical Being, and, consequently, that of nothingness to Being as well. It is neither Being nor nothingness that Difference undertakes first of all to save as against the Dialectic and the Logic; it is their essence to which finitude belongs essentially: to preserve their essence is to save them themselves and to put them on the way of their 'appropriation'.

3. The On-coming (of Being) surges forth beings or unveils them. In the same way the Absolute is not content with annihilating the finite, it is the 'source of finitude'.

Yet, still here, the 'source of finitude' must receive a Heideggerian sense distinct from the Hegelian sense, and first of all because the notion of 'finitude' is not the same. The Idea is the source of finitude only inasmuch as it itself is not or is no longer finite, but in-finite with a positive infinity that has suppressed its opposition to the finite. To the contrary, Difference is the source of finitude on the condition that it is itself finite: Finitude is source of itself, its own essence, because straightaway the 'finite', that is, beings, have not been sacrificed to the Idea, instrumentalized as intra-ontological cut without reality 'in themselves', as simple intra-ideal diversity that would no longer be the index of any 'thing in itself'. At once, beings have ceased to be finite, and it is Being that has become so. Yet although finite, it has, as Being, the resources for coming into its essence or its ownness and of thus raising finitude to the transcendental status of essence.

4. Manifested beings are sheltered in their very manifestation or non-occultation and thus endure as present beings. In the same way finitude conquers the being and consistency of the Infinite inasmuch as it does not cease to annihilate itself and identify itself with this depth without depth.

Yet, without speaking of the preceding reservations, the identification of beings with what manifests them or with the source of their presence cannot but be derived and deferred in the first case, and immediate (not in the sense that the immediate excludes and supposes mediation, but in the sense that it excludes Difference) in the second, a levelling and nihilist identification. There subsists between beings and their presence a real distinction or, more exactly, Difference as the in-between of real distinction and distinction of reason; between the finite and the infinity of its annihilation, on the contrary, is a distinction that we might parodically call *identically* 'of reason' and 'real', in the sense that it is Reason that *knows itself* (to be all reality) positing its distinction with itself.

5. Finally the complete proceedings or the Same of Being and beings, of the Infinite and the finite: in the two cases the opposites are unified 'at the interior' of a conciliating Dimension, of one and the same *Versöhnung* that is supposed to re-spect their difference.

Yet we know already that 'the Same' is not . . . the same for Hegel and Heidegger, so much so that the Same is the Concept in the one case and Difference in the other. The dialectical identification of opposites, their being-suppressed, is at one with the intra-ideal exclusion or nothingness as negativity, the pure and not empirical essence of objectivization. To this identification is opposed the Same that is no longer the real identity (to be sure as proclaimed 'real' by Idealism) of opposites proceeding through their *reciprocal* suppression and interiorization, but a (co)-*belonging*. This latter assumes the suppression of opposites *as* opposites, no doubt, but it suppresses rather this very 'opposition' in a setting-forth that is no longer recip-rocal and not even simply reversible. To this exclusion is opposed the gap of the differends, no longer as opposites in the element of ideal-ity, that is, as already interiorized, but as disjoint in the manner in which this time the real and the ideal would be. Whereas absolute Idealism undertakes to resolve the amphibology of the real and the ideal, that is, to suppress it purely and simply by installing itself in ideality, Finitude conserves and reinforces it in the form of a Differ-ence that no longer suppresses but maintains it as one-tension that sets forth each of the differends. Heidegger raises the amphibology to the height of a principle or transcendental syntax while Hegel sup-presses or denies it. The Dimension, the Conciliation of opposites (conciliation that itself discovers *and* shelters) is not a dialectical reconciliation, but the amphibological *and*, the essential *and* that remains irreducible in its real transcendence, essence of Finitude and Finitude as essence.

The process of the unification of identity and difference is still called 'Absolute', but Finitude makes of real transcendence one of the terms or differends and thus introduces a general distortion into their relation and its invariance (indivision of a division and a continuity). Instead of the difference of the differends being lifted in their relation and finally suppressed, it is simply 're-affirmed', in its real transcendence, as not created by thought, as Greco-Occidental difference of the meta-physical that affects even the Logic to which it is anterior and which this latter must 'receive' or experience. Such an experience of *finite* Being is the 'deconstruction' of metaphysics and of its Logic in particular.

Difference – above all in Heidegger – understands itself to set forth *Finitude, that is, a 'synthesis' of contraries that would not result in their ideal or ontological identification, the identification of Being and Thinking as in Hegel or Nietzsche* – that would maintain the gap or, more profoundly, that would make, if not the affirmation of their gap at least of its pass-ive affect, the sole possible content of their indivision. This latter is thus never solely ontological, an ideal and transcendent identity that would sublate negation and make use of it as of a simple instrument ordered to the ends of the Idea. If Difference may claim to save Noth-ingness from its metaphysical and dialectical servitude, from the dialectical forgetting in which it is reduced to the instrumentality of negativity, and to recognize in it a certain essential positivity without proceeding to the negation of the negation ('Nothingness nihilates' is not a 'negation of the negation'; it is the affect of its immediateness as nothingness, as essence of nothingness), it is for the same reasons that it may hope to divide, cut into and defer the dialectical identity of contraries and to maintain their distension against any resolution. Without one thereby being able to object to it *any more*, in an Hegelian style, a bad finitude: Difference is not a thinking of positive Infinity that would liberate itself – because in itself it would have been already, in a prior way, thus posited – from Finitude, that is, from the *inextinguishable* struggle of contraries. Contemporary thinkers attempt to re-open the wound that Hegel would have wanted to close or to heal with a scar too soon, the generalized Occidental aporia of a thinking condemned to contraries that do not 'pass', to an in-between that is never resolved.

The challenge of Heidegger is the desire to liberate oneself from the inferior or metaphysical forms of the amphibology of ideality and the real, and to give as a task or as stakes to think the *essence* of the amphibology, amphibology as such. Heidegger does not shrink back, as do the idealisms of Hegel, of Husserl or of Nietzsche, before what these latter thinkers all consider to be unthinkable: Finitude and the real in itself, which they immediately suspend as devoid of philosophical pertinence. He does not declare it any more thinkable, but is content to give it as 'to be thought', the withdrawal-(of)-the-One or One-as-Withdrawal contenting itself with holding spellbound and 'in check' the thus finite thinking which is asked only to experience itself as finite, not to lift its finitude, but so as to order once more the thinking *of* Finitude to Finitude. The failure to think is in effect a failure *of* thinking if thought is understood in the idealist manner as identical to Being, or if Being and thinking are 'the Same' in a non-finite manner, if 'sameness' is here that of infinite Difference. But it is a completely possible and non-contradictory undertaking – not *logically* or *rationally* contradictory – if it knows how to remain faithful to Finitude as to its principle and does not claim to lift it, if it experiences it in a way that does not suppress it, since Finitude as possibilizing, real or determinative essence is inalienable and cannot be suppressed except through illusion.

THE HEGEL–HEIDEGGER CONFLICT AND THE
IMPOSSIBILITY OF A DECISION

1. Finite Difference thus cannot be compared *solely from the syntactical point of view* to the Concept and, in general, to the whole Greco-Occidental tradition: syntax alone is an abstraction and each grand manner of thinking is incomparable and singular, at the interior however of the invariant of philosophical Decision as reciprocal and circular determination of contraries. Of Difference one may say in all rigor that it is a tempered and limited *Aufhebung*, both *less and more than Aufhebung*. It is not because there is a synthetic Unity of contraries that there is *Aufhebung*: this may be a 'dialectic' in a broad and originary sense, but is distinct from this even in its Hegelian effectuation. The Dialectic as System is a logical restriction of the unity of contraries, an ideal and idealizing version of what in Heidegger remains at any rate thought in a more open, if not more extensive manner. Difference is a dialectic without synthesis: in the very precise sense that it does not know for itself, but only as a logos to be fractured, an idealized identity, a purely ontological unity of the real and ideality that would *a priori* lift the real as ontic, programming the real suppression of contraries and the correlative reduction correlative of Nothingness to a simple instrumental function. In general, Difference, even in its Heideggerean form, 'eternalizes' the Greek dialectical and aporetic spirit, gives an immediate positivity to what the Dialectic, as System of the Idea, can only wish to 'lift', to 'sublate', finally to 'suppress', treating it thus as an instrument for higher ends: that is, the Other. While Hegel places *the* dialectical at the service of the 'rational-positive' and by this fact devalorizes it, complementarily, by assigning it to the understanding, Difference affirms the immediacy and positivity of the dialectical and the aporetic which it makes shine one last time and once and for all for themselves. It is in this sense only that it is a dialectic without synthesis, which does not mean: negative, since correlatively it is a nothingness without negativity. It is thus the real transcendence (of) the One that allows us paradoxically to say that Difference saves 'the' Greco-originary dialectical from its suppression in the Dialectic as System and Logic, and that it conserves mediation *as* the immediate or *with* it, whereas its abandonment to ideality would signify just

as much the degeneration and instrumentalization of Nothingness, as it is only the absoluteness of the One in itself, in its autonomy of essence, that is able to save the Idea from the self-contempt into which it never fails to fall as soon as it is carried to itself or forms the ultimate element of thought.

2. In its Heideggerean usage, Difference is an enlarged dialectic, more originary and Greek than Hegelian, *a finite and no longer logical dialectic*. Yet in any case a new repetition of the primitive dia-lectical essence of Occidental thought, of its habits of duality and coupling, its incapacity to free itself from the mixtures in which it is perhaps definitively imprisoned. By *real* finitude, it introduces a distortion into all the Hegelian articulations – perhaps what would have to be called, considering the problems of a Marxist form of dialectic, a cut of Finitude in the Greco-Occidental dialectic. Finitude prohibits *a priori*, in its very posing of the problem, the possibility of a closure through the Concept, Idea, or Rationality that would know itself to be all reality. It is obviously not a matter of holding up against Hegel a finitude of the empirical or of the understanding, but of metamorphosing or appropriating Finitude itself to its most proper essence, of carrying it from its empirical to its superior and tautological form: *finitude finitizing* . . . Since for what there is of the empiricist, indeed empirical, concept of finitude, Hegelianism is precisely the accomplished reprisal of the traditional effort of rationalism to lift it up, to overcome it in the sense of its interiorization in the Concept.

3. Here still, Difference does not install itself straightaway on quite the same terrain as dialectical rationalism and absolute Idealism – this is what renders any comparison nearly impossible. It produces an elaborated, reduced and transcendental concept of finitude that 'forms a system' with the fact of metaphysics. But, it is so reduced in relation to errant-finitude, it refuses straightaway, with what is still perhaps a philosophical gesture, the idealist = ontological reduction of finitude understood empirically as affection by particular beings. It contents itself with seizing it already in its Greco-Occidental essence of *a priori* or tear-proof correlation of Being and beings, then it assigns it, rather than to the particular being, to the being 'in itself'. The Greek fact of meta-physics is not solely an intra-historical fact – under this aspect it

is needed especially strategically against modern metaphysics, more and more idealist in its reduction of Finitude or of exteriority to the operations of the Idea. It is an *a priori fact* or a finite *power-to-be* (of Occidental *Dasein*), an already philosophically elaborated finitude. It is this in-between of finitude that Heidegger undertakes to inhabit and of which he takes stock as of an inevitable locus, contenting himself with little by little, better and better, glimpsing the identity of the in-between and Finitude. With this difference in their point of departure, Dialectic and Difference become incomparable, also at the level of the production of their effects upon the closure or non-closure of metaphysics. Heidegger does not take a position towards the Hegelian closure of the System in order to surpass it; from the beginning he does not position himself towards the same 'marks'. The Finitude of ontological Difference is straightaway either denied or posed as *a priori* – in both cases moreover by what is always and still even in Heidegger a philosophical gesture. It is this prior reduction of finitude, the idealist reduction that denies it (Hegel, Husserl, Nietzsche) or the Heideggerean reduction that 'lets it be' as essence or *a priori* of metaphysics, of the Greek *factum* of metaphysics, that must be interrogated when the time comes.

It can hardly be doubted that Heidegger received from Hegel his well-known critiques of Kantian finitude. But we would respond that the mainspring of Heidegger's thinking ceases to be empirical or subjective, that it founds itself upon the *real* and not merely *syntactical* irreducibility (indivision) of the One to the Idea, that it becomes *a priori*, indeed transcendental, finitude. However, that absolute Idealism does not here relinquish the detection of an insufficiently reduced avatar of the empirical, is also evident. Perhaps we finally lack any criterion of choice between Hegel and Heidegger? Certainly we may say that the absolute autonomy of Logic and Logic as the content of the Absolute are founded upon a denial of contingency, of inauthenticity, of the quotidian which we have shown to co-belong to the contrary to Finitude as one of its two continuous aspects, the continuity which is the condition of authenticity as of inauthenticity, and which must ground at the same time the autonomy of the philosophical gesture, the internal possibility of an inaugural cut and the respect for errancy inasmuch as it ignores or forgets itself. Is this not a sign? Must not Finitude be taken – *but from another point of view, that of the real essence of the One* – as the index of a reality that Finitude itself still refuses to recognize in its absoluteness? This other point of view is no doubt the only one that would be capable of throwing off the yoke of these complementary positions which turn in a circle and where Hegel and Heidegger respond to one another interminably . . . , as do all the unitary thinkers who call this war a 'dialogue' . . . The finitization of dialectic does not fundamentally modify the age-old Occidental conception of essence, namely the supposition of the existence of a syntax within the One and of a real/syntax disjunction. What must perhaps now be invented is a thought stronger than a cut and which would not be a simple changing of syntax – *Difference is syntax par excellence, the minimum syntax of nearly every Occidental thinking* – nor a destruction of Hegelianism through a specific articulation of Finitude, but the renunciation of every possible syntax and an abandonment to the immanent givens of the One.

CHAPTER FIVE
Derrida

DERRIDA BETWEEN NIETZSCHE AND HEIDEGGER

1. The present study of Derrida is fitted into the analytic of Difference. But we could have placed it in the critique or dialectic of Difference, because it comes here by way of a countercheck to the theses undertaken in the following chapter as much as in those preceding: namely insofar as Derrida, even more than Heidegger: (1) avows what there is of inconsistency, and accentuates what there is of latent self-dislocation in Greco-Occidental philosophical decision, whose originary dehiscence, its primitive incapacity to assure its real and rigorous unity with itself, he points out; (2) refuses to unknot this decision and conserves it despite everything as aporia that does not resolve itself except through sheer movement as an unreal, wished for, hallucinated unity: this headlong flight is the very essence of incoherence, of impossible Unity, and so *wished for* all the more. Derrida is the thinker who carries philosophical decision to the limit of aporetic dislocation pure and simple and who yet, through a virtuosity of the endangered tightrope-walker, undertakes to seize decision again one last time and to maintain its possibility and truth, refusing to take the final step. Philosophical decision not only accommodates itself to this risk and this contact with the abyss, where it forgets more and more the problem of the essence of its internal unity, but

in this experience it actually confirms its unitary essence, it finds new forces: the final step will not be a fall into the void. This is nothing else, once one measures it against the finite One, than the practice of in-coherence which knows and wants itself as such. It is a practice that has relinquished the most radical theoretical exigencies and science itself for an enchanted and magically mastered chaos. The deconstruction of metaphysics is the 'truth' of metaphysics, the magnification and radicalization of what there is of the definitively insubstantial, unreal, purely fictional and indeed hallucinatory unity within philosophy in general. Keep this thesis well in mind in reading the following study – both this thesis and its complement: *the self-dislocation of philosophical decision is at the same time its becoming-unitary, its self-ensnarement, its intrinsic self-inhibition – its paralysis.*

2. How with the means now at our disposal are we to render intelligible Derrida's enterprise and undertake its genealogy?

The method cannot consist in 'applying' Deconstruction to itself, in letting it be affected by its own procedures, in registering the effects of this affection: this is what Deconstruction itself does. The method consists rather in evaluating from a non-deconstructive point of view the mechanism, thus suspended in its validity from the standpoint of the One, of 'Differance'[1] and of the affection of the logos by differance. What strategy shall we follow? The first point – but it is only the first and will have to be reinterpreted – consists in showing, perhaps paradoxically, that *Differance* (or the other Derridean 'marks' of this sort which possess the same syntax) *is syntactically a sub-system of Difference*, understood at once in the most general sense in which we have grasped this invariant (as this empirico-transcendental parallelism which has appeared to us capable of rendering a consistent account of the greater part of Occidental thinking), but also in the more restricted sense of Greco-Nietzschean 'Difference' which is the principal mode of the preceding invariant. What Derrida calls 'Differance' is one of the three types of Difference, alongside Greco-Nietzschean and Deleuzean Difference and Heideggerean *Differenz*, but it is at the same time a mode derived from the former rather than the latter while it belongs, through its effects, to the tradition of the latter. The second point consists in recognizing that Difference introduces an important and original variation – and precisely what kind – defining the specificity of

Derrida, his irreducibility within and relative to the philosophical field. The thesis undertaken here is thus double, *and is not valid except as double*, since it consists in making salient the specificity of Derrida relative to the poles of Nietzsche and Heidegger through the introduction of a third term – a Judaic component.

a. The problematic of Differance (of Deconstruction, of the Double Band, etc.) may be read as being still a mode of metaphysics, of Difference in its essence such as Nietzsche reprised it, in order to intensify it. *Derrida's 'positions' are, solely from the syntactical point of view, in the neighbourhood of those of Nietzsche rather than of Heidegger.* But the topological term neighbourhood can only be strategic and provisional here.

b. This neighbouring is not, in effect, a simple continuous proximity save only for a mere deformation or torsion. 'Between' Nietzsche and Derrida, there is more than a continuous torsion; there is a cut by inversion – we will analyse this later –, an effect of rupture but as exercised upon the same type of syntax, whose structure it thus inverts. This inversion has a non-Greco-Occidental origin, an origin that may be called Judaic. After having elaborated the 'Greek' finitude of Difference, we must elaborate the 'Jewish' and no longer Greek finitude of the same invariant. In quite external terms that still remain to be demonstrated: with means that are more those of Nietzsche than Heidegger, Derrida rejoins Heidegger in his type of the critique of metaphysics. In other words:

α. Derrida is initially 'closer' to Nietzsche than to Heidegger, since he uses the Greco-Nietzschean syntax of Difference and indeed nothing else, yet he provides this with an interpretation in terms of finitude, in a Heideggerean fashion, as soon as he transmits to it a rupture or inversion. This rupture or inversion is doubtless, as we will insist, strictly ir-rational or un-intelligible, yet it becomes relatively intelligible when it is 'rectified' in Greco-Nietzschean terms. This rectification, to which we will proceed, amounts clearly to re-inscribing Derrida – *save for a certain remainder* – within the circuit of metaphysics. We are not taken in by this re-version (he himself would refuse it, it is not his point of view), but it is strategically intended to make apparent that the Derridean inversion, which is necessary for assuring the unity of his project, continues to presuppose metaphysics among its conditions of existence (and not merely as an *object* to deconstruct . . .) and that the Judaic variant of 'Difference' has no autonomy precisely without this latter, without at any rate the Greco-Occidental of which it has a pressing need if only in order to invert or deconstruct it, with which it forms a system for all eternity . . . or for history;

β. It is precisely the type of discrepancy – Judaic – between Derrida and Greco-Nietzschean Difference that produces in Derrida a 'Heidegger-effect' and legitimates the impression, often felt but seldom explicated, that Derrida works at once 'by extending' Heidegger and yet remaining nevertheless irreducibly foreign to him. The Judaic inversion of the syntactical relation that is Difference cannot but 'simulate' Heideggerean 'deconstruction' (*Abbau*) and questioning, though without using precisely the same 'procedures' nor the same 'positions'. The 'specific' difference of Derrida in relation to Heidegger is thus not specific, but Jewish, which means that despite everything it is still 'specific' or must pay its debts to the Greco-Occidental.

3. We thus interpret Derrida through the highlighting of an element which has hardly, perhaps never, been taken into account, neither by him nor by those who make use, whether closely or at a distance, of his project: a certain Judaic component. Without taking this into account, it would be impossible to situate the locus, the 'non-locus' rather, from which he places himself in relation, in non-relation rather, to Nietzsche and Heidegger; nor inversely the still very Greco-Occidental locus from which he places himself in relation to, for instance and to take the other, anti-Nietzschean and anti-Greek, pole of contemporary thought: Levinas. To the extent that he also uses the procedures of Difference, Derrida is Levinas's Greek Other and, in order to have signed the contract with Being and affirmation, without any common measure to Levinas. Inversely, by emphasizing, at the very heart of Greek immanence, an alterity of inversion of all the 'logocentric' hierarchies, he becomes foreign to Nietzsche and even, though in a more limited way, to Heidegger. Every philosophical decision always carries with it the allure of a seemingly impossible challenge: at times, as in the metaphysical systems, there are the Greek-like *aporias*; at times, as in Derrida, truly unique in his kind, there is *the difference of Greek and Jew* or, as we will say, *the Judaic mode of aporia*. Derrida's entire enterprise takes place within

this enunciation that puts him 'between' Nietzsche and Levinas (the two extreme poles) and in a *simulated* proximity to Heidegger: *a writing that is neither Jewish nor Greek, at once Jewish and Greek.* It seems to us impossible to analyse anything of his work while remaining silent about this *Judaic component*, this *de-composition of the Greek* the effect of which will turn out to be at once essential and limited. Derrida himself has read Levinas by showing how much Levinas still 'suffers' from a Greek symptomatic. Perhaps it will be necessary in the future to read Derrida in an inverse or nearly inverse way: by showing how much he 'suffers' from a Jewish symptomatic (if and how this formula still retains a sense).

THE GRECO-JUDAIC AMPHIBOLOGY AND HOW TO TREAT IT

1. It is this Derridean 'mixture', not a Greek mixture but a more unstable mixture of the Greek and the Jewish, of the immanence of the logos and its becoming-Other in a Judaic mode, that must be explicated or, more precisely, interrogated in the following sense: to what extent is such an amphibology or rather differance of the Greek and the Jewish *possible*, meaning here merely: coherent with itself *despite everything*, as philosophical though also non-philosophical project or decision? What kind of unity, perhaps non-logocentric, belongs to it in the last instance and is capable of holding together the Greek and the Jewish? To what extent does it avoid the risk of passing for heterogeneous, syncretic or inconsistent? And if it is thinkable, or let us say intelligible, neither under Greek or rather 'logocentric' conditions, nor under Jewish conditions, namely as unthinkable, to what extent is it not an enterprise that 'holds' only as a forced yoke, through the genius, that is, the violence of a single man? Through the practice or the force, as always the power of synthesis imposing itself through its self-evidence – here the force of writing? The differance of the Greek and the Jew not being 'possible' as either Greek or Jewish, will it suffice not of course to 'say', but to practice neither . . . as Greek nor . . . as Jewish, in order to assure for it an 'at once', a coherence? We mean the following: the greater part of the systems of philosophy, and not only of metaphysics, make use

of a mode of the amphibological unity of the real and the ideal – precisely Difference – that is to say of a mixture of immanence *and* transcendence that remains unthought *in its real unary essence* and that from then on compensates for this emptiness, this fragility with a headlong flight, an infinite postulation, a fury to realize itself that is meant to balance the inconsistency and non-reality of its beginning. Yet Derrida accentuates in an extraordinary way this in-consistency or exteriority through which metaphysics self-deconstructs in a limited manner – compensating it for its lack of a proof of existence with recourse to an 'interminable' work. He attempts rigorously a particularly unstable and contradictory combination that he counterbalances *at times* through the 'Nietzschean' recourse to an ideal immanence or to Affirmation, absolute in its own way, and *at times* through a 'Judaic' claim of alterity, itself also absolute, *although in another way,* in relation to the logos. What then is this 'at times . . . at times' of absolutes worth, this oscillation that is neither that of Nietzsche-Difference nor of Heidegger-Difference? It too grounds itself *in any case* upon the practical violence of philosophical decision in general, upon the traditional blow of force that wins every time, that passes (without passing . . .) from one technique to the other (to the Other), that holds together through its virtuosity two in-coherent idioms or writings – a unique and split writing. To say that Differance is just the simple alternative of Greek and Jew that holds through the virtuosity and haste of a writing, is not unjust: this haste is what balances the latent incoherence, noted here, of every philosophical decision. Yet this practical unity, precisely because so much is solicited and asked of it, makes Differance stand out with more force than the others, bringing it to the fore, and all at once bringing to the fore how much in the others and in Differance it is called or requisitioned without being elucidated in its possibility and its reality.

Philosophical decision – as we have seen in the case of the two interpretations of Difference – either recognizes itself, that is, recognizes its finitude, its exterior possibility, a residue which serves as its motor, or tries to deny itself as decision in an autoposition or *causa sui* that is ideal in the last instance. Yet even in the former case, it is not a matter of an absolutely radical exteriority but an exteriority still and in the last instance wished for and assumed despite everything by the decision that it is supposed to initiate irreducibly. Derrida himself does not escape from the latter case, beyond which there would no longer be any 'tenable' and possible philosophical decision. All the deconstructive vigilance, its worry, its surveillance of self and others will be inscribed in this ultimate naïvete, this abandonment to deconstructive practice and its undecidable decision. This latter and its violence are thus self-legitimating – we will be offered this as an answer. And in effect, these do receive a certain coherence since they postulate, still much more clearly than absolute or infinite Difference, an absolute reality or actuality of the future, and since 'interminable' writing is an 'ontological' proof of the existence of writing.

In a sense there is indeed no *relation* possible between on the one hand the Greek, logocentric immanence, and on the other hand the type of absolute alterity that must inhibit it. Will it be said that Difference is effective only if it does not come from any determined locus, any logos? But we will answer that in order to be so, must it not also be taken in terms of the logos? This is already a crucial problem in Levinas but which Levinas himself eliminated: 'the Other *and* the Same' is in Levinas an impossible utterance and a false symmetry. The Other, in reality, has the indivisible I for immediate 'correlate' that it transfixes, but it does not affect or touch the Same, for if it did the Same would affect it in return, which is excluded. So much so that the entire discourse of Levinas on the Same is either strategic, ornamental or denying, mere ephemeral concession to the Same, a sewn-on yet symptomatic anti-Greek patch. Either the Same perhaps exists, but 'to the side', as paganism exists 'to the side' since otherwise it would be possible to lend it a status at the interior of the experience of the absolute Other – experience that precisely has no interiority (there is no communication of idioms in a system of election by the divine Other). Or, if the Same does not exist as such, it is because it is in fact already Other and the Greek is thus the neighbour of the Jew, existing as none other than my *neighbour* and not as Greek participating with me in a unique Cosmos or a unique Polis. But as for Derrida, he neither makes a simple concession to the Greek as judged to be without importance nor does he deny it: he is affected by both idioms and wants to assure their communication despite everything. He is thus twice without identity while Levinas is so only once, but only the Jew who has secretly handed over his weapons to the Greek is capable of being twice without identity. Levinas will have wished to make Judaism philosophize, but without paying its debt to philosophy: it is Derrida who pays that debt with all the aporias of a necessary but impossible exchange. And Levinas wants above all not to be confused with Derrida, since Derrida is Levinas's truth, his becoming-Greek.

2. But this is still here to take up again Derrida's own point of view on himself, or *the self-postulating of Difference as already actual* (in the only mode that it can be so). Thus from this side, inasmuch as we remain in Derrida's own 'positions', we must say *simultaneously and alternately* that Deconstruction is coherent *and* incoherent, that the Greco-Judaic amphibology must be taken from both sides 'at once'. Derrida asks only that we abandon ourselves to this oscillation where he has already partly won. But this abandonment itself he can neither thematize nor elucidate (it has its root most likely elsewhere than in itself) and we have made no headway thus to suppose – with him – the problem resolved. This pre-deconstructive naïvete is the secret of Deconstruction, and it is in fact this that it is necessary to elucidate in order to see there in all likelihood an effect of the One. The discourse of Deconstruction concerning itself cites its own effectivity as a plea to legitimate itself: this may satisfy a philosopher – even Kant for whom *quid juris?* would be nothing without the support of *quid facti?* – but cannot satisfy those who, straightaway, regard Deconstruction in One. We want to examine the amphibology of Deconstruction from a heteronomous point of view, and to leave the enchanted circle – inhibiting every resistance – where it holds us, still more imperious and 'anticipatory' of its resistances than psychoanalysis. We must re-introduce at the very heart of Deconstruction the point of view of the One that, in a sense, will not destroy it, but, more profoundly, will allow us to operate its 'Transcendental deduction' (in a new style, non-Kantian to be sure), an undertaking that, in that very way, will not destroy anything but the philosophical illusion or this illusion's remainder in which it has magically entrapped itself.

How then?

A unity must be found in the real functioning of Differance. How to discover it? By making of Differance a completely Judaic inversion of the indivisible relation that constitutes Difference, an inversion that, consequently, remains partially ensnared by the latter. Apparently, in effect, Deconstruction does not have at its disposal the minimum of internal unity necessary to the coherence of any philosophical project. *Except if, proceeding otherwise, and with the aim of extricating the kernel of real unity, of indivision that renders it autonomous and viable,* one observes that the repulsive and inhibitory alterity, the experience of the cut as absolute is not simply juxtaposed to logocentric immanence, which would be at once absolutely dissolved as such (the logos is not logos, statute or Law, it is itself also my neighbour), *but obtained from immanence and through a process of inversion.* Why examine Derrida rather than Levinas? Because it is neither Levinas's Judaic rigor nor his philosophical non-rigor that draws a balance from philosophy but refuses to reimburse this debt in order better to reimburse another. Because, like Nietzsche for Platonico-Occidental metaphysics, Derrida 'tips the hand' of the Jewish philosopher and he shows this by the very fact that Levinas denies, namely that the Judaic Other, in its inviolable transcendence, is only an inversion of the Greek and does not exist except *with* the Greek – *with* paganism, that is. A Jewish philosopher is an amphibology who, with ruin threatening, has no other option than to deny himself radically (Levinas) or else to suppose himself, to posit himself (Derrida). It is thus in fact the operation of *inversion* that assures the sought after communication of idioms, the internal unity of Difference, that is, its inevitable moment of indivision ensuring that it is not the simple juxtaposition of two ways of thinking without any communication whatsoever. This inversion of the Greek, an inversion that Levinas denies, is for Derrida what allows him at once still to be Greek and, nonetheless, to be able to deconstruct the Greek himself. This is why it is necessary to begin by placing him in the neighbourhood of metaphysics and above all with Nietzsche. When Derrida deconstructs Levinas, he says what he himself is *and* is not, the 'truth' of Levinas, that is to say, his very 'own'. Derrida is Levinas *come true*: while Levinas is absolutely unthinkable, or juxtaposes the thinkable and the unthinkable without communication, Derrida is still thinkable *as* unthinkable even when he experiences the absolutely unthinkable at the heart of thinking.

But this inversion, confessing the Greek despite everything, is perceptible only through the strategic procedures outlined above. It is this internal coherence of Deconstruction that we will seek, a coherence that is still 'metaphysical' or derived from Difference to be sure and *which appears to us as the only one that would be intelligible*. Instead of acting like Differance itself which presupposes and anticipates itself incessantly as actual in order to 'suspend' its own risk: being nothing other than a *precipitous* juxtaposition, we shall reduce Differance to being a mode of Difference, but each time adding – this being no more than a precaution, the precaution allowing us to place Derrida back within the circuit of metaphysical destiny and to make him arrive at the destination despite everything –: 'save for an inversion'.

Differance is thus a mode of Difference – 'save for an inversion'. It is a matter here of a Transcendental Deduction from Greco-Nietzschean or metaphysical Difference of the absolute or Judaic Other. A challenge, no doubt, but it is Derrida himself who invites and leads us to it. He strives to preserve the tension of the logos (of the inevitable 'return', of repetition, etc.) and of allergy or alterity; the tension of the Same (-as-differance) and of Differance (-as-Same): the balance of Greek and Jewish elements through the partial loss of their idiomaticity. This equilibrium, this *at times . . . at times*, this matrix of the *neither . . . nor-at the same time*, this superior 'tension', are these not the Greek par excellence, the regularity or invariance of a superior and universal law? In reality, always the same alternative: *either* Judaism cannot but simply and purely ignore the Greek and philosophical and relinquish philosophy (can philosophy be Christian? it cannot be Jewish), which Levinas does not do, Derrida thus being able to denounce this inevitable double-dealing; *or* the Greek idiom will always prevail at the final accounting, that is, through its finite conception of the infinite, over the Jewish idiom. This is what we intend to demonstrate here: all the effects of the alteration/difference/deconstruction of metaphysics presuppose the latter and remain relative to it still and despite everything. No doubt the procedure through which they are obtained, that of inversion, *has the particularity of denying itself,* and the Jewish idiom must deny the Greek idiom, a structural and finally quite obvious denial. So much so that the inversion cannot fail, *at the same time*, to be relative to what it inverts and also to posit itself as immediately absolute or to deny its entirely relative origin. Derrida, as we will show, in no way exits from this Judaic form of duplicity which he exploits in every one of his utterances. His strength is to reveal this, whereas it would remain apparently, perhaps even quite *apparently*, dissimulated in Levinas – thus to reveal it a second time.

We shall examine the theme and the practice of the 'relation without relation', of the relation (?) of relation and (?) non-relation where the problem of Differance is concentrated.

REDUCTION OF THE AMPHIBOLOGY

1. Here and there, at regular intervals, Deconstruction poses local and relative evaluations of its force.[2] It has, it will always have – we do not contest this necessity, not here and not yet – the form of a double discourse, a thesis of weakness, of relativity, of limited calculation, of micro-economic and tempered vigilance, and the insistent thesis, never abandoned, of an effect of absolute difference, of a point of irretrievable loss, of a collapse from which one never recovers, of an incalculable which *still must* finish by being absolute . . . It is impossible to separate these two discourses. *Their relation alone, the relation of this relativity and this absoluteness of Differance is our object, the delicate point perhaps where Deconstruction itself becomes symptomatic in its turn and must be analysed.* It could be that the necessary duplicity of this strength and this weakness would be interpreted in an 'interesting' and ambiguous manner: precisely because it has to do with a double *self*-evaluation of force or 'politics'. Furthermore, the characterization of Differance as relative and as absolute is not understood by Derrida as a phenomenon of syntax to be meticulously elaborated. He has the tendency not to think the coexistence as such of the theses of the relativity and the absoluteness of differance. Less than others, but regularly, he in fact dissolves the complex relative-absolute, its unity of process (but what unity?), playing *at times* with one *at times* with the other. Nonetheless, somewhere, these two characteristics likely co-belong to one another in the following sense: *Deconstruction is an absolute process* (in the sense of autonomy: deconstructed texts + borders or margins + practical-technical means, operations, codes and procedures) *by dint of relativity; it is not absolute altogether, but relative-absolute.* In order to understand this intimate association, it does not suffice to say of deconstruction that it is relative to texts, to the logos, to representation, to editorial,

economic, ideological machines, a relativity to a determined state of forces, and then, moreover, that it *must still* also be an absolute, inadmissible blockage. There is a law of this relation, still a law, and it is perhaps this that points towards an ultimate *plane*-of-dehiscence.

As for utterances of this kind, they outline a matrix or syntax of the differance-effect:

> what I am proposing here has once again and always the form of the double bind: neither simply this nor simply that, this and that being contradictory, *one must* [*il faut*] (weakening, fault [de-faillir, defaut]) have both this and that and go from this to that, etc. (. . .), contradictory 'one musts'. (*Ja* 64 [111] – trans. slightly modified [RG])

And *relation* in the same fashion: 'a clinging/de-clinging dual unity, inhibited at the origin' (BB 7 [99]). Elsewhere: a 'relation without relation'; 'hooks that unhook'; 'grab in order to loosen the grasp'. Such is 'the crafty logic of this "topical structure"' (BB 9 [100]).

The craftiness of this logic begins in fact with the hesitation with regard to its craftiness [*son retors*], its retortion, its return, with the affirmation of the *at times* 'more or less' *at times* 'absolutely' inadmissible character of alterity; with the distinction, or non-distinction, of a differance that cannot but delay, distance, defer and thus tolerate a return and a certain admissibility, and a differance that opens an irreversible wound in the side of the logos.

Here we must cite an assortment of texts that are *more or less* ambiguous: 'to accumulate all the conditions of non-receivability' (*Ja* 42 [93]); 'that point where calculation gets absolutely lost' (*Ja* 42 [93]); 'the non-receivable for itself'; 'the delay of differance will have always precipitated the other, toward the other, the wholly different' (*Ja* 49 [99]); 'one sees oneself (or does not see oneself) shaken off by the inflexible force of a simulacrum [. . .] some skidding off the track from which one cannot recover' (BB 19–20 [107]); 'this text can only *interest* the reader if, beyond all the cunning and all the impregnable calculations, he or she is certain that after a certain point I don't know what I am doing and cannot see what is staring me in the face' (BB 21 [109]); 'on the border, neither in the text nor outside of it, and yet both at the same time, defying therefore all the presumptions about the limit of a corpus' (BB 25 [111]); 'the relation of the *déjà* to the absolute ancestor, to the past that has never been present' (BB 26 [112]); 'an outside which it fails to make *its* outside' (BB 27 [112]); 'it can always go wrong – to a certain degree, even, it goes wrong every time' (*ibid.*); 'heterogeneous (almost inadmissible) forces [which] one cannot resist [. . .] or rather one resists them, but in such a way that the resistance creates a symptom and is set to work on the body' (BB 16 [105]) – 'The inadmissible {*irrecevable*} – that which at a determined moment takes the formless form of the inadmissible – can, it should even, at a determined moment, find no reception whatsoever; it can and it should escape from the criteria of receivability, be totally excluded, and this may occur in broad day-light, even as the inadmissible product circulates from hand to hand [. . .]. The inadmissible (as well as the ungraspable) is also that which may never be taken, that can be dropped, that, even, can only be dropped. Like the rest. This incalculable remainder would be the "subject" of *Glas* if there were one [. . .] and when it is explained in its undecidable economy. The syntax of the word *reste* as well. The ungraspable – remain(s) ("the skidding that forces a certain letting go" ["Dissemination"], a certain de-clinging of the dual or dialect-ical unity) is the relation without relation of the two columns or colossi or bands' (BB 17 [105–6]); 'not yet encodable, in any class' (*Ja* 45 [96]).

The hesitation between the economic relativity of the loss (more or less, to a certain degree, the maximum possible . . .) and its absolute-ness is no doubt constitutional. *But according to what 'superior' relation are the economy and the an-economy of Differance adjoined in order to form the unity-nonetheless of Deconstruction?* How is one to reconcile, to organize rather, and according to what hierarchy, order or syntax, the without-return of destruction and the crafty character of its co-extens-ive functioning with absolute torsion? The relation (to) the Other is to be both the stakes and the matter of Deconstruction:

> something would remain inaccessible *to me*, inaccessible in any case to these approaches, eluding any becoming for itself – and that would be, precisely, 'my' idiom. The fact that this singularity is always for the other does not mean that the latter accedes to some-thing like its truth. What is more, the idiom is not an essence, merely a process, the effect of a process of exappropriation that 'produces' only perspectives, readings without truth, differences,

intersections of affect, a whole history whose very possibility has to be disinscribed or reinscribed. (*Ja* 52–3 [101–2])

In this syntax of the-one-for-the-other, is it the other who hides, who steals away furtively? Is it in turn absolutely impregnable? Or rather must one not complete, *prolong and continue infinitely* this relation: *the one is for the other, which is in turn one for the other, etc.*?

Deconstruction thus evaluates, at many times, in many modes and from different points of view, its own power and that of its effects. The 'disseminating' style refuses to bind and unite these evaluations; it tends to juxtapose the discourse of the relative and that of the absolute – and from this a certain obscurity results. Yet this is itself nothing but an effect: not only through a lack of theoretical thematization but more profoundly due to a certain conception of their relations which would *itself* have to be programmed, included and derived in turn from a more powerful argument.

What is at stake in this global evaluation that Deconstruction cannot fail to make of itself at the same time that it analyses itself, exposes-and-inhibits itself, is its significance as both political *and* anti-political, *relatively and absolutely* anti-political. Not the recognition in it of certain Marxist formations or instances, whose analysis according to the law of differance would have to be weakened from the start, nor the claim for itself to be a 'political' Deconstruction, but rather the intra-, over-, anti-political effects co-belonging immediately and across its entire surface to Deconstruction. The Greco-Occidental symptom of Deconstruction is in the fact that there is a symptom, that is, a denial of the political in the form of its deconstructive inversion. Here it must be asked if Deconstruction is capable of cutting into and weakening not political positions, but 'the' position of 'the' political itself. It is quite evident that the answer is no and that Deconstruction does not believe it possible to proceed as far as an absolute displacement of the political, for instance by ethics as in Levinas. Deconstruction puts its relation to the political at stake – *still at stake*, thus political in the superior sense of the word. Even if this 'relation' is one of inversion and consists in inhibiting the political *even if it means* reviving it, or rather (the Nietzscheans will understand this nuance . . .) inhibiting it *in order to* revive it.

2. What are we to make of this strange 'relation' and what exactly is our operation here? Something like a putting-into-argument of Deconstruction, its universal 'argumentation', an *animadversion* destined to *turn* once more the deconstructed and the deconstructive towards their common operation, towards the relative-absolute process that they maintain, but a turning that is itself no longer deconstructive and sceno-graphic. Even so, this turning is not yet of the order of affirmation, of the 'unlimited yes' said to differance. A single concept is here justified by the nature of the attempted operation: *it is a re-activation, an attempt to render Deconstruction active, and not merely affirmative*, with the network of critical effects and new evaluations that this operation projects onto Differance. Why primarily 'activity'? Because it is a question of the power of synthesis that must indeed 'act' somewhere in Difference. We would ask of Deconstruction by what miracle it might call itself 'affirmative' without first calling itself 'active'? In effect, the problem may be posed as follows: Derrida mixes, as we have said, a sense of absolute alterity that is easily said to be 'Judaic' and which brings him close to Levinas, and a sense of relative alterity whose temperament keeps rather closely to 'Occidental' thinking, for example that of Nietzsche. The one does not agree very well with the other: from this follows a serious equivocation of the term 'absolute' (of absolute inadmissibility, etc.), precisely at the moment that, wanting in turn 'to affirm difference' in order to render it absolute and irreversible, apparently without return, he invokes an 'unlimited yes' that presupposes a synthesis or an 'activity' that cannot but render it definitively relative-absolute, and first of all relative. The two go together badly, which is why it is necessary to clarify the problem by re-inserting, redistributing this double evaluation in the sole universal economy, that of relative-absolute systems or syntaxes (Difference). In order to see how these self-evaluations are not incoherent, how there exists a clear law of this obscurity, it is necessary to take hold of the regularity – the Argument – which Deconstruction still obeys even in denying it through its 'inversion'. This would permit for example distinguishing, this is a mere indication, between the forms of Representation that are said to be local and determined (by whom? for whom? from what point of view?), that would be in effect destroyed without return by an irreversible torsion, and Representation as such, which re-turns as such, of which the as such would be

the return or retortion of this entire logic – even logic 'in general' yet under Judaic influence –, recurrence of infinite presence, constitution of a *field of alterity's presence*. Not everything returns, but 'this' would re-turn most perfectly, as dehiscence, as *Judaic plane of alterity*. Even though this does not correspond to Derrida's own view – we have here posited the principle of the matter – such a correlation of the relative and the absolute allows us to render coherent (in its own way, still without elucidating the internal essence of this coherence) the double discourse of deconstructive effectiveness and thus to understand Differance as a derived mode of Difference, derived through its inversion.

It is thus a matter of inscribing these texts of Derrida on the alterity and inadmissibility of Differance, on their evaluations of the relative or even absolute character of the 'other' within the universal scheme of *Difference*. It renders them intelligible, analyses them and puts them in place, it arranges the procedures of Deconstruction according to their relative or absolute strength. It can arrange them because they themselves – this is the entire initial thesis – are so to speak withdrawn from this general argument, no doubt as isolated and reinterpreted by Derrida, but are still in a sense programmed by it. I call this procedure: the activation of Differance, its active rectification through its reduction to the synthetic syntax of Difference.

THE RECTIFICATION OF DIFFERANCE: AS DIFFERENCE

1. Here is a diffuse sensation, little argued but persistent: Deconstruction – in addition to the use made here and there of Nietzsche and Heidegger – accelerates the constitution of contemporary thought, its most insistent and visible phylum, in a combinatorics that is in the midst of drawing out its final consequences, even if it may draw these out infinitely, of producing its final effects and fulfilling itself, even if it may fulfil itself in the form of an unlimited becoming. Practically all contemporary undertakings, including Deconstruction, including Nietzsche and Heidegger, make recourse to a univocal scheme which they unfold, fold up and auto-affect in order to make themselves produce effects that are more and more expansive and brilliant, affects

that are more and more intense, variations that are more and more, one might say, interminable . . .

Derrida notes a 'general disinvestment' (*Ja* 47 [97]) with respect to writing and Deconstruction and he explains this by way of a sort of reactive exhaustion of the scheme ('the reproductive exploitation of writing') and the general symptom. But is not an interpretation in terms of resistance and symptom here a bit hasty? Does it not resist in turn another threat that would affect the very existence of Deconstruction by showing *to what* its existence holds? Another danger that would be the risk of turning into if not a combinatorics, at least – but is this really all that 'different'? – the 'superior form' of every possible combinatorics as represented by the absolutely universal – thus Greek – invariant of Difference? If one takes it in the totality of its texts and works, Differance has always the form of the symptom, not in the psychoanalytic sense of a formation of compromise between Differance *and* its avoidance, but as the universal or 'superior form' of the symptom in general, that which puts Differance in a compromising relation no longer with *what* resists it, but with what *it* resists, namely the syntax of the relative-absolute as Difference. It cannot fail to claim sometimes to be absolute, sometimes relative, playing strategically sometimes with one evaluation, sometimes the other, but leaving in obscurity the link of inclusion or continuity of these two 'sometimes' which are *despite everything* none other than the moments of a continuous process. Otherwise put, the requirement of absoluteness, once it is manifest in Deconstruction, takes the form of the general synthetic form of the symptom, which is never an immediate given.

Reproductive exploitation and combinatorial placement do not work their deception merely outside of Deconstruction. Not only do they produce themselves also 'at the interior' of the already constituted deconstructive field where the risks of sedimentation, recentring, re-appropriation co-belong to the work of differance: all of this, it has already programmed and attempts to prepare for, more or less as always. *But more profoundly there is another risk:* not that of '*paralyse*', but that of '*enlyse*', why not, that cannot be perceived except through the re-activation of Differance, a risk that would come to it *both* from the interior *and* the exterior, that would even perhaps be nothing but the unity of this *and*. The risk or destiny of seeing a universal scheme reveal itself in this *and*, as what wishes to reaffirm itself. Not only to affirm Differance, but to re-affirm in a limitless way this affirmation of Differance. The risk of seeing constitute itself – we have seen this already – a sort of unlimited deconstructive continuum that no doubt is not what is called 'combinatory', but which, to be sure, has the universal *a priori* form of every combinatorics: the reversible syntax of continuum/cut – precisely 'Difference' . . .

That Deconstruction staves off its reconstitution in a finite and closed combinatorics of invariants is quite clear, this is not what is at issue here, nor any inferior combinatory forms. *It is a matter of its inevitable constitution in an invariant re-affirming and re-producing of itself unlimitedly in, by and through its variations.* Not a combinatorics of invariants (though it would be this too, as a result), but invariance as such, identical to the infinite variation-of-variations, the scheme and economy of every sort of combinatorics. Deconstruction is at one with reproduction; it lives off repetition, albeit in the mode of the faux-bond. It attacks the inferior forms of reproduction without seeing, even while seeing it but without drawing all its consequences, that reproduction in general, in its essence, co-belongs to it and that invariant combinatorics, universal logos, is still what, perhaps from afar, save for a certain inversion, orders it. *It is the critical genealogy of this invariant structure of the 'elsewhere', the constraint of the external/internal 'Other', that will perhaps have to be traced.* Combinatorics in its purest form appears in the system itself of an-economy and dia-graphics. The fact that it hetero-affects (itself) does not prevent the relative-absolute Other from reforming a system and hetero-affection from re-forming a pure invariance, that of infinite variation. There is the intra-representational combinatorics where Deconstruction can always re-turn, a combinatorics of essences that would no longer be processes, and the supra-representational combinatorics with its invariant being the unlimited process of variations. Derrida's solution is the headlong flight in advance, the rebound of differance, the *paralyse*, repetition or *Kehre*. 'This *other thing* that orders, commands (with a whip), where heteronomy is the rule, *the implacable*' (*Ja* 47 [97]): but how can heteronomy be the rule? Either it is a false heteronomy, or if it is a true one, then it is the concept of heteronomy that must be abandoned since it is always built up against an autonomy and an auto-affection. Such is the destiny of philosophical decision.

Take for example – but this is no longer just any example, but rather the universal regularity that Deconstruction argues for and that leads to its fulfilment – the proposed criterion for an effective deconstruction: effects that are *more* disrupting, *less* encodable, *more or less* (than) re-appropriable. What kind of thinking puts forward such criteria, plays now with a 'more or less . . . ', now with a 'more or less than . . . ', turns in the displaced-displacing circle of the couple re-appropriation/ non-receivable (= non-appropriable), makes use each time of *all* the conditions of Differance and thus possesses a moving and infinite locus, and identifies the unlimited whole of its conditions with the Absolute? Is it solely a matter, as we believe, of that final word, that ultimate avatar of the scheme as programmed by the scheme? And is it possible to pose the problem of the 'beyond' (of Differance) in some other way, without once again some 'scheme' entering to include its repetition as a step/not, a *Kehre,* a *reversio,* an *unlimited yes,* always some form of transcendence more or less inhibited and never an 'otherwise'-than-transcending?

Such is the destiny – the invariance of Deconstruction. Not so 'inadmissible' as all that, programmed already in its variations and its difference-effects, through *the universal form of the plan(e) or code,* something that we would have to find necessarily in Deconstruction and that would be only too obvious at the rendezvous, *worn-out and broken but there nonetheless,* something like a plane of inscription. If not Deconstruction's plane of consistency, after the fashion of the Nietzschean Eternal Return, nonetheless a plane of dehiscence: *a Judaic plane, no doubt, but still a plane* and so even if it denies itself as such.

Perhaps this, this *and,* is the deconstructive continuum. Even if Deconstruction does not reform a closed and finite whole, it becomes an infinite whole, broken *and* infinite (we will call this the enterminable . . .). This adjunction reforms a structure of 'sameness', if not of identity. Non-evaluable due to its interminable and broken character, inverted, yet all the more so restrictive or implacable. It may indeed always be broken; it is what we shall have to call the *universal equivalent* (one does not say 'general') of the effects of differance, the infinite debt invested each time in Differance: this chimera that would be called the *Judaic-universal equivalent.* No doubt fundamentally non-evaluable at a homogenous quantitative level of power, its strategy refers to a non ? strategy internal to, an incalculable proper to the improper of Deconstruction. But the power of Differance, of its being staged here and there is equal to the sum or the reconstituted unity of its *economic and an-economic* effects (effects *of 'critique' or of displacement*). And this summation that is neither 'arithmetical' nor 'economic' still signifies, solely, an otherwise-economic, at best an otherwise-than-economic: but how can the Other of economy be of help to us with regard to economy, above all if in other respects one still affirms economy? What does 'in other respects' mean here and how would this be possible?

> This is why – the Absolute alone knows – one must cease deconstructing.
> It must not be, the Absolute.
> One must thus no longer cease deconstructing. It will not give you what you already have.

2. It is thus a matter of finding again, in the Deconstruction that denies it, that never dismantles it except to presuppose it, this special coherence of 'process', in order to evaluate what is relative and what is absolute in Differance. If there is an 'originary' or a matrix, it is here differance as thus the syntax of a 'relation that is taken away as relation', syntax of the *neither . . . nor . . . at once*: 'that which remains stuck in the throat as other, neither-received-nor-expulsed (the two finally coming down to the same thing): that is perhaps the desire of what has been (more or less) calculated in *Glas*' (*Ja* 43 [94]). This is not an identity that would exclude contradiction, and all the same differance does not place two opposites face to face. It is a syntax of asymmetry, of unilaterality, in which the contraries (*at least in principle*, since unilaterality is perhaps not at this point really absolute – this is precisely the whole quarrel here with Derrida): *a)* are each mixtures of the logos and of heterogeneity or cuts; the one is the logos more or less pure and dominant, the other equally a mixture but which carries rather the effect of differance or alterity; *b)* are no longer face to face in equilibrium, in the element of a mediation, but each from *one* side. There are not two equivalent sides, but one side that accumulates the logocentric or representational effects of continuity and synthesis, *and* (?) one side – more or less, perhaps absolutely ? – irreducible to the other, asymmetrical, irreversible, more or less unilateral and communicating to the entire system its power of unilaterality.

What then could be the invariant of these syntaxes? It is necessarily the matrix: continuum/cut, relation/cut, etc., *where the cut is in turn a new continuum, every continuum representing a cut for another continuum,* etc. It is just as powerful for analyzing the 'dual unity without relation to self' (EC 106) and 'inhibited', the 'relinquishing seizure', the 'relation without relation', etc. Relation is perhaps the element capable of bearing this astonishing syntax. To suppose – it is a necessary supposition, the minimum of logical structure and intelligibility that is required in order for there to be a logic (and a topic . . .) of Differance or the Other, however twisted, precisely in order for it to be twisted – that the real content of Differance would be this invariant, implies that differance is indeed a cut inhibiting or slowing a relation, continuous by definition, a division arresting and paralyzing the continuity of relations. Inhibiting them – but conditioning them too: Differance as source, cut-source of a new continuity. It is impossible to separate, to abstract the cut from the unique and divided relation that it inhibits/revives, the immediate synthesis of contraries (relative continuum/cut) being thinkable in both senses at once. Continuity does not exclude the cut, to the contrary, and the cut requires reciprocally a continuum.

Differance's effect-of-absoluteness or effect-of-inadmissibility must thus be re-inserted in this economy in which it is the continuum, that is, a relativity that in a certain way now prevails over or constitutes the essence of the cut. At least in being concrete like the stone or the earth – this piece of lava on the moon spoken of by Fichte, and descending, erratic, into the logos – *Differance is itself or in its essence a relation, save only for an inversion.* Derrida however defines it as 'a relation without relation' (to itself). But this can only mean that juxtaposed here as empirically as possible are two 'simple' non-contraries. On the one hand Differance is not only the 'without relation', but the complete or continuous syntax of the 'relation without relation', the unique (and split) band which makes the two bands. On the other hand the continuity of the relation extends always, by definition, beyond and across (over . . .) the cuts that it traverses and associates, the infinite always 'finishes' by prevailing over the cut and by carrying it further. Finally, and most importantly, at least for being conceived as an effectively absolute alterity without relation to relation (which is perhaps 'conceivable' for example in Levinas, a risk to be run in another context than that of Deconstruction and the most general presuppositions of Derrida, where this attempt can never be anything but a temptation, an imagination or a fantasy), *the differing-of-relation still has the inalienable structure of relation*. But it is a relation the values of which = 0, differance being the cut, the bar or the angle = 0 delimiting the logos without itself being simply interior *or* exterior; the *parergon*, if you will, which is *at once*, as effect of differance, *both* interior *and* exterior. And [*et*] . . . and [*et*] . . . etc., the parergon would perhaps have the structure of the *et*(c).

3. *Thus the Derridean thesis becomes problematic – the thesis which no longer has, all at once, any sense other than that of the Judaic – that of the absolute inadmissibility of Differance, absolute without remainder, or absolutely absolute.* For in this syntax, Differance is 'absolute' only *for* the cut flux, for the inhibited relation: relative absoluteness, simple differance-effect produced by Difference over the inferior and determined logocentric forms *with which the deconstructor him/herself identifies, and this solely from the point of view of these logocentric forms themselves and their 'subject' thus affected.* Here is the answer to the question: for whom does Difference produce a differance-effect? Even if it inhibits originarily the relation of duel unity, if it is a 'without relation' and experienced consequently as an absolute by the inhibited relation, this does not prevent it from being the differance *over* and *of* this relation, a determined and relative cut. Its claimed absoluteness is thus an abstract phenomenon, merely the point of view of the logos as affected, all the jouissance of which is concentrated in this expropriation, this self-dispossession. Deconstruction no doubt stands from the very beginning, this being its idiomatic affect, in this jouissance of being-affected as absolute, of being-absolutely-affected. Yet Difference, in excluding by its account this affect, will have designated for us at once its true origin – non-Greek. Since, for Difference, we have here a partial, separated and 'engineered' point of view, and the only concrete point of view would be that of the whole syntax which is able to furnish this inasmuch as it produces a process or continuity through the traversal of its differance, *the syntax that is absolute only inasmuch as it is relative-absolute.* The immediate unity of contraries is still a unity despite everything, though it be divested of its mediations by Differance. Its 'haste' towards the cut that strips it bare, that takes away its protections, is

clearly no longer the unity or identity of the inferior forms of representation (for instance the signified), however it remains an intentional continuity, and even one so pure that it might even be *the* continuity or transcendence par excellence, that of the Judaically experienced Idea . . . The Idea too *remains*, and not only differance. The *remainder* is complex and has a continuous structure. What resists is the continuous unity of *a flux that represents a cut for another flux*, this would not be destroyed but rather reinforced by this inversion lending it a supplement of stubbornness . . .

4. Differance is thus not an absolute 'without relation' as *opposed* to the relation of logocentric essence; the effect of absoluteness would be in this case abstract in a new way and separated from its obtaining conditions. It is a state = 0 of relation, relative to relation and itself 'relational'. Differance is Difference (I will come back to this tragicomedy, the 'reduction', *more or less operated by Derrida himself*, of Differance to Difference) not of the logos and its absolute Other in an immediate way, but of the determined and inferior local forms of logocentrism and the essence (in becoming) of the logos, the logos itself as limitless flux. If Differance is relative, then it remains 'intra'-logocentric, exterior perhaps to certain of its forms or states, but identical to the *essence* of logos, making one body with it. And the essence of logos, logocentrism's becoming what it is, is the relation 'to' difference, the relation/cut, the 'relation without relation': *Differance is the superior though 'Judaic' form of logocentrism*, the relation that divides *itself* or disseminates itself *both* interiorly *and* exteriorly. Indeed, Differance is nothing but the *and*, the copula par excellence, the superior form of the copula experienced in a radical transcendence. Differance, thus 'rectified', if not 'transvaluated' at least reactivated, thus does not attain a point where it is *absolutely inadmissible*, where the logos is lost altogether, because it has never really been in a state of absolute *being* or *becoming* (but these terms already annul its claimed absoluteness). Effective because it is an arrangement or montage of relations, it remains, and definitively, a relation in the pursuit of its absoluteness, an economic loss seeking the collapse of all economy. The danger of a formula like 'relation without relation' is its generality, which seems to convince us that *all* relation and thus the very essence of relation is, could be, or must be annulled. *Differance only cuts into*

relations of inferior order, those with which common sense and metaphysics identify, and not just this, but in order better to save logocentrism or its essence, its excellence, its infinite centrality. We will verify here a thesis already upheld with respect to Nietzsche and Heidegger.

5. Let this be the 'law' concentrating the whole technology of Deconstruction: 'One only undoes the urgency of a striction by compressing the other side of it' (*Ja* 35 [88]). 'Rather simple' (*Ja* 35 [88]) no doubt, but impeccable, putting the finger 'precisely on where it is necessary' and 'not necessary' in order to demonstrate the relativity of the striction. In order to exceed in turn or to overcome striction, in order to un-clutch from a relation the non-relation of the striction, it is necessary, this time an *unfailing necessity*, that there be the supplement of another striction which does not exclude but precisely requires a relation. A new cut unbinds the former, renders it relative, requires that it *too* be a relation. The absoluteness of a striction is an entirely relative phenomenon because the striction is itself always relative to another striction.

These are the strictions, the cuts that reciprocally determine one another, relativize themselves or produce their relation. As in all the thoughts of Difference, there are those here which deploy their infinite relations, even as the logos *unbinds* them, extends them, prolongs them. Yet the mechanism is such that the strictions, if they 'produce' the relations, by the same stroke relativize themselves. Deconstruction finally conceives Differance, despite itself, as a phenomenon of reciprocal determination that fulfils, effectuating it while denying it, the ideal that it cannot truly assume from unilateral determination. In these systems, as always, the prior conditioning of this unilateral determination is posited yet missing. Reciprocal determination annuls or betrays this latter because it is already, *a priori*, conceived virtually as a relation and the absoluteness of the difference is *a priori* missing. The Other, the already which arrests every relation, is already contra-promised, foreseen and programmed by relation as such. Not absoluteness, then, nothing but strategy and conflicts of force all the way up and into the in-calculable and non-strategic. Deconstruction attempts to hold together, in a duplicitous way, a pan-strategic discourse of conflict, of double and contradictory difference, of relations of force – and a discourse of absolute Alterity, of the absolutely in-calculable and non-negotiable which is a kind of 'furtive' and reticent homage to Levinas.

6. The problem is to evaluate the respective 'relations' and, despite their co-belonging, the primacy or hierarchy of the *neither . . . nor* and the *at once*. This *neither . . . nor* (delay, differance, arrest) is an instrument, a process that works for the associative flux that quickens over it and over itself, a synthetic quickening that is at once produced by it and launches it further. Moreover the form of differing, of reversal, is already synthetic, is already a repetitive operation: neither . . . nor . . . (etc.), thus: *both* neither . . . *and* nor . . . The Other acts in the effects of repulsion of the given, the given that almost always takes the form of contraries more or less ideally closed. Yet this function (slowing, delay, differance, repulsive hindrance), as exercised upon the inferior empirical givens of representation, is in turn one with a continuous flux that it 'secretes' and which traverses the terms. This is the *and . . . and . . . etc.*, or the *'at once' that associates the neither . . . nor . . .* There is a yoke, an *active* synthetic or associative power of the effects of differance. The synthesis of the *at once* is worn away at, broken down by the *neither . . . nor*: it *must* be so (*both* this *and* that, from this *to* that). The synthesis is no longer primitive, given or empirical; it is in second place, as it were. But one is still necessary and consequently there will be a 'superior' form of synthesis. If there is a pertinent and critical logic here, it is that of the *inclusive disjunction*, the *dis-junction (Aus-trag, Dif-ferenz)*. Defined always as against exclusion, against the either/or . . . , it establishes a superior relation, a re-lation and a re-ferral: 'the necessity of this gap by which each of [the texts] is already placed in relation to itself' (BB 12 [101]). This relation to self as inclusive of an-economic differance must, by tradition, be called the Same, inasmuch as it distinguishes itself, as *inclusive of* differance, from identical Being deprived of differance. The Same or repetition, re-inscription, etc., the power of the etc.

Thus the strictions are absolute or first only from their own point of view. What is complete or relative-absolute is the superior relation, Differance as logos *and* logos as Differance, their *simul*. The strictions are perhaps cause or determining essence, but the logos is at least their existence and together they form the game of *a Judaic plane of immanence*. The logos is di-vided or differed into intra-representational logos and supra-representational logos, this latter is the *co-*, the *and*, the *simul* which enacts in the last instance the entire process, as a foundation or a presupposition upon which, one may be sure, slide the interminable fluxes of critique, of analysis, of all the analytics, of Deconstruction without thereby cutting into it. This *'at once'* is the logos in its accomplished essence as supra-logos, the continuous associative element that reigns throughout all the technologies of Difference. So long as absoluteness is an effect of first place, it has every chance to be reactive. It only ceases to be so – in this system or this law of Difference in general – when it becomes an effect or a process. A statement such as this: '[t]he 'already' with which one would here be put in relation, a relation that only relates by removing itself . . . ' (Ja 38 [90]) cannot but acknowledge the divided nature of the relation that relates itself to itself despite everything in an infinite continuity where differance as inhibition is no more than a means. The powerful law of what may be called *andcosimultaneity* [*etcosimultanéité*] is what continues to reign all the way up to the point of its inversion by differance.

It is this inversion that we must now examine: the non-syntactical moment of the general syntax (of Difference).

THE JUDAIC INVERSION OF DIFFERENCE: AS DIFFERANCE

1. In conformity with our planned strategy, we went previously from Derrida to Nietzsche, going back to the condition of possibility or the Greco-occidental *a priori* of Deconstruction. We must now take the inverse trajectory in order to achieve what we have already[3] called a Transcendental Deduction of Deconstruction and to derive Deconstruction from Difference.

Derrida always interprets the complete syntax from the cut that slows and stops, from the cut-effect rather than from the flux: a delay that is clearly no longer that of a mediation and that renders the Other *more or less* (. . .) immediate. An interpretation which, without neglecting the revival or the recommencement, the relay function in the delay, tends to forget the flux-structure and fails to bring out the synthetic and active character of the process, its associative and productive character (from this derives its allergy to the value of 'production'). Derrida has a tendency to isolate the 'cut' effect from its real conditions, to index it to an absolute alterity, to dissimulate its relativity. He insists upon the 'critique' or rather, since it is more powerful than critique, upon the deconstructive force that becomes the *whole* of the operation at the expense of its synthetic-connective aspect. Above all, he will look to 'recapture' this latter aspect or to compensate for its deficiency in the theory of the double-band by saying, through a long-expected return to the Nietzschean style, that an *affirmative difference* as object of an 'unlimited yes' is *necessary*.

He fears, with good reason, having absolved differance, that the 'double-band' (DB) does not 'cadaverize', does not congeal and does not halt itself in a repression = 0, a universal destruction of all the textual games and forces. From this follows the necessity of appealing to an unmoved mover, an unlimited affirmation. There would be much to say concerning this fear. On the one hand, for syntactical reasons internal to Difference, *this still cadaverizes*, the cadaverization is a universal function of the system; but it may (Nietzsche and Deleuze) or may not (Derrida) be a means, a procedure (which Derrida will recover later as disinterest or distraction) at the hands of affirmative Difference, this latter being necessary as well (but not so for the disquieting reasons given by Derrida: in order to *compensate* for the halting, since its necessity is more positive and grounded in the continuity of the DB). On the other hand this fear confirms that it is indeed the cut-function that has been absolved from the continuous process and that serves thus as argument or guiding thread, always threatened with reactivity, for interpreting the whole of its functioning. And then to assign the risk of cadaverization to the double band is either to absolutize the cut (as we have seen) and to forget the fact that the DB is still at work, the cadaverization belonging to another structural moment than that of the relation/non-relation system which, precisely, *still* continues unlimitedly without ever running the risk of halting itself by itself; or surreptitiously to recognize the unfailing continuity of the DB with this other structural moment of the deconstructing process – what we will soon call the *Body-without-writing* that conjugates *both* cadaverization *and* vivifying affirmation. Finally, in order simply to be able to hold up the necessity of this compensation, which is not theoretically impeccable unless it amounts to making relativity and continuity the very content of the Absolute, one would have to begin by saying that Differance is solely a relative and not an absolute phenomenon. Or if not, it is because the word *affirmative* conceals something else: quite simply the unlimited character of Differance that entails all its consequences and goes to the very end of its effects. But in this case, that is, as 'applied' to the DB deprived of activity, it is no longer affirmative, but infinitely negative, having as real content not an affirmation of affirmation, a double affirmation, but the affirmation proper to the negative. The 'limitless yes to difference' risks being a limitless yes to the negativity of difference as cut, a negativity necessarily reconstituted through the summation or reproduction of differance as absolute Other. This risk is at one with the subordination of the relative to the absolute; it does not entirely neglect the relative-synthetic side of Differance, but it subordinates it to its absolute side, sought thus necessarily in the cut.

2. *Yet this subordination indeed appears to be the reversal or the inversion of the true situation, a reversal that expresses the point of view of the cut and its primacy, a reversal of the primacy of 'activity' (tätig, active =* synthetic*).* From this follows a tendency to reverse the hierarchy of the relative and the absolute and to make of Difference an inadmissible absolute, an alterity that is consequently hypercritical. Within the configuration of the various thoughts of Difference which have wished to distinguish themselves from Dialectic, this will not be the first time that the positivity of the philosophical operation and the possibility of resistance – deconstructive resistance to the powers of the logos and/ or of institutions – will have been sought from the side of phenomena of the cut rather than the side of phenomena of continuity or relativity which are at any rate, though this argument remains insufficient, indissociable. For example M. Foucault's theory of the 'plebs': this is a still *rather* reactive interpretation of resistance as attributed to the cut of the fluxes of power, whereas the essence of resistance is given through the fluxes of power themselves – if not solely through these, at least in their co-belonging with the cuts. There are two kinds of resistance and they are not equivalent: a resistance-cut, of inferior type (hindrance, delay), and a resistance-flux, a resistance of the *over-*, that resists the cut and dominates it. A sobering distinction: the sole structural, real hopes for resistance, namely those of unlimited

becoming-revolutionary (Revolution as affirmative difference, as unlimited summation = etc. of phenomena of resistance) are hopes for universal hierarchy and domination; power par excellence, dominating and subjecting itself . . . ; Differance as unlimited or continued logocentric dictatorship, built upon the continuous ruin of its most immediate forms . . .

3. The absolution of the cut is an effect most likely of Judaic origin. To it corresponds an endeavour for fixing and halting the process, the essence of which is held rather in relativity and continuity, in transition or connection, in what Dialectic would call the 'Unity of contraries'. A meticulous examination of the techniques for thinking Contradiction, Differance, Difference, relieved of their political declarations of intention so rarely fulfilled, shows in every case that the famous Unity of contraries ends up prevailing over their scission or their division. It could be that Difference is stronger, sharper or simply more irreducible than dialectical contradiction. *But the Greco-Occidental syntax and the age-old problem of the Unity of contraries are still not abandoned.* It is still the same project and the same technology, only more refined, more positive, with a sharpened sense of inhibition to be brought against the process of re-appropriation and interiorization. What changes is the power of the scission, of such a kind that Derrida is able to 'deconstruct' *Aufhebung*: more precisely, its most 'negative' and idealizing forms, since a continuity subsists through and beyond the de-limited interiorization, so much so that Differance never ceases to render homage in its Greco-Judaic mode to the topic of the Unity of contraries that is *Aufhebung* in its universal form. One of the contraries effectuates the Other yet continues to be at one with the logos-function; it does not appear to be *sublated* by this latter nor does it sublate it in its turn, nonetheless there is indeed relation and synthesis, a split relation sublating and prevailing over itself. *One confuses, as always, the destruction of the negative and of exclusion with the destruction of dialectical syntax as such. It belongs however to the dialectic to be the dialectic of Difference at least as much as of Contradiction* and one hardly sees what – not only in Derrida, who is particularly vigilant concerning the problem of filiations, chains and constraints, but in all the thinkers of Difference (Deleuze) – would indicate a truly new value and a new mode of thinking, aside from an acceleration or intensification of the

process that will have been initiated by Nietzsche. Although Differance would no longer be a contradiction resolved dialectically and would no longer contain the contraries 'interiorized/excluded', its problem remains, in its Greco-Judaic mode, that of the 'synthesis' of contraries, of their proximity and their distance. The *epoche* of Deconstruction, which amounts and re-turns to destination or sender despite everything, which still amounts to a destination even as it unbinds the postal effect, will thus be at once that of the softening and of the angularization of the Dialectic, the Dialectic having become accordingly implacable. It brings a supplementary step/not (not so much a 'step/not this side of . . . [*pas en-deçà*]' since it is rather a screw-step, the step/not of a screw and a supplementary turn of the screw) to the wish or the universal possibility of an essence that, at a determined moment and also continuously, is called the 'dialectic'.

It is not without emotion – rather this is manifest in its own way with an intimidating strength – that we must here give back to Deconstruction its own crafty retortion [*retors*], nor is it without hesitation (this is not done for those who resist Deconstruction unreservedly) that a thesis is put forward: Deconstruction is the most subtle, the craftiest [*le plus retors*] (in another sense that is also the same, a supplementary effect of the same) procedure that logocentrism, drawing new forces from Judaism and its affect, will have invented – bailing out its most immediate forms, burning interminably its vessels, consenting to a loss proclaimed as absolute but which is merely relative – in order to preserve itself, re-affirm its excellence and its own type of mastery, the mastery necessary, and *necessary* only quite relatively, for deferring and expropriating.

THE BODY-WITHOUT-WRITING OR JUDAIC PLANE OF IMMANENCE

1. To oscillate unendingly from one band to the other, Deconstruction cannot fail to wish either to avert the risk of a sterile pendular movement and to revive movement definitively, or to place one term at the risk of relativity and re-appropriation by the double band and imprint upon it 'an other end', an end that would be truly other, absolutely

and nothing but other. Not an (other) end, but the other (as end), perhaps, *but this is not exactly certain*, the other otherwise than as end. These two projects amount to one and the same, each time infinite movement must serve as a term, yet an unlimited term, in the indefatigable play of contradiction.

From this follows the passage to a second moment, another structural phase of the deconstructive work, the call to the 'unlimited *Ja*' of Zarathustra and the surprising return of Difference within Difference. 'How to give *affirmation* to an *other end*?' (Ja 51 [100]), of an end other than that which programs and normalizes for example the work of mourning? How shall Deconstruction work its mourning of the logos, and consequently its mourning of mourning itself, putting an end, an *other end* to the 'normal' or re-appropriative end of the logos?

> [To] speculate then on an 'end' of mourning-work which would not be the 'normal' completion of mourning, but something like a beyond the mourning principle. This is almost unimaginable [. . .]. It is the unimaginable, even unthinkable logic of this step/not [*pas*] beyond which interests me. (Ja 52 [101])

The conditions of the problem are, as ever, quite fully analyzed:

> the beyond of mourning can always put itself 'at the service of' mourning-work. Very soon, then, one would find oneself back in the necessarily aporetic movement of the pleasure principle's beyond. It is the unimaginable, even unthinkable logic of this step/ not [*pas*] beyond which [. . .] lends at least a contour to the able-to-be-thought. (Ja 52 [101])

There is here a regularity in Derrida's work motivated and exemplified by the second structural moment of Deconstruction: *the requirement of a truly absolute cut-point, of an effect of differance absolutely without return*, of an un-thinkable remainder that delimits in the end (in-the-end, still as an end, un-endingly as without end, in the end unending, in the mode of an infinite end) (without remainder?) the contour of thinking.

2. Yet how at the same time that one is at work, shall one 'speculate' concerning an end in the end absolutely an-economic, of a beyond of

nevertheless interminable contradiction, which would truly be a 'beyond'? How to distinguish between a normal or re-appropriative completion and a totally other completion, a boundless ex-appropriation? Splitting and betrayal: how will this second completion not be defined as interminable or unlimited, nothing then distinguishing it any longer from the completion or the incompletion of the work of contradiction? And defined also as a term, a term put to work in this work, nothing then distinguishing it any longer from this work always threatened with arrest? The work of the DB is at once 'indefatigable' (interminable) and threatened with arrest (terminable); in its own way it obeys the law continuum/cut-continuum, etc., the law of the *et* (cetera). *But this law equally regulates the 'unlimited yes': it is everywhere the same scene, that is, the same syntax, and the 'hope' for another end does not look good.* For an end inasmuch as it is other and above all inasmuch as it is otherwise than final. Since as for ends, Deconstruction does not find itself lacking; its very principle is the infinite end, the unlimiting limit. It will be difficult to avoid equivocating over the word 'absolute', at times taken in a 'Nietzschean' sense as the simple unlimiting of continuous or relative sequences, at times equipped rather with a Judaic charge of alterity. And in this latter case, the absoluteness of this *yes* cannot be, at least here in Derrida's Greco-metaphysical context, anything other than the same effect of abstraction examined previously (the absoluteness of the cut). Moreover, it will be necessary as counterpart, antithesis and corrective to the threat of cadaverization, a threat which we have seen results from a unilateral interpretation of the *etc.* Its character as the absolute 'beyond' of the double band or of differance is finally of the same kind, obeying its same constraint, *an absolute of alterity that results from a dismemberment or an inversion of the real syntactical conditions of its immanent 'production'.* The 'unlimited Yes' still risks being nothing other than this effect of alterity (this time positive, affirmative and infinite) in which is prolonged the balance of the DB as one of its echoes or effects and what it produces in a decidedly finite spirit which refuses to conceive or to think the positivity of the infinite. Derrida has elevated Finitude to the status of the 'essence' of thinking, not only with the practice of Differance or the DB, of the inseparability without mediation of always reciprocally correlated contraries (differance or originary finitude of the logos); also with this unlimited *Ja* of which he privileges despite everything the side of 'height', 'transcendence', the side of expropriation (most certainly affirmative), the absolutely unthinkable absolute(ly).

3. But how is an affirmation, an 'unlimited yes' possible without a prior *activity* attributable to an alterity obtained through inversion? to a finitude of the sort just described? To understand this, let us repeat the analysis with respect to other statements seeing as he will have written and thought 'difference' firsthand as a Nietzschean.

> The double band: when it is tightened to the limit, there is indeed the danger of a cramp; it cadaverizes and empties out between the two incompatible desires. This is the condition of possibility (and) of impossibility of erection. Play is then paralyzed by the undecidable itself which, nevertheless, also opens up the space of play. (BB 24 [110])

> But if this double band is ineluctable (whether in me as an idiom and/or outside of me), *it is necessary* – a completely other *it is necessary* – that somewhere it not be the last word. Otherwise it/id would stop, become paralysed, become medusa-ized immediately – I mean even before it/id stops because, of course, it/id is going to stop in any case. It is necessary that, beyond the indefatigable contradiction of the double bind, an affirmative difference – innocent, intact, gay – manage to give everyone the slip, escape with a single leap and come to sign in laughter what it allows to happen and unfold in the double band. All at once leaving the double band in the lurch [*lui faisant d'un coup faux-bond*], suddenly no longer coming to terms with and explaining itself with the double band. That's what I love, this *faux-bond*, this one here (not to be confused with a missed rendezvous, nor with any logic of the rendezvous), the only thing I love is the moment of the *'ungeheuren unbegrenzten Ja'* of the 'vast and boundless Yes' which comes at the end of *Glas* [. . .]. It is the 'come—yes' and the 'desire to roll toward the sea in 'Pas'. (*Ja* 64–5 [111–2])

But is the insistent opposition of a diligent and working-class difference and an affirmative, gay and fully joyous difference pertinent here? There is already *jouissance* in expropriative differance, this latter is already, or always, a relation and a synthesis *which tends to remain unaware of itself as such*, and the 'unlimited yes' cannot extend, continue, *in-terminate* the DB (at once en-terminating it and rendering it interminable) unless it is co-present to it from the origin as reproduction in/outside of production, being its term only because it is its interminable continuation or its indefatigability. The affects of the deconstructor appear to be born from the repeated separation of the continuous moments of a completed process which, however, inasmuch as it is a process, cannot but be finite/infinite, a cut producing, reproducing and consuming itself infinitely. *This isolation of differance in Difference is at one with the forgetting of the synthetic (active) moment* that appears undoubtedly in the text, but more often at the level of theme (possibly to be deconstructed) than at the level of 'operative' condition of the process. With the immense, unlimited locus where writing spreads, it is not, contrary to what Derrida would have us believe, synthesis which effects the relay of differance, nor even the infinite the relay of the finite or the interminable that of the arrest and inhibition. The syntax of the *unlimited term*, let us say the en-terminable, is universal and arranges just as much the mechanism of differance as that of affirmation.

4. *Cadaverization* and *affirmation* are two syntactical or structural functions that co-belong to one another. They both belong not only already to the system of the DB and of its work which they extend, but to another system, co-present from the origin within and outside of the DB, a system that has no particular name in Derrida, that is designated rather by its effects or functions, and that I shall call the Body-without-writing. These functions are inalienable, they cannot fail to appear in deconstructive theory and practice. *On the one hand* (Ja, 88, 95, 96) a function of universal repression, of the cadaverization of writing, of the signifier as much as the signified, of Differance itself which impedes and inhibits itself. Secretion by the DB itself of a Body-without-writing, of a band infinite and homogeneous yet heterogeneous to all writing, of writing's degree zero, of a limit of repulsion, of textual de-inscription or indifferentiation (the whole thematic of disinterest, of distraction, of infinite slippage, let us add too of disgust with literature, an entire misoscriptism, the hatred of deconstruction as structural moment of Deconstruction), that is the

condition for a new interest in . . . for . . . *On the other hand*, precisely (Ja, 96), a function of economy (fin-al or in-finite: of an economy affected by an-economic repression, overcoming and including it in an infinitely displaced circling) of interest in . . . for . . . the unthinkable, the inadmissible (fin-ally: of interest including and overcoming anti-textual disinterest and distraction). This function forms the reproductive moment of Deconstruction, re-producing in turn the two functions of the DB. The Body-without-writing is itself also constructed in two series or two bands, this is what makes of it despite everything a plane of immanence: on the one hand the cut, but having becoming unlimited, universal; on the other hand the continuum, but having become infinite. Or, since it was already infinite as band, infinitely infinite. The true opposition between the DB itself infinite and the unlimited Yes is that of the Universal or the Idea and the All = System = Same = Unity, Uni-(ty) of universals, re-affirmation of interminable, general economy of partial but unlimited 'perspectives'. The Body-without-writing (BWW) is the Greek plane of immanence of which Judaic alterity remains despite everything capable – if it does not simply deny it.

As 'unmoved mover' (which gives a movement without producing it from itself or without being animated by it inasmuch at least as it is a movement of return to self, of reproduction), the BWW is a *reserve of inscription* that stores up and condenses the energy, intensifies the work of differance and re-affirms the infinity of the DB. This energy is not created by it, the energy comes from the DB, but the BWW divides it (function of repulsion, disinvestment, anti-inscription, textual anti-production) and multiplies it from itself, redistributing it across all the effects of the DB. It is necessary to distinguish between the energetic source (the differance-source, not only as differance but as source or continuum) and the phenomena of infinite displacement, of intersected trajectories, of divergent and emergent becomings, of impetus, of interest, these having the BWW at once as locus and as object, articulated according to a veritable *being-towards-writing*, this distinction itself of course being made by this atextual body. The Body-without-writing is a kind of double band tape recorder, a recorder and reproducer of writing, but which is in its turn double or split. This system too has its *neither . . . nor* and its *at once*, but in a higher dimension, more powerful, the dimension of

power or intensity par excellence, combining cadaverizing depoten-
tialization and revivifying potentialization, arranging the DB, which
remain nevertheless universal, in a superior machine that imprints
them with the erect beam of its gallows [*sa potence*].

5. Yet the system of the BWW just as well *cannot,* any more so than
that of the DB, *be simply absolute, but only relative-absolute, constructed
over a space of relations.* With this difference however, that it relates
all the split and contraband bands to itself and relates itself to itself,
that it is this relation-to-self of the DBs across their differance, their
slowness, their delay. A delay, above all if it is relative, has never
prevented, and we will come back to this, a return and even a destination, and Derrida's sending may well too, and this is what we
are trying to demonstrate, arrive only too much at its destination.
The absoluteness in which the 'unlimited Yes' finds itself invested is
none other than this return, but a return denied by the pathos of
this absoluteness, the pathos of absolute alterity and the dread of
the 'postal effect' not being renormalized. As if the effect of absoluteness produced by and as this return which gives to Derrida's
idiom the only possible form of selfhood and of interest-in-literature
were once again abstracted from the process, rendered autonomous
and transcendent, and used to deny its own essence, namely its
relativity, its continuity, its ideality. *Re-affirmation of activity, no doubt,
but abstract.*

Derrida never fails to unravel and pull the threads, to put tradition
in chains, to mark the lengthy historico-systematic constraints organ-
izing the scissions, secessions and oppositions. But this whole technique of continuous and crossed relations, this art of the interminable
chiasmus which knows how to divide and envelop, to bog down and
paralyse the textual and other effects of power, is still placed at the
service of a pathos of absolute distance, a differance whose absoluteness would itself be no longer quite that of which the logos is capable.
Or which would not take the form, even if it be infinite, of 'return'.
Yet just as in the DB the synthesis prevailed over the cut which it
'associated' or connected, in the Body-without-writing economy and
distribution prevail over repulsive heterogeneity, on the one hand
because the heterogeneous band is still as such a mode of synthesis,
on the other hand because its interminable volte or revolution *includes*

heterogeneous synthesis and scatters its effects of disinscription over the entire body deprived of writing.

What does affirmation do? It is interminable perhaps, more precisely en-terminable. It cannot prevent, we have been awaiting this, what else is there to await? *coming back to sign* that to which it makes the faux-bond. And it is Derrida who signs this, faithful despite everything to the rendezvous with the BWW, itself faithful to the rendezvous with the DB. A fidelity of Differance to Difference, precisely because Differance is never anything but a mode of Difference. It is difficult to avoid such rendezvous, above all once they are programmed by the laws of the problematic. This is the return of prodigal difference, perhaps disappointing but structurally inevitable, and differance just like the rest arrives always at its destination – unless it denies its origins as in Levinas, which Derrida refuses. However much it slips infinitely, renders itself interminable: precisely because it would be from the origin nothing but an interminable term, an unlimiting limit, a continued and continuing cut, it remains dedicated to repeating itself save for differance, entering under the irrepressible law of the same, sustaining a new coherence, one which is capable of *including* and *overcoming* the incoherence of the DB.

Here again Derrida's argumentation, as elsewhere that of Deleuze, amounts always to absolutizing the most immediate forms of circularity which are to be destroyed (for example those of the signified, the signifier, or the 'symbolic', those of the representation, presence or identity of objects) and *to projecting the absolute character of these forms, correlatives of finite consciousness, upon the operation of their destruction and still further upon the instrument of their destruction* (Differance, Difference). In fact these latter are turned against presence and identity but are in turn filled by the infinite essence – merely purified – of presence and identity. But their becoming-unlimited is not, quite to the contrary, their without-return but rather the necessity of their return. Deconstruction secretes little by little a field of presence without the present, a field of logos without logocentric objects – a Greco-Judaic plane of immanence. The BWW never fails, within this system, to constitute itself and thus never fails either to 'make one body', and rather heavily at that, with the DB, the DB with which it breaks so minimally that, instead, this monstrous clutching is rather 'wished for' or 'desired' by the DB itself. If it had really been able to make the faux-bond and to become pure cloud, pure horde . . . But it never fails to come back, its faux-bond succeeds only in being a true faux-bond or a false faux-bond. The faux-bond succeeds only to fail: yes, of course, failure of this premature success; but such failure is a superior success or the superior form of success: still a rendezvous. All at once, at one bound, the faux bond is re-bound, the BWW affirms and confirms incoherence once again and *includes* it just the 'same'; it 'recovers' differance *in extraemis* as one recovers a 'blunder' or a 'gaffe'.

6. Derrida refuses the reduction of the deconstructive double band to a 'Moebius strip' (*Ja* 51 [100]) which would hold as a model only for the successful work of mourning, for the economy of re-appropriation, for the end of mourning, but not for the *other end* of deconstruction. Whereas it is characteristic of the Moebius strip to return to itself, there would be in Differance a caesura or hiatus preventing 'what in effect resembles such a band or strip from turning back on itself' (*Ja* 51 [100]). That in Deconstruction the Moebius strip would be affected by a tearing, this too deferred, that its topological and mathematical properties would be a partial effect, a local simulacrum in the larger economy of the DB, this necessity (which cannot be lifted except through a non-repetitive, non-deconstructing mode of thinking) clearly implies that parcelling out, breaking into bits, dissemination are laws inalienable from the system, *but does not at all imply that these would be nothing but absolute* and that the bit would be simply neither-swallowed – nor-rejected, since it is conceded that it must be *also* and *at once* swallowed *and* rejected. Deconstruction does not form a topology like science, agreed, but it still forms a transcendental topology even if this is itself parcelled out, and there is a Judaic plane of immanence whose topological properties auto/hetero-affect themselves simultaneously (this simultaneity: the transcendental character of the BWW, the relative-absolute immanence of which relates Deconstruction to itself, save only for differance).

Like nearly all modern forms of thinking as soon as they inhabit Difference, Deconstruction too secretes a plane of immanence (no longer Being, but the Same = Being + differance + the One) which makes one body with its interests (dis-interested or not, dis-invested), with the permanent retro-reference of the effects of differance to themselves. For example Derrida capitalizes (save for their division, save for their re-cutting and cross-checking) the effects of displacement that he recalls through an entire system of self-citations, self-references, auto-localizations (an auto-topic, a self-staged setting). He draws from these a unique regularity that situates, orients, delimits the gash each time through a set of *neighbourhoods*. This would be impossible were it not that in and with the course of deconstruction a principle of capitalization or incorporation of its works emerges, a locus obviously without consistency, formed in turn by displacements, paths, lines, chains, but which has an *other* consistency, that proper to differance. This 'objective' memory of deconstruction (the second function of the BWW) is Derrida's 'universal' phantasm, his first object (zero and first, zero and thus still first like first philosophy and the prime mover), the objective appearance of Deconstruction. Deconstruction extracts from the work of the DB a surplus-value of differance that it places in the service of reproduction and 'return' and that is therefore nothing but one more value, not a more-than-value.

7. *It is this – the BWW – that is the sole truly 'absolute' moment of deconstruction. But this Beyond of differance is itself none other than relative-absolute.* Quite simply it is absolutely relative-absolute, a supplement changing both much and little with respect to differance. Much, since Deconstruction finds in this 'beyond' a principle of suture despite everything, excepting only differance or cut itself. Little, since this supplement still has the same syntax, the *beyond* of mourning is still constrained by the structure precisely of supplementarity and the Absolute – in this context of the modes of Difference – is absolute only through and for relative phenomena. Derrida attempts to 'compensate' for the risks of the differance, the inhibition, the originary finitude of the logos by calling for an affirmative difference, an 'unlimited yes' of Nietzschean hue. But exactly this call betrays the risks definitively – absolutely. Differance loses all chance of becoming 'absolute' in the sense Derrida wants precisely at the moment it *becomes* so. Its absolute character, that which the theory of the DB assigns to it at least as an ideal or a necessity (but of what order?), withdraws definitively with its 'signature' by the 'unlimited Yes', its magnetographic recording by the BWW. 'Repetition' only renders differance absolute by re-affirming its relativity, by effacing its radical absoluteness and by

delivering differance over to the law of the Same. Or even then the absolute that is recognizable through differance (reactive absolute, transcendent without relation, apparently without relation, contrary to the affirmative absolute) risks being cut off from its relative and thus active essence. This is what *Machines textuelles* already tried to show: that there would be affirmation, but little activity, synthesis, relation. This is true to the extent that Derrida, obviously without being unaware of it, does not recognize in the *relative* character of differance its very essence.

RELATIVELY UNDECONSTRUCTIBLE

1. The syntactical scheme of Difference, on the condition that it be infinite, that the cut be in its turn a new continuum – this scheme is thus capable of analyzing Differance, of problematizing its logic and its topic, of denouncing its endeavour, the endeavour to immobilize the process in a differance that would be immediately absolute, an alterity absolutely without mediation, an immediately Inadmissible and Incontestable. It is endowed with an inalienable transcendental value that Deconstruction cannot but manifest and betray, betraying its own defence to it by turning into a symptom, into what always takes the form of a turning, a return beyond repetition, into the symptom's superior form. This scheme is the logic of its logic, the topic of its topic – the index of the pan-logicism and pan-topologism into which it escapes from only the most obvious and immediate forms of the logos. *Machines Textuelles* already, although without going beyond, without posing the problem of a veritable beyond of Deconstruction and of Greco-Nietzschean Difference, reinscribed its techniques and its problematic in this relative-absolute syntax of Difference. Above all, it would not be enough to *affirm* difference; one must try to *re-activate* it.

If there is no longer any general equivalent that would fix the values and remunerate the work of Deconstruction, it must recognize, simply in order to exist, that there is despite everything a 'universal equivalent' that grounds a superior economy, that which takes as its object the aneconomy of Difference, or the superior form of economy in general, that which formulates itself still in the form of Representation: *every continuum represents a cut for another continuum, a logocentric phenomenon represents differance for another . . . ; no 'inversion' of this relation to the profit of the cut is able to inhibit this process itself, except of course – but this is hopeless – to deny it.* To elaborate a universal scheme, that of the complex Representation/Difference is not to recast Deconstruction in a logo-speculative style that one might oppose to the mise en scène, and the scene-of-language. First of all *a deconstructive invariant* is also a simple effect of scene, a fragment, a broken piece in a breaking-broken machine. However this fragment, by the very fact that it is relative(-absolute) and not an immediately absolute part, that it repeats a long chain of others, does not prevent but to the contrary necessitates that Deconstruction 'possess' a (relatively) 'undeconstructible' law; that it make one body with this law, with its variations and its invariance. So much so that the mise-en-scène, *the work of Differance, we now suspect, is the logo-speculative having recovered its essence across and beyond its Jewish experience.* The effective work of Differance obeys the syntax of this invariant and the variations introduced into it by textual conditions, diverse institutions, instances of writing, of political, economic, university, editorial power. *Deconstruction is of itself, to itself, for itself an Undeconstructible:* a formula worthy of eliciting laughs from the deconstructive audience who have long thought, believing so without daring to believe – let us give them this at least – that 'the' Deconstruction has never existed . . . Alas, it is the universal law, the law of law, one always exists too much . . . It is hard to finish (with) deconstruction . . .

This first Undeconstructible is thus wholly relative, like an invariant, and if there is another, one that is really absolute, it will be irreducible to the work of differance. Undeconstructible as 'internal' to this work, at once internal and external, *but this simultaneity (that of Representation, rather of its essence that differance takes upon itself) defines exactly the type of immanence proper to the deconstructing process.* The meeting takes place, the volte is nothing but a revolt, the leap a re-leap, the variations-of-variations of hetero-affective differance are limitless, this limitlessness is their invariance and its 'auto'-affection. 'Auto' no longer designates identical Being, but the synthetic same that includes the work of differance and over-comes it by coming back to such an unmoved mover, steering wheel or spring of the machine. Unlimiting-limitless unity of an infinite regularity *and* its staging effects, the over- and counter-determinations which it organizes despite everything. Deconstruction, through its functioning and its systematics, is thus an ideality, but it is the chimera of a Judaic ideality. This ideal border of an *epoche*, limitless border, line of rupture in the philosophico-political scene, encloses itself in itself and stands in the current wake that it traces and where it draws its invariant Greco-Judaic consistency. Even Difference forms a continuity, *topos* (Derrida's phantasm) and *typos* (whether you want to or not, by your identifications and your resistances to it, you *become* subject-of-deconstruction, a subject in progress). Deconstruction is the univocity of the system-of-the-Other, the Judaic plane of immanence, it exploits an infinite possibility of variations on a scheme to which this infinite possibility belongs. One part logos, something like an intra-logocentric, no longer overlooks the scene, but rather distributes itself there. But another part, the same except for the scene itself – the scene's except-ional presence – overlooks it, forms the over- of the scene itself coextensive with its effects. Over-look in another sense and despite everything. *Despite everything*, unique-split formula of the 'same', of this *deconstructive continuum* that elaborates itself patiently in us without us and through us outside us.

2. The unlimiting of the deconstructive continuum is none other than logocentrism itself, save for an inversion. Deconstruction cannot hold separate and isolated the supposedly absolute destruction of immediate logocentric forms and the interminable character of their deconstruction, nor impute interminability to the opposed logocentrism, to the representation to be deconstructed. *The interminable is not an accident, nor even the logos infinite outside of Deconstructio; it is the essence of Deconstruction*. Logocentrism (Difference) is the essence of differance. Certain of the innumerable texts speak of the return of the logos 'over and above' the cut, and of differance as the simple delay of its advance. Yet insofar as differance fails to be itself conceived not only as 'a relation without relation' (the 'reactive' interpretation), but *also* as a 'without relation' that is nonetheless *still* a relation (the 'active' interpretation), *the logos is not perceived as the very essence of the work of differance*. A too narrow, too limited idea of logocentrism is fashioned, and this local logocentrism is absolutized in a way that is at times a bit Manichean, that gives up recognizing its interminability but finds

interminability in comparison, as extra, and above all without clearly, without structurally admitting that it is not solely exterior to deconstruction but interior to it as well. Deconstruction is the Same as it appears in a Jewish way, a relative Undeconstructible. Why relative? Because its undeconstructibility is identically its deconstructibility.

Differance analyses (codes, presuppositions, closures, etc.) by using, only as displaced, all the analytic procedures of philosophy, linguistics, psychoanalysis, etc. But it does not analyse the *present* forms of presence without paralyzing itself within the *essence* of presence, which is hardly a non-present essence since it representifies itself in an unlimited way. Derrida invents a word and a thing, *paralyse*:

> *Paralyse* is a new *name* I make use of (elsewhere, in *Pas*) to announce a certain movement of fascination (fascinating fascinated) that itself analyzes what prevents and provokes at the same time the step of desire/no desire in the labyrinth which it, *pas*, is – not. (*Ja* 37 [89])

Yet this is not, so it appears, in order to perceive in Deconstruction a process, in the form of an invariant or a relatively undeconstructible, of self-*paralyse*. Rather he sees here, always on the basis of its identification with certain local forms of logocentrism, a *paralyse* of the logos by Deconstruction. The other face of this problem seems to be what would have to be called ensnarement or *enlyse*, the self-ensnarement of differance, not by presence but by the unity in progress, the unlimited fusion of differance and presence. You deconstruct; the distance of the logos from itself will no doubt grow, but in another way and with another movement – relaunching the former along the same trajectory; worse: assuming it as a vehicle but in a contrary sense . . . – it contracts itself. The unique flux of an unlimited deconstruction will surprise you in its own way with its necessity of water and stone. While you suffer and enjoy being made and doubled by all the work of disappropriation, it itself is remade in the last instance; it ensnares itself in its vigilance – by dint of recouping itself, of overbidding itself, by dint of oversnarement [*surlyse*] – and takes upon itself all the weight of the logos that it prevails over, that prevails over itself, lifts and sublates itself, assumes itself once more.

3. There is a decline of Deconstruction: this has nothing to do, or finally only a little bit, with any loss of audience. To the contrary this

decline is at one, is *of the same contrary movement,* as it were, with its flourishing; Deconstruction declines in itself and in its triumph even where it falls into the wells of its truth. This Undeconstructible is at once Deconstruction's decline and its limit of declination. It is the success 'despite everything' of its failures to succeed. By dint of practising, systematically, the failure of logos, presence, etc., it succeeds all the better in foiling and missing the absoluteness of Differance. It confuses itself with the abyss that it digs out and fills with its own steps. Its headlong flight, which recommences always faster, farther, more vigilant and omnipresent, which accelerates its speed, that is, its differential relation to texts and institutions, causes it to lose little by little the original, well-charted ground from which it had given the impression of pushing off in order to take flight. From then on it has come 'unstuck', it has 'taken off' in the sense of an economic, epistemological, etc., lift-off or unblocking – but an infinite lift-off, an interminable unblocking . . . Like every self-starting process, which has always already taken off, it never ceases to soar over and survey itself. Not to soar over experience, which it stages, but to soar over itself-and-experience. It is not 'over itself' that it resides, but over the trajectories it maintains with respect to the givens of presence, which it reduces, multiplies, intensifies, intercuts and overbids as it pleases. It has no substance, but it weaves itself one. Even in dividing itself, above all in dividing itself in an unlimited oversnarement, in counter-determining itself, in inter-determining itself, its work remains such that in itself it is immobilized to the point of its alacrity. A kind of self-bogging, self-burying beneath what it digs up and brings to the surface, as the very surface of the exposition of the logos. Deconstruction does not repel the limit that logocentrism imposes upon it without reconstituting it somewhere else, namely in itself. Bedazzling itself, like Argus, with its phantasm, or, like Argos, with its infinite variations – its self-reference, its infinite oeuvre, its self-contemplation. The more Derrida analyses and works, the more he contemplates an infinite agglutination, an infinite collage, a synthetic surface where the *andcosimultaneity* soars over and surveys itself. How would the infinite, the unlimited deconstructive continuum fail to revel in itself to the point of dying of it? For lack of objects, the embittered might say – but this lot becomes absolutely common once it is Difference that sins and lacks, and there are still too many objects.

DERRIDA'S CORRECT USAGE: HOW THE GREEK LOGOS
OVERCAME ITS JEWISH EXPERIENCE

1. Derrida makes with respect to 'the' Metaphysics a work that is
nearly as metaphysically unintelligible, logocentrically ir-rational (it is
obvious all that we can still 'intend' when we say that it is un-intelligible: to the extent that all philosophical intelligence is Greek and . . .
Nietzschean, Nietzsche being infinitely more intelligible in this sense
than Heidegger) as that of Levinas. But it is much less 'strong' than
Levinas's and represents a strategic compromise with the Greco-Occidental. So much so that, despite its irreducibility to Nietzsche as to
Heidegger, Derrida remains ordered to the invariant of Difference.
Contrary to Levinas, to his provocative rigor, Derrida continues to
honour Difference in the name of critical effectiveness and procures
from it the Judaic variant – the Judaic pathos of the aporia. That this
necessity of critical effectiveness has no value in itself and expresses
solely the fact that Derrida is himself already and straightaway situated 'in-the-midst-of' metaphysics, that there would be here quite
simply a vicious circle that intimidates none but those – the philosophers – who are themselves *already* placed there, matters little here.
Repeating – precisely . . . – Greco-Nietzschean Difference save for an
inversion, which produces the 'deconstruction' effect, Derrida returns
again in a manner otherwise-than-Greek to the Greek nebula of Difference and polishes up for himself the reasons that will allow for his
inscription in the same ramified system. The will to deconstruct metaphysics may very well inhibit or rein in itself; such inhibition is still
the best 'perverse' argument for a co-belonging to metaphysics.

2. Yet Derrida draws a 'critical' profit from this belonging, he brings it
to its greatest force, revealing it all the better, the transcendence and
exteriority, the intimate in-consistency of metaphysics: this is what he
calls its deconstruction. It is this in-consistency, this (still . . .) philosophical refusal to interrogate the One and its essence that requires
this absolute primacy of the future destined to compensate for them,
this brute existence of writing existing solely in the actuality of its
traces (all Derrida's auto-citational capital), in its effects and their
exteriority. Yet despite this, Derrida does manage to finish off the last
bit of idiomaticity in philosophical decision and in Difference. More

than Nietzsche or Deleuze who still 'logocentrically' limit the exteriority, the differance of Difference, more too – though every evaluation of this kind is risky – than Heidegger for whom 'finitude' remains still at so many points bound to an entirely Greek sense of the transcendence of the real (of beings and the One), Derrida is here the index of a fundamental 'tendency' of philosophy towards dehiscence that he himself would have accentuated and yet tried not to reveal.

However, the injection of Judaic allergy into Difference does not fundamentally modify the situation of metaphysics, contrary to what happens with Levinas, whose attempt may be judged at a stroke as strictly *impossible*, really inadmissible, completely devoid of essence and condition of possibility and reposing entirely in the exteriority of a religious tradition that refuses straightaway the minimal conditions of rationality and Occidental intelligibility. To introduce into Difference the Judaic idiom of alterity and inhibition, to force the penetration there of a non-Greek experience of the cut, gives rise, on the other hand, to an attempt which solicits this rationality without completely destroying it, since it postulates it.

3. Of the invariant of Difference one may say that: (a) Nietzsche has given it its absolute or idealist metaphysical form; (b) Heidegger has given it a form that is finite and real or ontico-Greek, that is, anti-idealist; (c) Derrida has given it a finitude that is no longer ontico-Greek or real, but Judaic, by inverting the 'terms' of the relation that it constitutes, and has thus recognized in it indirectly a necessity: beyond, it must be said, its simple presence as historical text to deconstruct. Greco-Nietzschean Difference is not only a 'present' and closed text, it is not only what must be inverted, it is also the element at the interior of which this inversion produces itself. The destruction of certain inferior forms of the logos is not that of the Logos, of the Representation that victoriously overcomes the ordeal of its deconstruction. Precisely, in the name of Differance what acts is not such and such a mélange of the logos with its objects, but the pure logocentric power, the pure power of synthesis that has overcome the Jewish obstacle. Deconstruction is an amphibological process of infinite fusion or inclusion, not only of the logos and Difference, in the Nietzschean manner, but of this latter and its Jewish experience or ordeal. Derrida is the attempt to assure the

superior fusion of Greek and Jew for the greater glory, finally, of the Greek and of philosophical decision. Just as there would not be, in reality, any purely Greek finitude of Difference (this latter excludes every exclusive choice . . .), there will not be any purely Jewish finitude of Difference: Difference is already a Greek concept and compromises in advance any insertion into it of the element of alterity that ceases being absolute or of which the absoluteness thereby changes sense. From this follows the uncontrollable ambiguity of the Derridean passage to absolute differance: at times it has to do with an absolute of transcendence and alterity, at times an absolute of immanence. But rather than an ambiguity, it is a matter of the constitutive amphibology of the work. This is proof that Deconstruction remains dependent upon a practice of 'Difference' and is content to submit this latter to a non-Greek experience, a Jewish experience, that it will have overcome.

To be sure, from our point of view, Derrida's Greco-Judaic amphibology would be still less grounded, more unstable than the amphibology of Platonico-Nietzschean metaphysics, if one does not try, as we have done, to re-inscribe it in Difference. *But this is merely to attenuate the amphibology without doing away with it.* The problem is precisely not that of suppression; it is that of looking into the non-amphibological requisites that ground in the last instance its very reality as amphibology. Yet these transcendental requisites are those of the One as non-reflexive experience or immediate givenness (of) Indivision that is non-thetic (of) itself. It is clear that the Judaic treatment of Difference does not 'save' Difference, and does not save itself either, since it postulates Difference and does not possess any autonomous existence outside of logocentrism (and its work upon it). *Judaism, once it takes the risk of making itself into philosophy, is always constrained to sign (even in Levinas, though he denies this) contracts and compromises with the Greco-Nietzschean and is thus worth no more than it for a radical positioning of the problem of philosophical decision.* That there might be a mode of thinking that would not have to sign such contracts with 'the' Greco-Nietzschean metaphysics (which does not mean that it would have nothing whatsoever to do with this latter, here we have another problem: that of the *second* principle; we suppose at this moment the reality of the first principle, the One, the essence of which is not definable by metaphysics) is clearly an intolerable claim which has already compromised itself with the adversary (through the simple fact that it thinks an adversary exists).

NOTES

¹ I shall write *Differance* in order to designate the global system or Derridean type of Difference; and *differance* to designate the moment of alterity, cut, slowness of the continuities specific to the "system" of Differance. The same goes for Deconstruction (the type) and deconstruction (the procedure).

² We will cite only two texts, but these from among Derrida's most apparently "theoretical": "Between Brackets I" (BB) and "*Ja*, or the *faux-bond* II" (*Ja*) (in *Digraphe*, 1976) [both available in Peggy Kamuf's English translation in *Points . . . . . . : Interviews, 1974–1994*, ed. Elisabeth Weber (Stanford, CA: Stanford 1995). All citations follow these translations in what follows – Trans.] These are sufficient to permit an exhaustive analysis of the *problematic* of Deconstruction (and also that of the "Double band": DB).

³ *Machines textuelles*, Le Seuil, 1975.

CHAPTER SIX
Critique of Difference

OF THE ONE AS FOUNDATION OF CRITIQUE

1. We seek a non-philosophical critique of philosophy in general and of Difference in particular. We have called the integrally real experience rendering such a critique possible the One, in a sense that is, at any rate and before any other precision, non-Greek. The One is the immanent Unity – but radically immanent, in a non-thetic form that philosophy has been unable to program – of philosophy *and* the science of philosophy, as well as of philosophy's real critique. We do not have to seek out, in a traditional mode, *if* such a non-philosophical critique of philosophical decision is possible: with the One it is real; the real critique of philosophy is as certain as the One itself. Thinking cannot begin except with and by the real – it knows straightaway and immediately as science what the real is, that is to say, what posture to take with regard to it. Its sole concern must be to think in conformity with the real and with its essence. To do this, it takes the immanence of the One as its guiding thread, without wanting or desiring it as philosophy does, contenting itself instead with 'cashing out' this initial certitude which, to be sure, no longer takes that form of *certitude* called metaphysical; which is rather the element in and from which we now think without being able to transform it in return, which is thus too absolute and irreducible still to be a simple presupposition.

What does it mean to say that the One would be an immediate given? It is not a given in the empirical sense of the word, as nothing empirical is really immediate, but instead in the sense of *a transcendental experience that is non-reflexive or stripped of transcendent contents*. Metaphysics, including contemporary attempts towards its overcoming or its appropriating destruction as well, is the history of the interminable encumbering of the One and of truth with objects and ends that are not necessary to their essence. However to 'open the void' within the One, to accomplish the sobering up of truth's essence, can hardly signify yet once again that the One would have to be thought with nothingness, and nothingness *with* the One. This would return to a still philosophical kind of solution with its diverse modes in certain Neo-Platonists and precisely in Difference. The One has an absolutely positive content: and it is the One itself as Indivision. There is nothing here of formal identity or transcendental tautology. The One whose imperishable exigency and all-preceding reality (preceding even philosophy) we are trying here to make understood has nothing of the Unity that one might attempt once more to oppose to Difference in order to re-establish the ontological identity of the real, of beings amidst one another, of beings and man, of man and God. On the contrary there is too much of this idealized and transcendent unity in the usage Difference makes of the One. The gnosis of the One, yet completely transformed and stripped of its mysticism, having become transcendental rather than theological science – such is the sense of this abandonment to the One through and beyond Unity and Difference: the essence of science is the dissolution of centres and, soon enough, of mixtures.

2. Indivision is an absolute phenomenal given that must no longer be experienced in the mode of an ideal essence and transcendent law, or even as an internal and external limit to division, as is the case with Difference. That the One would be the object of a transcendental experience that is non-thetic (of) itself, absolute and without remainder, this would signify that it is given immediately (to) itself as what it is. Indivision is given (to) itself in the mode of indivision: it is 'non-reflexive' or immediate. This is why a thinking of the immediate givens of the One and the space of multiplicity specific to the One thus lived in immanence is opposed to the philosophies like

those of Difference which posit, after Hegel, after the entire tradition, that is, philosophical decision, that the One or the Absolute is given *through* and also *with* scission, given in loss and in the mode of nothingness. As if the immediate could be given through and with mediation, as if the immediate would have neither sense nor truth save in the speech of mediation to itself. Yet the One or truth knows neither withdrawal nor forgetting: it is only philosophy that forgets the One. Not for reasons as contingent as the contingency of the emergence of the ontological fact – the *parousia* – in the Greco-Occidental field, but for reasons of transhistorical and 'eternal' principle, as eternal as the One itself.

3. To deliver the *transcendental truth* from the aims of metaphysics would perhaps be the means for retrieving the irreducible 'mystic' condition of every philosophy. In introducing the term 'mystic' we do not intend to link thinking once again to aims that would be alien to its essence, but to restore to thought the sole object worthy of its contemplation. Perhaps we should distinguish carefully what is at issue here, not the 'mystical' ['la' mystique] but the 'mystic' ['le' mystique] inasmuch as this latter is the essence of philosophy – itself nothing but a technology of thinking that would like to take itself to be thought's essence – and to distinguish the 'mystic' precisely from the 'mystical' and still more from 'mysticism'. Each of these three cases has to do with a recourse to an immediate givenness, or some claim to such. But by the 'mystic', we understand the immediate givenness of the One, as well as of the Other *in* this radical immanence of the One, the givenness of Indivision as such and as separate from the All; by the 'mystical', the claim to the immediate givenness of the Other in what remains here despite everything a theological transcendence; by 'mysticism', the claim to the immediate givenness of Being or the All of reality. The 'mystic' such as we understand it here is the token or guarantee of the radical autonomy of the most 'individual' thinking and, through this, of philosophy with regard to what is not philosophy. But on the condition of separating this from every technological part of philosophy, among other things from Difference as thus deprived of every constitutive function with respect to philosophy. It is not a matter of claiming to dissolve or to destroy Difference, for example into two principles, but of thinking

the technology of Difference from its real essence, precisely what Difference on its own account has never been able to do.

THE REALITY OF THE CRITIQUE OF PHILOSOPHICAL DECISION

1. Difference cannot be attacked on its own terrain. But this is no obstacle, since we have already renounced *once and for all (is this possible? this is no longer the question)* to 'repeat', 'turn' or 'overcome' it. We are constrained, by the One rather than by Difference, not so much really to change the terrain as to know that we are already on another terrain. To pass *but is this really a passage?* from the terrain of ideality mixed with reality to the terrain *but is this really a terrain?* of the real in a transcendental sense – which is not necessarily to ground some 'transcendental realism'. The One in its essence is not transcendent, it is *absolutely* separated from beings and from Being and is so *solely through its real immanence in itself.* This means: in reality it is not the One that is separated from Being, it is Being that is separated from the One; it is not the One that is the Other of Difference, it is Difference that is the Other of the One. In the real critique of Difference, we do not proceed through any passage, escape from . . . or re-entry into . . . philosophy.

In order to break cleanly with the infinite prestiges of Difference, Being, Text, Desire, Power, Perception, State, Neuter, etc., we must thus renounce 'leaping', 'rupturing' or 'interrupting', 'turning', operations that belong to the logic of Difference and to the continuity of a calculus: since we must make a rupture with Difference itself, with transcendence itself. Would this not be the most invisible gesture, to abandon – this step has never been taken except through hallucination – all transcendence, that of Being, for immanence, that of the One stripped absolutely of 'opening', of 'scission', of 'difference'? Truly immediate givens cannot take any form other than transcendental; they cannot also be metaphysical or still use the inaugural and supreme operation of philosophy, transcendence. The real does not tolerate any operation and is not an operation itself: *we do not exit from philosophy into the One; we describe the vision-in-One of philosophy.* Philosophical activism, no matter how mitigated by Difference, is here only an object or an experience to be described; it is no longer *also* something to be done: nothing of reduction, of doubt, of operation-of-transcendence, no overcoming, turning, etc., is able to contrive *access* to the One, which knows nothing of such measures.

2. On the other hand, if there is difference or distinction in general, if for example Difference is the Other of the One, then this very distinction must be experienced and tested from the One. Also, we do not rise back here from Difference to its foundation in or its requisition of the One, but instead we follow an irreversible order going from the One, which in any case we are, to Difference, which we are not. Consequently, a real critique of Difference from the beginning does not ground itself – since this becomes a simple effect – upon the fact that Difference presupposes the One in the name of *requisite* and yet denies or forgets this. Such an argument is still of a philosophical kind. However it may prove useful. In effect, Difference produces, as we know, such transcendental tautologies as 'Nothingness nihilates' or 'desiring machines desire' or 'Difference differentiates', etc. Yet these are never – despite their most secret hope, which they remain capable of denying locally but outside of which they would possess neither life nor thought nor movement – immediate experiences of essence, absolute or absolutely irreducible experiences or tests of essence (of Being, Desire, Text, etc.). Difference is a game of paper and ink postulating the most non-reflexive immediateness by drawing a balance from the One, but without placing itself in any state where it could possibly repay. We find here, reaching up into its ideology of the debt, of debt rather than exchange, the profound irresponsibility of Difference. Difference requires the One, but the One is not recognized as the true 'differentiator' of Difference; Difference claims to be its own differentiator and to form a process capable of an auto-production and reproduction that would no longer be merely ontico-ontological but also unary-ontological. Yet without the One as susceptible to being used for grounding the unicity and co-belonging, the continuity and multiplicity of the throws or gifts of Being to thought, without this transcendental factor, universal Being would founder, as essence itself, in the contingency of empirical or intra-mundane plurality. We thus do not criticize Difference for failing to assume a supreme Identity

in order to bind together the disparate – it necessarily does assume such an Identity and in any case cannot do otherwise – but rather for assuming that this function of unification exhausts the One's essence. It is not an originary differentiator that Difference lacks, since Difference does require the One, but the transcendental truth of the One itself inasmuch as this truth is in no way constituted by and as Difference. More precisely: Difference is ultimately 'grounded' as such in the One – which is to say, in the non-reflexive transcendental experience of immanence – but Difference makes use of the One in such a way that this experience is denied; Difference is thus obligated to render itself infinitely 'iterable', to become its own stakes in its own game, the becoming-difference of Difference that *must* 'be' itself as Self (*das Selbige*) since it has after all taken up the mediation of the One, the Self's source. That 'Being itself' (*Seyn*) would be its 'own' process and the process of its becoming-its-own at any rate presupposes the One in its truth, but it still denies this.

3. However this argument is merely a consequence and cannot found a rigorous critique of Difference. On the other hand it may at least indicate certain tasks, even if it is unable to resolve them. For example: if Difference knows how to distinguish the One from the Idea, it is still in its necessary unity with the latter, in its role as limit. *It has not reached the point of founding itself upon a terrain other than that of the Greco-Occidental and Neo-Platonizing, on a non-reflexive = indivisible immanence that would have as 'object' Indivision itself as essence.* Difference does not know how to 'reduce' the One to the state of non-thetic given or lived immanence, but has always experienced it at worst in its mélange, at best in its co-belonging, with the Idea – in the pure mixture of Being. It has known not only how to draw out the maximum effects of Being as of the most fundamental Greco-contemporary mixture, but it has known how to 'intensify' this and place it in the position of continuously augmenting its critical effects. No more however than with the Dialectic or with Structure, no more than with the entirety of Occidental thought, has Difference been able either to dissolve or simply to ground the mixture of Being itself. It would be content to purify Being of the inferior forms of Representation, to generalize or universalize it as supra-historical, supra-mundane, supra-logocentric, etc. But a purification is nothing other than a universalization; it is not a

real and positive destruction, but is quite *nearly* the contrary. As soon as the One in its essence is no longer confounded with its effect within ideality, with a superior form of ideality, with the unifying system of Ideas or of the plural *a priori*, as soon as the One is no longer an Idea superior to the others or *is no longer a mode of transcendence in general*, it is freed also from the historico-global, supra-human, supra-political, supra-logocentric labours to which Difference, after the Dialectic and so many other epochs of thought, has dedicated it.

In a general way, like the philosophies that preceded it, Difference neither can nor wishes to go to the very end of its presuppositions, to their 'unary' or absolute form; it halts itself if not before the mixtures, at least before the essence of mixture, mixture par excellence or mixture's superior form. It halts on the one hand at the experience of the One as given by Being, and on the other at the experience of Representation as given by Greco-Occidental history (*Parousia*, *Anwesen*, identity through exclusion). And moreover, it would destroy itself if by some chance it were able to extricate the unary kernel of ontology and if it were to reach the absolutely ultimate 'presuppositions' of the One as immanent transcendental experience and of Representation as a non-thetic type of transcendence 'before' or 'opposite' the One.

4. Must the limitation of the philosophical critique of Representation be made still in the mode of self-critique or rather in that of another experience of truth, still other than that of a 'withdrawal'? And is to say that the One is something still other than a limit without being for all that a logocentric interiority to fall under the limitation still exercised by the philosophical One? We here abandon precisely any philosophical kind of 'critique' that would proceed through a supplementary limitation of Difference, which at any rate is already every possible philosophical critique. But in compensation we 'postulate' that the limitation by Difference of the logocentric interpretation of the One does not hold by its own condition within the specific *essence* of the One. The circle of interpreting-interpreted or of deconstructing-deconstructed no longer holds as soon as it is a matter of the real essence of the One rather than of its ideal modes. From Being to the One – this indeed no longer marks some 'leap', some always continuous cut needed for thought, or a 'shift of terrain', or a

change of order or dimension, or a *Kehre*. It is a shift that has no name and is without concept since it sets thinking within the non-lieu of the One and does not proceed by following a boundary or a limit, neither 'proceeding' nor 'retroceding' in general.

If thinking is able to traverse the cycle of the systems of Difference, a cycle perhaps moreover infinite in extent, but which may still be grasped in its invariant essence, if thinking understands the essentially vicious character of this philosophy and not only this philosophy – its nature of decision and auto-position –, it is not so as to 'exit' from metaphysics or to claim naively to have destroyed it, but to recognize the eternal and supra-historical necessity of metaphysics from the standpoint of the One which, in this way, justifies it further than philosophy itself ever could. It is hardly a matter of dissolving the mixture of Difference: this would be to prolong and universalize, thanks to the One, the mixtures of metaphysics. It is rather a matter of holding separate, without communication, at least without any communication or exchange that would be reciprocal, which is possible only through their vision in One, the 'opposites' that are on the one hand the One as immediate givens of truth or of immanence, as transcendental criterion of truth given with truth, and on the other hand philosophy, all the metaphysical technology of Being and Unity, as well as that of the destruction of Being, of Logos, etc. It is not a matter of claiming naively to place Heidegger between parentheses, nor indeed of cutting a Gordian knot in order to 'choose', but rather of distributing entirely otherwise – from here on without having to operate, sever or cut – what is severable (philosophy) and what is not (truth), of rejecting philosophy outside of the essence of truth in the sense that, while philosophy of course has need of truth, it does not constitutively determine truth's essence, an essence that neither is nor can be constituted. This solution clearly has mystic and gnostic tints. For it is perhaps possible, if not to 'exit' from metaphysics, and from Heidegger as well, by 'entering back' into the One, at least to comprehend that we need not enter metaphysics in the first place and that gnosis is what, of itself, separates the principles.

5. In reality what is able to pass for paradox in the eyes of philosophy, a supplementary manner of contorting the same concepts, is understood as perfectly simple once we have recognized here the posture of

science with respect to the real or to its object: science does not constitute its object, but knows itself straightaway and non-thetically to be identical (to) this real even as its reflection. *Science is a representation that is non-thetic (of) the real, altogether distinct from what philosophy imagines as Representation.* Given its strictly immanent and transcendental nature, its essence as fundamentally non-positional (of) itself, we suspect that the One provokes a perplexity and resistance within philosophy: this latter imagines that the relations of the two principles are of enormous complexity and subject to countless paradoxes, if not aporias. To be sure, it is necessary to take these aporias seriously but to place them at the account of philosophy rather than of science and the scientific critique of philosophy.

Is it necessary to know how to interrupt a philosophy, and philosophy itself? An interruption, however, is still a matter of calculation, of strategic delay; it is a manner of prolongation. Is it thus necessary to interrupt interruption: not to interrupt in general? Rather: to render contingent, but absolutely so, which is to say, beyond its simple continuity or continuation, the philosophy one would propose somewhat naively to interrupt, as well as philosophical decision in general. Above all, not the logic of interruption, the unmoved mover of all Greco-Occidental philosophy to this day. Instead, the logic of immanent gnosis, which is to say, of science correctly understood: to raise philosophy to the status of 'eternal' *principle* that is nonetheless devoid of 'reality', devoid and contingent to the extent of its eternity and necessity.

What is alone capable of rendering a philosophy at once necessary and also empty or vicious, at once absolutely necessary and also perfectly contingent? The One alone. Only an absolute science allows for the 'exiting' from Nietzsche, Heidegger and 'Difference' in general since science makes it understood that man may never be, at least through his essence, determined and comprehended by philosophy. Philosophy is the Other of man – to describe this will suffice.

THE POWERLESSNESS OF DIFFERENCE TO BE ABSOLUTE

1. The aim of Difference? To become absolute. By what means? By detaching transcendence from its relativity to beings, to the presence

of beings. What Heidegger means by the 'absolute transcending' of Being is obviously wholly distinct from the absolute transcendence of some being, of a divine being for instance. It is rather what, to parody Nietzsche, we would characterize as follows: to make transcendence and immanence coincide at the summit of contemplation. A summit infinitely renewed where thinking finds rest in one *epoche* only in order to pass in transit (to) another. The inscription of transcendence within immanence is possible only if immanence is, if not the energy of transcendence at least its unmoved mover. This is the 'Turning': of man towards Being, towards the One in Being, towards Difference; but where it is not man who turns 'himself', where it is man who is turned by, for, as the One and who lets the 'Turning' be. 'Complete' Difference is the unary essence or arc that tends, all in one movement, from each of the contraries (to) the other, and deploys these *as* contraries.

Let us take the case of Heidegger in order to exemplify this law. Rather than Forgetting being stranded and disappearing in itself within the claimed positivity of presence (as *factum a priori*), Difference ensures that *forgetting continues or prolongs itself 'as forgetting', but in the sense that it is the One that now claims the withdrawal or the forgetting instead of the withdrawal claiming to withdraw or the forgetting to forget.* When the One claims withdrawal or immanence claims transcendence, when forgetting or transcendence 'turn' in the Turning (of) the One, then the forgetting *of* forgetting changes its sense, its truth and its locus: it 'goes up' as far as the One; it becomes this forgetting (of) forgetting in which the transcendent intentionality of the 'of' is lifted *by* and *as* the One. The forgetting or the withdrawal becomes relative to itself or absolute; this is still an intentional relation or a transcendence, but in the sense that intentionality, as transcendence inscribed *within* immanence, is now also a non-relation, an indivision.

2. *Yet does this effort, this tension towards and of the supreme condition suffice to lift the initial relativity of the a priori or of metaphysics to the object-being with respect to which it is thought from the very start? What does Difference achieve in its tension towards the Absolute?* How is one to render 'absolute' a transcending which by definition is always relative to what it exceeds and to that from which it separates itself? The

conditions of the task to be resolved are clearly contradictory. In order to try to save the *a priori*, the withdrawal that co-belongs to it or the nothingness that distinguishes it from the empirical or the 'real' (*res*), in order to rescue these from the ontic facticity relative to which they are nothingness or withdrawal and in order that one might say: 'Nothingness nihilates', or even, why not?, still according to the same logic, 'withdrawal withdraws', it will be necessary a second time, this time as transcendental, to re-affirm them. But to affirm the co-belonging of the withdrawal (of the universal) and the One, as a withdrawal from this point on 'proper to' or rather identical with the One, is to introduce relation, division and relativity into the One. On the one hand withdrawal is saved or retained as withdrawal, but the relativity to the empirical is in its turn retained as relativity and, in this sense, the fact that the One claims the withdrawal or the forgetting does not abolish the essence of relation, its relativity, but solely the forgetting of this essence in the positivity of beings. And above all, the relativity that is the essence of withdrawal or transcendence is from here on reaffirmed by and as Absolute; relativity penetrates into the essence of the Absolute with the help of the Absolute: transcending cannot be absolute except when it is still relative, but relative to itself; Difference cannot conceive it so except as relative-absolute. Unitary transcendental thinking has need of a motorizing couple, and in this case it is that of the ontico-ontological multiple (the *a priori*) and Unity (the transcendental): like every couple, it cannot fail to shackle itself in its own functioning. What is said to be transcendental is not so much the One itself as the operation of passage, overcoming, appropriation, turning of the multiple towards, by and as the One. The One is not experienced except in the mode of the transcendental All; it is placed in the service of Being so that Being may be saved from the empirical-and-rational forms of the totalization of beings. The One is indeed required as what distinguishes itself absolutely from empirical diversity, but it is sufficient that this distinction be experienced as a passage, as an ontological mediation, as an opposition despite everything or a relativity of the All and of essence to the particular and its multiplicity, in order that the transcendental essence of the One be missed once again. The One, which is the *absolutely* other of object-being, can no longer be anything but relatively other to it once it is effectuated within the element of ideality. The duplicity of Difference is to make use of the One, to capture it to Difference's own profit, in order to render Difference absolutely other than its ontological form, but yet to contradict at the last moment the transcendental truth of the One.

In order for a category to receive a tautological = differential usage (*Brauch*), it must fulfil a negative condition: to become in-determinable in both ontic and ontico-ontological (metaphysical) modes. But 'indeterminable' is an ambiguous term. What is excluded is no more than determination in the empirico-ontic sense of a 'determined' = particular object-being, in the sense of ontic multiplicity. Not only is object-being in general not excluded, but Difference is capable of none other than an entirely relative mode of determination, albeit, at least partially, a positive mode of determination. Supreme or transcendental determination comes from the One, and the One would not be transcendental if its determinative power were not 'identically' its power of 'auto'-determination, its positive power of determining itself solely and immediately through itself without passing through the element of Being and *a fortiori* of beings. But Difference itself makes a restricted or ontological usage of the One. It thus loses the positivity and specificity of unary determination as soon as it experiences this in the mode of loss or division, of ontico-ontological or meta-physical determination. No doubt this loss itself becomes relatively positive: Nothingness itself receives a unary or immanent usage, Non-Being itself becomes a mitigated and tempered non ? being. But the One does not lend its transcendental positivity to the Nothingness or the Loss that it delivers from their meta-physical bondage without losing on the exchange, without being affected in return by the non ? being that becomes this monstrous partner that it can no longer 'unclutch'. In this way the positivity of unary determination is itself forever affected – if not really, at least in the hallucinatory mode of philosophy – by the non ? being, a Nothingness that is still relative to Being and, from there, to beings. Not only is Nothingness unable to be saved entirely from its relativity to Being and to beings, from its metaphysical usage – precisely because this philosophy claims to place the One in its service and to take care to guard Nothingness from its ontic and ontological usages – but, conversely, these effects being complementary, the One is no longer absolutely metaphysically indeterminable; it is compromised by a remainder of relativity to Being.

Scission, relation and relativity re-appear within the Absolute, within the One and *with* the One. Without a doubt Difference becomes a transcendental principle subjugating the major categories of metaphysics to itself, imprinting them with the form-without-form (the 'Form forming-formed . . . ', etc.) of the Same. But Nothingness is indivisible *and* separated from itself (this is why it 'nihilates') and the duality of contraries is found once again at the heart of their unity, even if each of them appears to have acquired its transcendental autonomy or its 'absoluteness'. An Absolute of this kind is hardly an absolute: it is only a *relativity to itself*, a *Selbst* at once divided and indivisible; only immediateness receding infinitely from the immediate *and* from mediation. It is indeed the *And* in its transcendental sense that Difference strives to think even while supposing it still to be unthought, the *And* or the *Same*: *but does not transcendental truth exclude outside of itself the 'And' and the 'Same'?*

The sense of Heidegger's project with respect to essence must be correctly understood: it does not signify, or not only, as Heidegger says at one point, that Being withdraws *inasmuch as* it opens into beings, but rather that withdrawal is self-withdrawing, and is so not as the operation of some new form of the metaphysical subject and a transcendent being, but as One or essence. It is even more interesting that Heidegger almost always places dissimulation's 'self-withdrawing' in relation with the operation of Being upon beings. There is nothing at all surprising here – Heidegger, Difference and philosophy in general pose the problem of essence in such a way that it is impossible to resolve to the benefit of essence itself and such that withdrawal, even thought as autonomous = immanent = unary, as an absolute self-withdrawing, remains relative to Being or to unveiled beings, to the operation of the unveiling not of Being itself, to be sure, but of beings by Being.

How would appearance or phenomenality be able, with such an essence, to be other than beings? The transcendent type of finitude definitively prohibits any thinking of the Absolute that would be something other than an absolute 'transcendence', an absolute withdrawal. The function of the Absolute is performed by the moment of division or forgetting, because this Finitude is the point of view that definitively relativizes Being and reduces its essence to transcendence – always relative – rather than to immanence; which elevates it to essence and also condemns both it and the One itself all at once to be thought according to this mode. Essence, because its positivity as non-reflexive and immediate given is straightaway lacking, is no longer able to be thought except as Non-essence, as still determined in return by the metaphysical type of essence to which it opposes itself and will continue to oppose itself, remaining relative to it to the point of its Turning which is still nothing but a mode of transcendence. As if the light belonging to essence had still *finally* to be related to the illumination of those beings that will come to dissimulate it.

If to think Being in its truth means simply that it is distinguished from any determinate being, then Difference suffices – in principle at least and setting aside the problem of Finitude – for this task. If it means that Being will be thought as having nothing to do with beings in general, one must answer: (a) Difference thinks Being as Being, *Wesen* as *wesendes Wesen*, according to the transcendental rule of tautology, and thus independently, in effect, of its 'contrary' of beings – or nothingness – and this is true in a sense even when nothingness is said on its own account to co-belong indivisibly to Being; (b) however Being as Same is immediately its scission with itself; contrariety is reintroduced directly into it: Being is also nothingness or being-One to the extent that it is *also* distinct from itself. Consequently, Being is indeed thought as 'itself', in its autonomy, but it is the autonomy of the Same instead of being that of a real identity (with) itself. Heidegger, in the treatment of whatever category, in this case that of Being, knows no other alternative than that of formal identity and Difference as transcendental tautology. The 'ownness' or essence of whatever category is not an immediacy, is not the immediation of unary essence, but solely Difference, which undoes only the inferior forms of 'ownness' and 'propriety', but substitutes tautology for these which, despite its transcendental essence, misses the One, misses the 'proper' absolute that the One is and, for this reason, is incapable of really thinking Being as absolute Other of beings in general or of nothingness. The potentialization of ontological Difference does not abolish its mediate/immediate character, its syntax of the chiasmus; it is content to transfer this continuously up into the One. This is why all of Heidegger's attempts to think Being 'itself' are immediately threatened with making recourse to a transcendence of Being where the Absolute is placed once again in the service of transcending.

3. In having liquidated transcendent terms and even the ontico-onto-logical relations bound to the ontic multiplicity of Being, in having imprinted upon these the non-formal force of the One, mediation has still not really been excluded outside of absolute Difference. The One in its essence is the positive absence of form. But in its usage by Dif-ference, the One is no longer absolutely without form; it is its merely relative absence of form – relative still to the meta-physical form that it repudiates – that is permeated by the absolute without-form, which thus loses its radical absence of formality. In just this way the contra-ries, here too, mutually permeate one another and mediation re-introduces itself within immediacy.

Will it perhaps be objected that Difference has succeeded in think-ing mediation *as such*, that it has learned finally how to appropriate mediation to its essence, to raise it from its metaphysical servitude to the Idea to the state of 'tautology' or transcendental principle, and that just as Nothingness nihilates, in the same way would 'Mediation mediate'? But on the one hand mediation is not elevated by Differ-ence to its 'superior' form or form 'par excellence', as differential and no longer dialectical mediation, except at the price of an ultimate but irreducible mediation this time of the One, not by such and such an empirical form of mediation, but, what is worse, by Mediation in per-son. Even when the One claims mediation without being, in principle at least, mediated itself, since it is then the immediateness *of* medi-ation rather than an immediacy for mediation and as offered to its work, it still does not prevent the One from being, for one last time but definitively and without recourse, mediated, no longer by such and such a particular mediation, but by the essence of mediation, mediation in general or as universal. And on the other hand, the tran-scendental essence having been lost in the operation, it becomes use-less, if not to turn in a vicious circle, still to relate mediation in its metaphysical forms to Difference: Difference will not lend to it – to it as to Being, Desire, Power, Language or whatever other 'category' – anything but an 'ownness' fundamentally contaminated by what is not it, a lacked essence, and more radically lacking than Difference could ever imagine and foresee as it does to a certain extent from its own side. Immediacy is no longer an absolute essence, immediately given in an internal experience; it becomes an attribute or a supra-attribute that is said of all the attributes (Being, Nothingness,

Language, Power, Desire), but particularly of Nothingness or of mediation. Instead of immediacy remaining in itself, it is alienated as relative to/relativized by mediation and is said of mediation. Difference believes itself able to render Being immediate by relating it to the One, but in this operation it misses the true essence of the One and mediates it. Far from excluding mediation, Difference excludes only its inferior forms in order to install itself within Mediation it-'self', as elevated to the rank of the very Locus of thinking and truth.

With respect to the relativity of Being and beings within metaphysics, the circuit of their reciprocal determination, a certain immediateness has no doubt been achieved. And it is true that the passage to unary immanence, even in this semi-immanent/semi-transcendent mode, allows for the destruction, the deconstruction of the most obvious transcendent relations of Being and beings, those of 'Representation'. But once again, the One cannot but place itself at the service of Being or transcendence and does not limit these in their metaphysico-empirical forms except so as better to save and preserve the reflexive and vicious essence of unitary transcendence. Difference is an instrument that cannot but infinitely approach – which is to say, retreat from – the immediateness of the One. Difference immediates metaphysical mediation, but only by mediating the immediate. There is here in fact no really immediate experience of the essence of Being, the essence of Nothingness, of Language, etc. Only a false immediateness, that which is experienced in and by scission or loss – alienation become positive. As the determination proper to the One implies the absence for positive reasons of every metaphysical determination, Difference cannot but lack it, sinking into this 'lack' and this failure, having failed it as such by its very existence as difference. The passage from its categorial to its authentic transcendental usage is confused here with the passage from its metaphysical to its differential usage. Difference does not save Nothingness from the category of negation, nor the essence of Language from the linguistic, nor the essence of Power from the political, etc. Is the task of the thinking that thinks essence to care for Power, for Language, for essence as essence-of-power, essence-of-language, essence-of-nothingness, etc.?

4. *The whole operation collapses then in the inessentiality of an interminable process, in a mitigated but unlimited labour that must presuppose itself in*

order to give itself reality and of which auto-position is the sole reality of sub-stitution and artefact. The mitigation of dialectical labour within Differ-ence does not cause us to exit from the ancient, Greco-Christian ages of metaphysics, but rather prolongs them. Heidegger's pathetic effort to think an originarily finite Absolute, an absolute Finitude, is a con-tradiction that cannot be resolved except by 'becoming what it is' through its unlimited repetition, through the introduction of becom-ing into Being and through the definition of essence as infinite co-belonging of becoming and Being, an aporia that can only become positive by being transformed into an infinite task. This effort belongs to the essence of Difference which tries in vain to think a withdrawal that would not be simply a loss. It cannot liquidate this aporia that it itself is rather through and through and which is born from its 'lack' of the One's essence, a lack more essential in every respect than its self-withdrawing-withdrawal. A certain naïvete of Difference – but this has been the greater part of the tradition, at the very least since Plato – has fostered hope that the Absolute is possible in the mode of transcendence or of precisely *passage*, that the One may be thought in the mode of Being.

'Absolute Difference' is an interminable desire. It is not the Abso-lute itself, but rather what causes the loss of its affect. Philosophy is in general the dissolution of the Absolute, the spirit of scepticism and war with respect to the real, the most steadfast attempt to corrupt and destroy the individual. On this basis, it compromises step by step all the other categories that are destined to be 'differed' and activates their tautologies. It cannot imagine a Nothingness that would not exit from itself, that would not alienate itself in order to 'nihilate', even if this were to be something other than an ontic exiting from self and production. No more does it imagine that essence would be able to remain in itself inasmuch as it would be unary: *das Wesen* must be *wesend*, Difference itself must be 'differance' or 'differentiating'. Medi-ation has been simply interiorized to the One, obviously not in the mode of a psycho-metaphysical interiorization, but in the only mode tolerable by the One when it is reduced to ideality.

5. The Nothingness that nihilates must be lived from the beginning in a strictly non-reflexive mode . . . Language speaks right from the beginning, before any lexico-grammatical context, before even any

sense, in a radical immanence, remaining there *in itself,* not only *next-to-itself* like the *phonē.* Language speaks without any repetition belonging necessarily to its essence, and we say all things 'in' Language. Through its essence, Language is straightaway *really-immanent* (to) the One or in-itself = non-reflexive. It has no need from the start to be an infinite attribute requiring a repetition or Turning in order to accede to its essence. Because Language is straightaway immanent, strictly individual, 'individual' in the transcendental sense of the word, because it is absolute in this way, it has no need to be this universal element carrying within itself the scission of language and the spoken (*Sprache/spricht*) and then overcoming or including this within a repetition. All this might be said equally of Being, Nothingness, Desire, Text, Transcendence, etc.

If Finitude and what it introduces into Difference prohibit any confusion of the Heideggerean project with a mere repetition of Hegel, it is still however not this – here is the last reservation, yet a decisive one, as little Hegelian as possible, constraining us to abandon Heidegger himself – that is able to claim *really* to have liquidated Idealism and its avatars in Hegel and Nietzsche. The One, even as an absolute transcendence, is experienced here still as a mode of transcendence in general; its reality and its immanence are sacrificed to what remains *despite everything* of a transcendence of theological origin in the 'thing in itself' and Finitude. No doubt it is also this that must be thought: the absolute 'transcendence' (of) the real, *this separation that the real imposes rather upon the World.* Yet perhaps one must accept for this the dissociation once and for all of the Absolute and transcendence, cease to be obsessed with an operation of scission, division, cut – even if this is disguised through 'Withdrawal' – and abandon oneself to the One without transcendence in the same way that it gives itself (to) itself and also just as much (to) us. Heidegger re-activates against Hegel a generalized Kantianism, but he remains dependent upon the thematic of an extrinsic Finitude. This latter, despite its transformations in order to become essence, remains a restrictive and timorous interpretation of the One itself, but also of its 'vis-à-vis', 'second principle' or 'transcendence'. Heidegger has no means for exiting from the confusion of the real and the ideal. His obsession with the idealist reduction of the real and the philistine remedy of extrinsic Finitude he proposes are complementary and divide up a unique theoretical field, that of the unitary mixtures whose essence he wishes finally to pre-serve, as well as the necessity this has always had for Occidental thought. There is perhaps something of more grandeur in the idealist power play. But there is a power play here too at the very interior of the region of mixtures, the only region in all likelihood where think-ing necessitates violence.

OF THE ONE AS GUARDIAN OF METAPHYSICS

1. Difference fails to attain its goal, a proper and sufficient internal determination of essence. The One is not sufficiently determined by it. Why? Difference fulfils, giving to it its perfect form, the oldest Occidental habitus: at worst, to philosophize is to mix and confuse; at best, it is to traverse the in-betweens or to trace boundaries. To think is thus to-think-at-the-limit: never has such contempt for the 'term' and the individual been so manifest, such obsession with 'relation'. Never has thought been such a master of the Limit, of its own limits, of its weakness. Never has it established with such metic-ulousness and relentlessness the adding-and-subtracting of its pow-ers and its powerlessness with respect to Representation and the possibility of pushing back the limits of Representation. *Yet is the One equally a phenomenon of the 'limit' and may it thus be placed solely in the service of the difference of contraries?* Are we condemned to return to logocentrism and Representation as soon as we refuse to think the One in terms of limitation (in terms of cut or 'analytic')? The essence of Being excludes Being from being pure manifestation or transpar-ent presence to itself: Difference in general dismisses this solution which it identifies immediately with that of logocentric interiority or the self-adequation towards which metaphysical presence tends. But does this objection, even if it holds for Being, still hold for the One and its specific essence?

Difference believes so. It posits: *either* that the One may indeed be experienced in itself; but then it is not a matter of the One and its indivisible, in itself and real essence in this idealist version of Differ-ence (Nietzsche, Deleuze), but only of the One's ideal immanence, understood finally in the mode of Being. *Or* that this One is real and supra-ideal (Heidegger, Derrida) but can never be experienced in itself, every 'experience' being presupposed as transcendent and idealized, susceptible to being divided and deferred; and that the One intervenes solely as unsurpassable Limit, as the indivision of a withdrawal or a division. *This alternative or dialectic allows Difference to leave the essence and reality of the Limit itself undetermined; Difference abandons any attempt to explain its usage of the One and abandons above all furnishing any proper and positive essence to the transcendental itself, since it reduces all positivity to that of beings.* Moreover, it has to place the positivity proper to essence no longer within the One, but rather on the other side of Difference, in the operation of division (the case of finite Difference: Heidegger and Derrida).

No doubt the limit as used by Difference is just as much unlimited and interminable as limited, and its finitude is just as much infinite as finite. But this unlimitedness is none other than the correlate of a relative limit that cannot save itself from its relativity except by making itself unlimited, by becoming absolute in this secondary mode that is more wished for than real. It is thus quite an impoverished Absolute, permeated as it is by a never truly destroyed relativity, that Difference articulates. An Absolute that is none other than a still limited unlimitedness, that will never free itself from the spirit and the technique of 'limitation', which is to say, of Decision. There is nothing more 'historical' and more perfectly corresponding to a certain state, for example of modern if not of contemporary mathematics, than to deprive thought of all *supposedly* intuitive content, of every given term, and to assign to thought a game of limits or cuts.

If this comparison has meaning outside of Difference, for a thinking of the One, while it has none for Difference, we would say that Difference has not learned how to elevate itself really to the level of substance and that it has remained a thinking of the attribute, of the mode-attribute coupling, of the coincidence, whether immediate or not (Nietzsche or Heidegger) of the singular and the universal; a philosophy that projects this synthesis, more or less deferred but always obeying the same schema (the mode's cut is also an attribute or represents an attribute for some other mode, and so on unlimitedly – Finitude would not really destroy this schema) on to substance, instead of thinking substance in its essence. Yet perhaps the true malaise of Difference, of which Finitude will have been able to change nothing whatsoever, comes from the fact that it still conceives the One precisely as a substance, as a universal of universals or the unity of the attributes, as no more than a sort of *supra-attribute* (the 'Same' as the indivision of differends). The One is not experienced in its essence by Difference. Rather, Difference makes it coincide with the universal (the metaphysical form of the *a priori*) in a manner either more or less immediate = logocentric or on the contrary deferred, and in either case thus demeans it in the inferior process of the limit.

Without a doubt, no limit thinks itself in itself; it is something unconscious that causes thought and that manifests the forms and loci of thinking. It thus cannot be a matter for us of thinking the limit 'in itself', but rather the essence of the One inasmuch as it *also* conditions, no longer being simply reduced to this, the functions of absolute limit fulfilled by the One, either within the element of ideality, since this latter from its side claims to project its divisions or limitations up into the One (Nietzsche), or against ideality and yet still in relation to it (Heidegger). With Difference, philosophy finally becomes this technology of limits that are transcendental in kind or more exactly semi-immanent and semi-transcendent – at times immanence prevailing (Nietzsche, Deleuze), at times transcendence (Heidegger, Derrida) –, this art of in-betweens and their primacy over their terms, this power to critique and to reproduce empirical mixtures that still does not know itself as the pure or *absolutely universal* force of mixture in the face of the One. Such knowledge assumes another point of view.

2. The systems of Difference belong to this constellation of the transcendental – the greater part of philosophy – that defines the transcendental itself through operations of division, synthesis, choice and non-choice, through an entire technology or syntax, through decision in general. That they have purified and universalized the syntax regulating the relations of the empirical, the *a priori* and the transcendental, that they have cleared this syntax of its exclusively scientific, historical or cultural objects marks a great and important work distinguishing them for example from Kantianism. But they have subjected the *veritas transcendentalis* all the more so to a philosophical technology that is still, although to different degrees, as much transcendent as it is transcendental. By refusing to substitute the transcendental as

experience and as immediate givens for the transcendental as syntax; by remaining at the border of the meta-physical and the transcendental; by reflecting so many of their meta-physical predecessors into the transcendental; by ceaselessly combining new mixtures, semi-immanent/semi-transcendent entities like Power, Text, Desire, Being; by instituting the coincidence of immanence and transcendence as the infinite task of thinking, they have perhaps lost the true summit of contemplation. The drama of classical and modern transcendental thinking is that it is torn between its aim, which is immanence, and its means, which are, as its name indicates all too clearly, those of transcendence; it is thus a Decision and has an aim and gives itself means instead of being a rigorously immanent contemplation.

3. Difference proposes quite obviously to save not the One and the *veritas transcendentalis*, but only the conditions for the obtaining or producing of the meta-physical, of history as the history of Being and of Being as *a priori factum*. Like the entire transcendental tradition, it puts the *veritas transcendentalis* at the service of the *a priori* or the meta-physical; it orders it with respect to the subaltern task of genealogy, 'to think' and 'to save' the metaphysical. Difference renders immanent, as One, the critical decision that produces the *a priori*. It places in its service a 'sending' or 'destination' which must form no more than the genealogical element of Difference's ontological form. Instead of guarding the truth in its essence, it concerns itself from the start with the *a priori* and uses the One for the 'inferior' task of conserving, affirming, continuing the memory of nothingness that belongs to the meta-physical and in order to struggle against this latter's relapse into the positivity of beings. The transcendental is experienced as the unary dimension that over-comes the *a priori*, but does not over-come this without 'interiorizing' it and continuing to turn around it. Turning, Reversion, Re-affirmation, etc., signify not only that the meta-physical must no longer turn around objectivized-beings – this goes without saying – or that it is saved from particular beings, but that the Turning itself, however 'absolute' it may be, pays the stiff price of this intervention and continues to turn around the meta-physical as reduced from its side to its very essence, that is, to scission.

Difference produces to its own profit a surplus-value relative to metaphysical Being or Nothingness, a surplus-value of Being and of

Nothingness that it appears – an objective appearance – to have drawn from itself in a somewhat miraculous way (it is Being that approaches man, that 'sends' the relation of man to Being, etc.), but that it has most likely taken from the work of metaphysics, that which is made in the Relations of Being and beings in their multiplicity. An objective necessity of the system demands that it deny this origin, that it attribute to itself this surplus-value of Being, of Nothingness, of Language, of Mediation, etc., that it confound – how could it do otherwise? in play here is its very mechanism – the transcendental truth which itself excludes every form of 'surplus-value' with the element or categorial organon that it puts to work (Text, Being, Desire, etc.). From this follows the mixed notion par excellence of 'surplus-value' and the reduction of transcendental truth to a phenomenon of value, or Difference, and even of Difference as the very essence of value.

As productive of surplus-value, that which Difference in fact places in the service of Being – meant in this case as the very element of philosophy – Difference would claim rather to have put in the service of the One. In effect the classical conception of the transcendental as superior attribute reigns throughout Difference: *the transcendental is indeed an indivision through and beyond empirical distinctions, but it continues to attribute itself to something other than itself, to the empirical and to beings, or even to Being.* This is to confound the essence of transcendental reality, the One which is transcendental through itself and in itself prior to being so for any experience, with its ontological version which makes a mere dimension of the transcendental, as if Being were its vehicle par excellence, as if the One had need of being supported by and finally related to beings. Difference is in this way the game that the One introduces into the relations of Being of beings, distending them – through and beyond their contents of negativity, exclusion or identification – through a different disparity, through an inhibition and a unity that are no longer empirical but transcendental or indivisible; Difference sets a differance into Being separating it from beings in a way other than metaphysics ever could in its exclusive/identifying or topological modes: it makes use of the transcendental and requisitions it in the service of Being. *Difference, in thinking itself, thinks everything that it is possible to think of Being as soon as one no longer wishes to think it onto-theologically. On the other hand it thinks next to nothing of the One and is content merely to make it 'function'.* It has learned how to limit the identity = convertibility of the *ens* or of Being (as *Seyn*) and the One or Truth, but it has not done so except precisely to limit and defer such identity. It works by delaying this convertibility, by breaking up the exchange or equivalence of the transcendentals, but only in order better to reaffirm their co-vertibility, their co-version, their re-version. As if Difference had injected into the convertibility of the transcendentals none other than a provisional and partial irreversibility, just enough delay later to restore the convertibility in the form of 'tautologies'. The contemporary philosophy of Difference is the operation transforming transcendental convertibility into transcendental tautology. It has thus learned how partially to raise the One above the other transcendentals, exacting from these a certain labour, the entrance into a process in order really *to become* transcendentals in the mode of the One. But it has persisted in making of the One merely the superior form of the transcendentals; it has not broken once and for all with the system of convertibility and acceded to the transcendental essence that remains in-itself even in its gift to Being. That Difference thinks in the form of transcendental tautology is no great sign of daring: there has never been philosophy outside of the transcendental dimension that is philosophy's sole locus. But that Difference exceeds convertibility only in service of tautological thinking is indeed the sign of its timorous essence.

4. The thesis undertaken here against Difference, in Heidegger and others, is that it does not save itself from the meta-physical in general as it would propose, but saves only the metaphysical itself from its most reified, inferior forms (Representation, Logocentrism) and thereby carries it back to its essence as scission or transcendence. Far from destroying metaphysics, Difference remains content merely to purify its essence, just as it purifies and safeguards the essence of Representation against its most empirical forms: by sacrificing the essence of the One. The transcendental or unary remains supported by the *a priori* relative to which it does its work. This is precisely its naïveté: to believe that when Nothingness becomes *the Same* which it *is* in its essence, and which it contents itself with 'nihilating', it finally has excluded outside of itself its relation to its contrary and has freed itself from it, thus having really become autonomous (an 'ownness', a *Selbst*). But as for the real non-metaphysical essence of 'ownness', is it

Difference? Is it 'distance' as indivisible, 'structural distance', etc.? As always the illusion proper to Difference is *to believe that having 'differed' the most transcendent inferior forms of Representation, the most reified relations, it has at one blow destroyed every mediation, every 'relation'*. It has done nothing but relate these relations to a Non-relation; it has hardly abolished them – affirming moreover that one cannot abolish them or render them absolutely contingent, but affirming this only because it ignores the essence of the One. The true positivity of Nothingness, Desire, Language, is able to come to them only from elsewhere than from themselves. All the efforts to 'come up' to these 'tautologies' and to let them 'turn' towards/as the One only over-come the most vulgar forms of identity and presence but continue to ground themselves in transcendence instead of abandoning themselves to immanence. For transcendence too, moreover, it is just as with Nothingness or Mediation: Difference extracts an essence of transcendence that is still improper and vicious in the form of what it calls Turning (*Kehre*) or Reversion; it gives to metaphysical transcendence the 'form' of tautology, freeing it only from its metaphysical servitude (to which it will still nonetheless contribute) without allowing it to know the joys of the most positive immanence. 'Transcendence transcends' – here is an axiom that offers the true sense of the 'absolute transcending' of Being and signifies a limitation of the metaphysical type of transcendence, but a limitation that yet unlimits transcendence as Same. The One obviously does not limit the representational forms of transcendence except in order to save their essence, to keep this close to it and to communicate its inexhaustibility to it.

5. The task will be rather to restore not the truth of Being, but the very essence of truth inasmuch as this is no longer ordered to the safeguarding of ontological Difference or metaphysics, no longer interested in a claim to becoming, no longer caring or concerned with Being. All of contemporary thought is drunk with Samaritan piety: some want to take care of language; others want logic to take care of logic; still others find themselves caring for Being and delivered over to the caretaking of the Greco-Occidental metaphysical fact; the analysts and the analysed are interested in . . . the unconscious. To this piety, which takes such pains to distinguish itself from its religious origins, we will not oppose, as no doubt Levinas does,

man's imperious vocation to turn away from these idols and to become his brother's keeper, to substitute for the responsibility answering to the call of Being, the responsibility for the face of the Other. That Language, Desire, Text, Being, Power, the Unconscious are idols of man the philosopher is certainly quite plausible. However, we are not able to oppose to these idols *man* or the *I* as determined still through exteriority as hostage of the Other, for it is also quite plausible that man the philosopher is nothing without these idols precisely because it would still be too much simply to oppose him to them. It would be fine enough to be able to restore man in his solitude as against the philosophies that try to appropriate him to them and to adapt him to their theological, political, economic, etc., needs. And to restore with him the essence of truth and of science. And it is solely the essence of truth as transcendental and the transcendental as givens non-thetic (of) themselves that are capable of saving truth from the tasks of the caretaking of metaphysics or of onto-theo-logy in which truth risks losing its essence by gaining a soul, a history, a desire, a language, etc.

THE PHILOSOPHICAL HALLUCINATION OF THE ONE

1. The Same, or Difference as tautology is content to deepen the intrication, which is supposed to be a primitive fact of the Occident, of Being *and* the One. It does not make of the One a separated transcendence susceptible to events, to ontic (or ontico-ontological) procession and emanation. What Difference supposes as immediately given is not a transcendent hypostasis but the very operation or work of transcendence, *division as such or as One*, which is however not that of the 'Intelligible' since it is *immediately* the One itself. From this point of view, finite Difference is the essence in which Neo-Platonism may be dis-appropriated and appropriated to its essence. It appears to parody Neo-Platonism, but distinguishes itself from it by not choosing between Being and the One, by positing as its task rather their coincidence or indecision, that of the Intelligible (division) and the One (the indivisible). Difference destroys the continuities and exclusions that still reign in the hypostatic type of thinking and makes of

the simultaneity of the One and Being the authentic essence of meta-physics. It inaugurates a thinking that is hypo- *and* hyper-static and, but in this present sense only, non-'static' or 'positional'. Heidegger's 'Turning' is indeed a 'return', but a return already in the One and as One rather than towards the One (at least in the sense that relations of exclusive transcendence would still subsist between Being and the One). It is only in this precise sense that the Turning is not a cosmic drama, a real exit outside and return to the One.

2. On the other hand, from the radically finite point of view of the One, Difference like Neo-Platonism may be interpreted as a desire for the One that would be satisfied in a purely hallucinatory way. Difference claims to possess neither centre nor focus, but already and at any rate it does have these as fantasies, as sources of desire and anxiety: the One that it puts into play intervenes here in such a way, as Unity, that the objective illusion is re-created that Difference would be capable of re-centring itself; a haunting, insistent and besieging appearance that is strictly complementary to its infinite (*endlos*, interminable, unlimited) iteration. Yet the objective mirage of a focus or a horizon is created only because the One is lacking, that is to say, more profoundly, is hallucinated in its essence. The One is immediately an absolute dispersion of real individuals for whom the problem of a unity, a regularity, a continuity, closure and re-centring is not posed, is never posed, any more than that of an inhibition or a delay that are obsessions proper to Difference. When Difference posits a third 'term', *ein drittes* (Heidegger) beyond Being and Thought (*Dasein*), a disparate and an aleatory point (Deleuze), a point of transmutation (Nietzsche), it is never a matter of the One as such and in its truth but only of Difference as unary Difference. The *Simple* (*das Einfache*) is never given by Difference which confounds it with the originary 'in-between' of differends, but only as the imme-diate givens of an absolutely simple immanence: non-reflexive. Difference is enchained too much to the scission and withdrawal of the meta-physical as such ever to honour this One which gives it its sole reality. At the very most Difference conceives the One as the mixed mode of a differentiating Unity that Difference doubtless no longer wants to be transcending but which remains partially so nonetheless.

Thus all contemporary philosophy of Difference offers despite everything a strangely Platonizing spectacle: the interminable procession of the most communal entities, Being, Nothingness, Desire, Power, Language, Text, raising themselves up from the ground of experience each in turn like shades at once bloodless and laden with chains, trying to lift themselves in infinite file towards a mirage of the One where they would believe themselves capable of being regenerated and saved from empirical hell as at a wellspring of life. It is truly a bizarre and certainly quite 'philosophical' merry-go-round, philosophical because it is simultaneously ascending and descending and playing itself out finally in a circle and in place. As if these larvae wished, by their hesitations, their stumblings, their skiddings, the allure of their approach continually spoiled, to abandon the weighty forms of being or non-being in order to yield and sink into their limit, to abandon their determined forms of existence, to prove to themselves that they still exist when in truth they exist only as fleeting larvae on the earth. They seek the One precisely because they have not found it, and they will never find anything but their own hallucination. They neither find nor become anything other than what they already are: them-'selves'. They possess no more than tautological life, but they still do not know that tautological existence does not exhaust the real, that Being, Nothingness, Desire, Text, Power, etc., all this is absurd and these tautologies are unnecessary. They have their aims, hatreds and desires, but they continue to be unaware that if they possess sense as relative to one another and truth as relative to them*selves* and as system of them all, all this taken together – and *taken together*, the system itself included as well, which cannot now exceed or escape itself and its destiny – is as absurd and unnecessary as a tautology. For the One, the World is a redundancy.

3. Such passion for transcendence is at one with anxiety in the face of Representation, with the intense fear that every experience (of) the One or every 'immediate givenness' or 'non-reflexive givenness' would still be nothing but some form of ideality. Such thinking would deposit itself faster and faster within the in-between of Presence *and* Difference, within Difference as this in-between because it is fascinated by the Representation it presupposes as real. It puts itself immediately in a posture of combat because it assumes that it

has a real adversary. But this fear proves only one thing: that it is already by itself of the nature of this dreaded adversary, that it knows this and tries to flee from itself. In this anxiety, the essence of truth still 'speaks' or makes itself effective, but in the service of what is not it. One must marvel no doubt at how the usage of the absolute with respect to transcendence, or of immanence with respect to withdrawal, functions as the denial of the latter in each case, as a haunting and laborious call to joy, to the loss-that-is-a-gift, etc. or to an un-thought-that-is-all-of-thought. Pathetic and emotional, Difference is like this above all through its bad faith, its precautions, its exacerbated vigilance, its critique of 'all horizons' or 'all presuppositions', its anguished rushing about to the point of claiming serenity. It believed it was possible for it to determine Being in an other than ontic manner: but by definition every determination of Being that does not proceed immediately through the One and through it alone, that leaves the essence of the One undetermined and makes use of it as a simple 'keystone' for resolving the aporia of the Being/beings relation, which is to say to render it interminable, cannot but remain held at the interior of this relation and continue to determine Being by beings even in its subsequent appeal to the One. This is why Difference has this hallucinatory, soteriological and theological conception of the One: the One is for Difference the last, the highest means of thinking, thought's ultimate power-to-be, that which also signifies the powerlessness of thought, to which Difference has recourse as to a last instance without having taken care to ask itself whether the One tolerates such a usage and is able to enter as such into this history . . .

THE AMPHIBOLOGY OF THE REAL AND IDEALITY AND THE SELF-DISLOCATION OF PHILOSOPHY

1. The distinction of Being and beings, once it takes the pure form of the chiasmus, is neither a 'real' distinction nor a distinction 'of reason'; it is rather, in its turn, the 'difference' of real distinctions and distinctions of reason. Difference is the contemporary solution to the problem of the relations of the real and the ideal, the coupling of which

defines the amphibology of both classical and contemporary transcend-ental thought and, most likely, of every philosophical decision, since this is inscribed in empirico-transcendental parallelism. How are the real and ideality capable of being united, reciprocally conditioning one another, what unity may form from such contrary natures? *Difference or Co-belonging is precisely the concept of the sole kind of unity possible for two natures essentially foreign to and incommensurable with one another. But this solution of the amphibology is in reality its simple repetition* . . . Against the *partial* idealist dissolution (Hegel, Nietzsche, Husserl) of mixtures of the real and ideality, ideality thus conditioning the real but not recip-rocally, finite Difference re-affirms the amphibology, if not always the identification and reversibility at least the 'sameness' of contraries, the 'sameness' of the distinction of reason and real distinction. It postu-lates precisely the One as the sole means for placing a term in tran-scendent separation from this 'sameness', of registering it in the form of an *a priori* hesitation between the distinction and the unity of the real and ideality. Difference is the One objectively hesitating 'between' this repulsion that Difference cannot suppress within unity and this unity that it can no longer annihilate.

2. Difference is thus the syntax that endeavours to preserve the amphibology *as such*. However it is clear that the absolute-idealist usage of this syntax (Nietzsche and Deleuze) risks undoing the very reasons for the amphibology, namely finitude. There is in effect an extended sense of finitude that holds for metaphysics itself, and it is scarcely possible to treat the empirico-transcendental amphibology without characterizing it as 'finite' in general. The necessary correla-tion of contraries is already finitude, which is first of all this non-sublating co-belonging of opposites. The idealist usage of Difference eliminates ontic finitude but retains this general finitude that is proper indeed to Being and which – this is what nonetheless opposes Nietzsche to Hegel – signifies the refusal of the 'finite' to be finally 'sublated' into the infinite with which it is nonetheless bound up. On the other hand, ontico-real finitude holds open and accentuates the amphibology. Heidegger characterizes metaphysics in terms of the confusion of Being and beings, but its essence too resides in a *chias-mus* and Heidegger recognizes on his own account that in any case Being remains inseparable from beings: he cannot contest the notion

that Being is always the Being of beings. It is when he thinks of the ontically finite condition of Difference as explicitly taken into account, rather than of the effects upon Being of an intra-ontological plurality (Deleuze's 'object-cuts' or Nietzsche's multiplicity of forces, which result from this ontic finitude but only as forgotten or lifted by metaphysics), that he is able to lay claim to a step through and beyond metaphysics. What Heidegger insists upon is the correlation of Being and beings as *really* finite: not only the passage from the Being of particular beings to Being as the whole of beings, which is also Nietzsche's insistence for example as well as Deleuze's, but the passage to a 'really' finite Whole. One cannot, according to Heidegger, remain content with a Whole or All in the transcendental sense 'in general', defined solely – in the metaphysical manner – by syntactical structures. The explicit introduction of finitude, its conspicuous indication, while it may destroy the idealist usage of the unity of contraries, namely the idealist usage of Difference (Nietzsche), thus does not destroy Difference itself, that is to say, the amphibology, but serves rather to affirm its irreducibility.

3. Whatever else one makes of the 'finite' modality of Difference, its aporetic and amphibological style – which extends far beyond the Difference of contemporary thinkers that remains rather of the essence of Greco-Occidental decision – neither resolves nor dissolves the problems, but rests content with investing them with a principial function of essence:

a. Difference in general is the ruse of a thinking that is obliged to ratify the amphibology and to raise it to the status of essence; that refuses to dissolve the main Occidental aporia and instead elevates it to the height of a principle. *This is once more to place the One in the service of the aporias of philosophical decision which is always developed 'within' and now 'as' the in-between of the real and ideality.* The aporias too of ontic or even ontological finitude can no longer have pertinence or constraining force for us. *It is the very notion of ideal transcendence as relative to a real that one must consent to abandon* if one does not wish to remain content, like Nietzsche, Heidegger, Deleuze or Derrida, with elevating the aporias of the Greco-Occidental metaphysical fact to the status of philosophy, in an effort of synthesis far too wilful not to flirt with the abyss.

b. We do not see what unity is possible within the amphibology of 'idealist' Difference (Nietzsche) in general, and still less within that of Heideggerean and Derridean Difference, between the real of finitude and the ideal of Difference, what possible unity that would not be a simple juxtaposition offset by a forced movement, a frenzied becoming and historicity elevated to the status of essence. To be sure this problem exists as soon as the amphibology does, thus already in absolute Difference (Nietzsche). But it becomes more acute in finite Difference, the real finitude of which leads to the very limits of dislocation, as we saw in its crucial form in Derrida. In order to avoid idealist critiques (not ours, which are of another type), finite Difference in the strong sense is constrained not only to cast back its internal unity into the infinite and to rest content with a becoming-difference or rather a becoming-finite of Difference, but also to postulate an infinity proper to the Other, for example to the Unthought, the Unsaid, etc. Even if, as we have shown, the unity of Finitude and Difference is that of essence and existence, of determination and overdetermination, there is in this no real, that is, none-other-than-indivisible, unity but only an interminable process, a desire for a putative unity that remains satisfied with itself only by way of real unity and that is grounded upon the unlimitedness of a withdrawal the reality of which is assumed as given. Finitude cannot communicate its reality to Difference, but conversely Difference cannot give its immanence to Finitude: the mixture can only be put back into play and become its own goal. Above all, the internal unity of this complex principle is so weakly assured that it is threatened with an incessant dissolution, a dislocation or ruin that it believes itself able to avoid through a forced movement, recourse to the Other supposed as given, towards temporality and historicity in order to assure the hypothetical becoming-finite or real of Difference and the becoming-differential of Finitude. Does 'strong' or ontico-real Finitude as the transcendence of real being in relation to present or object-being give to the transcendence of Being an *absolute* content and means the reality of which would relay the weakness of this simple ideality? But it is then finitude that becomes problematic to the extent that it is still conceived as a mode of transcendence. If transcendence still remains relative to something given, it could be that *the unity of Difference and Finitude in which Heidegger seeks the remedy for metaphysics* is no more effective than the partnership of the paralytic and the blind man. The reality of the withdrawal or of Finitude will be charged with the giving 'of' (real) essence to the ideal transcendence of Being and with distinguishing this latter in a real manner from metaphysical Being, but the mere fact that it remains ordered with respect to Difference perhaps suffices to deny it any real effectiveness. Neither Heidegger nor above all Derrida will have eluded this risk of incoherence and unintelligibility, which they balance out by means of the systematic recourse, especially in Derrida, to Nietzschean motifs one can no longer deem 'metaphysical' and 'logocentric' (the re-affirmation of Difference).

4. Difference, whether or not it receives Finitude as its essence, appears unable to attain its expressed aim and remains an unfulfilled intention – precisely because it is always 'to be fulfilled' and wrongly posits that every 'fulfilment' of its essence would be premature, 'representational' or 'logocentric'. This intention: that Difference would become essence or principle, that it would acquire reality, absolute autonomy and a strictly internal determination, remains powerless to procure *a sufficient determination of essence itself*. This is not, moreover, proper only to Difference, but belongs to every thinking that remains caught within the empirico-transcendental amphibology and does not perceive the essence of the One as immanent given that is non-thetic (of) itself or conceives the transcendental globally as 'syntax' rather than as immediate or non-reflexive givenness. Difference is THE philosophical decision that affirms the aporetic disjunction of syntax and reality and rests content to 'turn', in all the senses of this word, within this in-between. This failure is particularly manifest as soon as it thinks the One: it then renounces without remainder any attempt to furnish such a sufficient determination of the One itself or believes it has satisfied this requirement once it has made use of the One to produce the sufficient determination . . . of beings.

The authentic real distinction – real, that is to say, here, transcendental – is that which goes, irreversibly, from the One to Being: this is the uni-laterality with which the One affects Being. Difference is condemned to falsify this, to think it as a mixture of real distinction and distinction of reason, distinctions which it itself both is and is not. The in-itself and non-reflexive One is distinguished from the regions of the empirical and of ideality by a pure transcendental distinction that is immediately a 'real' distinction in a new sense of the word, the real no longer designating the ontic but rather the One's sphere of non-reflexive immanence. Transcendental distinction is here grounded 'in the nature of the thing', in its reality which is neither ontic nor onto-logical. It is no longer simply formal; this transcendental reality is alone that of the One.

5. We are not refusing Difference here, but simply describing its mechanism as objective illusion, namely a hallucination of the real, as a point of view still too narrow and vicious with respect to the One. The general economy of Difference, precisely because it proceeds by super-universalizing (Difference as 'Same'), is still a restriction if one measures it no longer with respect to a universal but to an Absolute, no longer to an operation but to an essence that is non-reflexive or non-thetic (of) itself and excludes outside of itself every operation. From this follows its usage of the One, whether 'affirmative', onto-logical and substantialist or finite and inhibiting; at any rate, its crit-ical pathos extending as far as the affirmation of an Undecidable, its recourse to the Absolute as simple limit, its technique of dividing up representation. The tragedy of Difference – and this marks the philo-sophical sublimation and interiorization of tragedy, particularly when it claims to overcome tragedy as such through 'the tragic spirit' (Nietz-sche, Deleuze) – is that either Difference becomes an essence that is self-determining in an internal fashion (precisely Nietzsche, and the entire idealist usage of Difference), but in an purely ideal mode that loses the sense or weight of the real; or it proclaims the real as Fini-tude (Heidegger), but cannot achieve this except as *indefinite* (*endlos*, Heidegger; 'interminable', Derrida) tendency, movement or becom-ing that is always held in check to assure its immanence and its internal self-determination. This dialectic signifies that Difference lacks the real which it believes itself to co-determine and that it is the victim – it too – of this transcendental hallucination specific to philo-sophy in general. Let us explain.

The systems to which Difference gives rise are forced to confront a dilemma. *Either* Difference follows Nietzsche's idealist path and reduces ontico-ontological difference to an intra-ontological differ-ence, which allows it to give back a certain positivity and autonomy to the One itself. Yet it is then a matter of the ontological autonomy of an ideal instance, an Idea that may always be divided anew. The Nietzschean system is destroyed or deconstructed to the extent that it effectuates Difference in this infinite and ideal mode. *Or* Difference identifies *ontico*-ontological difference with Finitude, rendering these irreducible and being no longer able, or still less than with the previous solution, to render positive and autonomous the One or the Indivision of opposites. Due to Finitude, Difference is condemned – even when Finitude becomes transcendental finitude, and precisely because transcendental truth remains ontically finite – to privilege the operation of division or transcendence over that of immanence. At the same time, it must make of concealment (*die Verborgenheit*) the essence (*das Wesende*) of unconcealment (*Unverborgenheit*), an essence that itself withdraws or remains 'lacking'. It must thus think as essence not the One itself, which moreover remains masked within the opening or unconcealment that it effectuates, but one of the opposites that it isolates from their coupling and that it sets up with the functions of essence. The Turning, the unary 'Re-affirmation' of transcendence or of Being remains fundamentally in Heidegger that of Forgetting or Dissimulation rather than that of Presence or Clearing: irreversibility, but as grounded upon an ontico-real transcendent that is more negative than positive, as that of the One itself would be. Finitude renders impossible not so much a positive definition as such of the essence of truth, in any case absent from Difference in general and all its usages, as its definition through its 'positive' side. Even tautology (*das Sein west*) signifies that the essence of Being is *rather* on the side of Forgetting, Withdrawal, Non-essence.

The omnipresence of the theme of Being in Heidegger has for too long dissimulated the object of the care and interest of his thinking: the question or essence (of Being). But this, Being's essence rather than Being, still does not yet explain why he does not place solely untruth within the essence of truth and withdrawal within the Clearing, but, refusing to take in a divine equilibrium the scales of the balance, why he makes of untruth as essential and unary the essence of truth. It is necessary here to grasp again all the dimensions of the problem: because *it is impossible for him, as for all philosophy, to pose the question of essence as such and of its purely unary essence* and because he is content to pose only that of the essence 'of' Being, he is constrained to bind essence to Being and to determine reciprocally the transcendental immanence of essence *and* the transcendence of Being. He thus does what this problematic of Difference obliges him to do in opposition to Nietzsche (or Husserl), who, despite or because of his anti-Platonic affirmation of Becoming, is content with *super-Platonizing Becoming itself or the real*.

The tragedy of Difference is that it is condemned either to fall into Idealism and to affirm the final primacy of reversibility and of Being; or to combat Idealism by resorting to the quasi-philistine platitude of a Greco-Occidental 'fact', or rather a finitude that it presupposes, the foundation and necessity of which it is unable to perceive (cf. the previous chapter). *Inevitably the factual positivity or what remains of this despite everything in the a priori fact of metaphysics has to co-found and saturate Difference.* By being constrained to the primacy of the cut or transcendence, of what there is of scission within Difference, Heidegger traces a path that will be that of Derrida, whereas Nietzsche affirms the primacy of (ideal) immanence and traces the path that will be that of Deleuze. The primacy of withdrawal, of non-essence that counts as essence, if it has found for example an opponent in Gadamer, in effect programs 'Deconstruction', without entirely determining it, as well as its later forms that privilege the moment of withdrawal, inhibition, delay over that of continuity. The systems of Difference are thus distributed according to which of the two contraries they give primacy as essence of the other, whether the operation of the cut or of transcendence, or that of the open, of synthesis or association, of immanence – but only ideal . . .

There is here a dialectical constraint for Difference in general: *the One has always been experienced in the last instance not in its essence but in the mode of scission in general and therefore inevitably in the mode of one of the two contraries or differends that it unites*: either in the mode of Being (of ideal immanence which prevails over transcendence and reduces it without remainder); or in the mode of a real transcendence that refuses ideal immanence, of nothingness no longer as nihilist and as metaphysics but as finite. Since the content of the disjunction or scission of unifying Difference is Finitude as real transcendence, it is inevitable that the One is manifest positively in the mode of Forgetting. But still more general than this 'finite' effectuation of Difference and finally of the One itself, beyond the One as withdrawal and finitude, there is the Greco-Occidental constraint, to which Heidegger remains beholden, of having to experience the One at any rate *along with* a scission and sometimes *by* and in the mode of a scission. By repeating the experience of the One in this latter mode, its own enterprise carries on. On the other hand the One as immediate givens and no longer as simple dialectic of an immanent-and-transcendent 'limit' can no longer be a supplementary avatar, metamorphosis or epoch of Difference, the latest dispatch of the question of questions, the question of the In?division of contraries. It is this unconscious 'dialectic' of thinking, *the* unconscious perhaps in its very possibility, that must now be abandoned. This eternal conflict of systems of Difference, the conflict of Nietzsche and Heidegger, of Gadamer and Heidegger as well, then of Deleuze and Derrida, is, as measured to the essence of the One, indifferent, since this alternating of primacies is a shadow-theatre playing itself out against the background of a global lack of the One, a deficiency of Absoluteness that makes such games of re-seizure possible.

THE POWERLESSNESS TO THINK INDIVIDUALS AND MULTIPLICITIES

1. Empirico-transcendental parallelism thus impedes a rigorous thinking of transcendental truth, that is, of the One in its essence. Does it free on the other hand a thinking of multiplicities since in a certain way it is because it reflects multiplicities within the One that it prohibits itself proper access to the One? This is only an appearance: the reason prohibiting Difference from acceding to the One is the same that prohibits it from acceding to the essence of multiplicities. It is its manner of thinking the One and the multiple through 'difference' that causes it to take these once again in their 'in-between' and constrains it to take this 'in-between' at times for a thinking of the One, at times for a thinking of multiplicities, whereas it in fact thinks neither this one nor these others.

We must distinguish two problems – and involve ourselves in an especially difficult analysis:

a. The law of the chiasmus, which is the essence of Difference in general. There is a chiasmus or a co-belonging of Being and beings as reversible in their unity. Even if this reversibility is limited, as for example in Heidegger or Derrida, it does not entirely cease. There is no 'Difference' in general without a co-(belonging), still less without a (co)-belonging.

b. The problem of the multiplicity of beings or of the real that enter into the chiasmus. This second problem is distinct from the former as soon as it is a question of contemporary thinkers, principally of Nietzsche and Deleuze, but also of Heidegger and Derrida: the stakes are the degree and nature of multiplicity tolerated by Difference, stakes that become those of Difference itself once it gathers itself together and draws its furthest consequences, exploits its ultimate possibilities and claims to 'overcome' itself. But in order to be treated correctly, this problem must be examined through the framework of the chiasmus of Being and beings, even if metaphysics' way of treating Being is still insufficiently determined through the general reference of Being to beings and their reciprocal relativity.

Beings are always already given as divided, particularized and multiple, as a 'diversity'. As to the nature of this diversity, the three conceptions of Difference diverge. There is no Difference without this moment of a given diversity, but this may be either *extra-ontological* (we will then speak of 'beings') or *intra-ontological* (we will then speak of 'objects'). In the first case, the diversity is empirical; outside-of-the-*a priori* or outside-of-Being there is a real that affects the ideality of Being, so much so that the *a priori* and its essence have need of it (Kant: the empirical affect of movement; Heidegger: beings, the necessary co-belonging of which to the opening of Being or its ecstatic horizon is shown through a phenomenology more Aristotelian ('the Soul is all things') than Husserlian). In the second case, the 'real' multiplicity can no longer be extra-ontological, or given outside of the *a priori*; it is the intra-ontological multiplicity of the plural *a priori* themselves (Nietzsche: the perspectives, the multiplicity inherent to perspectivalism itself; Deleuze: the 'object-cuts' specific to the 'desiring machines', cuts that belong only to objectivity or ideality, and not 'in themselves').

Whichever solution is chosen, as a function of the 'metaphysical' usage of Difference or of the 'deconstructing' subsets of this latter, Difference still programs the external and/or internal affection of Being by beings: by now we will have recognized in this chiasmus *the empirico-transcendental parallelism* of which the various usages of Difference are none other than mere variants. Whatever its figure, whether this diversity of beings or the real be recognized as the point of view proper to metaphysics (Heidegger), or as the essential partiality of the ideality or the *hyle* the very continuity of which presupposes cuts and multiplicity (Nietzsche) – it is an invariant fact, it would seem, that the *a priori* is always from the very beginning ordered in any case to a diversity baptized as 'real'. That it is affected by this diversity, that metaphysics begins always by positing an 'ontic' multiplicity of the ontological, that there would always be an ontico-ontological primacy of particular beings that would remain unexhausted by their objectivity, or that it would be in some way universalized as the partiality of object-cuts and detached from every being that would be transcendent or in-itself – these signify not only that Being cannot fail to be considered in its turn as a being (there is here a relativity that yet exceeds the fact in question, because it depends upon the chiasmus), but also that Being is itself particularized and divided. From the start, the determination comes to Being from a multiplicity, if not always an ontic multiplicity at least an external and still transcendent multiplicity. Not only are beings posited *a priori*, one might say, as pure dispersion in the mode of transcendence (ontico-real or ideal) relative to Being or the *a priori* itself, so much so that the only multiplicity ever in question is a *transcendent dispersion*. But this brutal and soulless dispersion is such that it will also rise back, *via* the *a priori*, into Being, that is, into the essence of Being. Metaphysics is the history of the failure to repel war and war's own proper kind of dispersion outside of thinking, and it is far from certain that Finitude itself manages to inhibit this brutal resurgence.

So then what necessary form does the confusion of Being and beings take at the first level (*a priori*) of Difference? How does this amphibology become structural? As infinite iteration of ontological Difference: the iteration of Difference itself becomes necessary because the multiplicity remains exterior to it. Being is in its own way and its own turn (a) being; more precisely: every mode of being represents a being for another mode of being; every being represents a mode of being for another being. There is nothing here of any deficiency that would be linked merely to a human incapacity to accede immediately to the whole of beings; metaphysics would not be meta-physics and transcendence if it did not provide for itself as its point of departure an *a priori fact* in the form of an ontic diversity of the ontological, a real diversity, be it extra- or intra-ontological, which however tracks a limit to the universal or to Being.

. But this level of the *a priori*, as we know – this being a law of any philosophical decision whatsoever in general – must be surpassed in the direction of essence or transcendental condition properly speaking. Yet this ultimate level declares itself in advance in the form of a need for the totalization or re-unification of the diversity of the plural *a priori*, the ontic diversity of the ontological. The passage to the All (of beings) or to the One is the passage to the essence (of Being). What, then, of its relation to real diversity?

Such an All, clearly, must at any rate be distinguished from a simple empirical or rational summation of beings, that is to say, still, of *particular* beings. On what condition is Being as All (of beings) the Other of beings – which implies: of particular and divisible beings – given that the All of beings is still related to beings? The transcendental 'mover' of metaphysics is found not in the couple Being/beings but in the couple All/particular, the couple of ontic wholes and the transcendental-unifying Whole or All as their Other. Heidegger does not reject the equation: Being = All of beings, except for when the All is determined metaphysically and not transcendentally. He does not reject this equation in general – to the contrary. That Heidegger would be tempted at times in certain hasty formulations by an idealist reduction of beings, contrary moreover to Finitude, the origin of which is found precisely in this consistent requirement, this constraint of all transcendental thinking: to overcome ontic or empirical multiplicity, 'diversity', in a unifying 'All'. This transcendence of ontic diversity towards the One is an invariant that functions equally in the Nietzschean usage of Difference and no longer allows us to specify Heidegger.

Whatever the case, in order to pass from ontic diversity to Being as All, that is, as *Other not of beings but of the diversity of beings*, there has never been but a sole means, a sole solution, and it is this that renders a philosophy 'transcendental': to pass from the plane of ontic diversity to the 'plane' of the One. The Other of the diversity of beings is the One, which is not the other of beings in general. Being is from the very beginning understood classically by Heidegger as All (of beings), but this All cannot and must no longer be itself an empirical all; it is a transcendental or unary All possessing its reason in the One rather than in the always divisible and exclusive parts that it unifies. The chiasmus allows for the transfer of the relation Being-beings onto the relation Being-One; the *real* reference of Being is preserved across its transcendental mutation. If Being as Other of beings were to be Being deprived of beings, this transcendent separation of Being and beings in general would be a metaphysical effect still bound to the primacy of beings as particular. Its indetermination or its nothingness would still be thought through correlation with beings as *particular*. It is a question of unlinking this indetermination = dissimulation from the *opposition* All/particular, *which is impossible – an All that would no longer be opposed to the particular, that would no longer be empirical – unless it be defined and borne by the One which causes it to transcend through and beyond ontic multiplicity without letting itself be simply once again opposed to this multiplicity or to become again a merely empirical All.* Consequently this transcendental All that is Being refers still to beings, but now to the real or to the One. And it is more intimately fused than ever to the real, if not to beings. That the One is still transcendence and that multiplicity remains ontic and extrinsic even within Being, these would be two complementary traits born simultaneously from the philosophical or unitary interpretation of the One.

2. The effect of the preceding merry-go-round of reasoning, inscribed in the 'differential' coupling of ontic diversity and the One, is to have rendered impossible the thinking of multiplicities inasmuch as they are multiplicities of the One, and to have made possible at worst no more than their *Aufhebung*, at best their *Affirmation*. One says in general of the thinking that cuts only to continue, that is separated out only to repeat or to re-inscribe itself infinitely, that it is 'in-the-midst-of . . . '. 'Being-in-the-midst-of . . . ' is the very structure of Difference or of *In?divisible Division*, the internal regularity that immediately coagulates the singular and the universal. *It signifies the necessary insertion of individuals into a universal, their integration into a general economy. This integration may not be to some pregiven All and may express a co-belonging of contraries, but it is no less real.* By virtue of this logic of the chiasmus or of reversibility, individuals co-belong to the attributes that are Language, Text, Desire,

Power, and which those individuals *are*. There is perhaps no longer any All-politics, All-textuality, All-desire, but there is a being-in-the-midst-of-politics, of the signifier, of the text, of desire which, far from freeing individuals, accomplishes their shackling *as* and *with* these universals. From this follows these infinite ritornellos, these singsong refrains of repetition-that-is-no-longer-a-singsong-refrain: speaking, you speak language, desire, power; desiring, you desire desire, language, power; empowered, you empower power, language, desire, etc. What is the ineluctable element, as one might put it, of thinking? The reciprocal hetero-affection of these universals, this froth, this wrinkling where your narcissism is dissolved and the resurgent flux of Difference is trotted out once again. You are thrown-into . . . desire, language, text, power, perception or whatever other shroud – this structure of the 'in-the-midst-of . . . ' is universal and affects all thought. The individual in its indivisible or non-reflexive reality is projected onto transcendence and sublated through a universal or, at best, identified with one.

3. The anonymous universal hallucinates individuals. Metaphysics, as well as the critiques that attempt to delimit it, are thus full of strange imagery; they speak of the highest essence, which is to say, for them, Being, as Cosmos and Movement, as River, Flux and Fire, as Flash or Blaze, as Dawning or Clearing, when it is not as Maelstrom, Circle of Circles or Machine. As soon as thinking abandons the One for the Same and the All, as soon as it gives itself over to displays of tautology, it experiences interminably the fragility and errancy of its truth in the infinite metaphysical games of language. Never having set ground upon the One itself in its truth, but rather upon Being and its avatars who use the One without thinking any more about it, thought accepts once and for all, even in its attempts to exceed metaphysical 'Representation', the delivering of the essence of truth and the One over to the games that are those of the All and the Same, the delivering of the Absolute over to the universal powers that know how to make use of it solely as a crown: World, History, Being, State, Power, Desire, Language. Metaphysics and its critiques are not, properly speaking, imaginary, but neither are they activities foreign to the imagination: they take hold within this superior form of the imagination that is no longer merely the All, but the All as One, that is Same or Difference as

the in-between of opposites, and it is from this standpoint that they hallucinate the real. The imagination acquires its superior or transcendental usage once it becomes a principle of the synthesis or the adjunction of contraries, as soon as thinking, abandoning the One itself, takes as its object the All that unifies opposites. With a lack of spirituality testifying to its vocation for fantasies and imagery, metaphysics-and-its-overcoming, Representation-and-its-difference have not known how to free themselves from what there is of the swampy, the inchoative, the incomplete, the *brutalitas animale* in man, of everything that attempts to rise to the surface as soon as one thinks in terms of totality, *of everything that has need of totality, of the weapon and the category of totality or of form in order to impose itself upon thought* and to prolong its existence, to justify its existence, to attempt to justify what is definitively absurd, to form a defence mechanism against the anguish of its radical contingency and all the more so to compromise the absolutely 'mystic' element which is the essence of thinking. Metaphysics as ontology, as well as the destruction of ontology and of Being as All by Difference, which is to say by the All-as-One, is the unique and double manner in which the mystic essence of the One is compromised, inverted or folded back upon these universals that are Text, Desire, Power, State. These are the substitutes, offspring or new heads of the old *Physis* and *Kosmos*; at root they obey the same logic, which is that of capturing the One to their own profit.

4. Such is the malaise of contemporary thought: it would have to liberate multiplicities and individuals; it would have liberated only universals, re-inscribing yet once again the modes if not *under* attributes and substance, the singularities and individuals if not *within*, at least, which is perhaps worse, *as* Text, Desire, Power, destiny of Being, etc. Malaise within Difference: here then is a thinking that entangles itself, ensnares itself, *enlyses* itself perhaps, turns over itself and in itself faster and faster, substituting intensity for life and the acceleration of motion for movement, yet which thickens heavily like a 'turning' doughy paste. Is it still possible to open a new thinking that would be something other than a space, other than a locus or a sitting-place, other than a universal, even one sublimated to the status of limit, even one that would also be a limit and a finitude? Difference places us at the foot of the Greco-Occidental wall and

forces us to an extreme solution: either to conceive individuals, singularities or multiplicities as immediate givens (in a mode obviously immanent = transcendental), destitute of every transcendence, *prior to* the Idea, Being and its modes, *prior to* Text, History, State, Desire, etc.; or to conceive them as a simple supplementary refinement of Difference. Difference constrains us to distinguish a thinking that still resorts to universals in order to constitute individuals through their overdetermination, from a thinking that experiences the non-constituted, non-produced character of singularities. The One and the multiplicities proper to the One thus form a peculiar *a priori*, purely 'transcendental' and not 'metaphysical' or universal, since they precede every species of universality and are the *a priori* not only of experience, as is traditionally the case, but of the universal forms themselves, consequently also of Difference.

Yet why awaken this alternative? Precisely because Difference does not want it, since Difference has no need of any 'supplement' of individuality, being the system of the supplement in general and of all possible supplements. But the logic of the supplement or of difference is such that the supplement is still a 'logical' concept and the 'difference' is merely that of one universal (to) another, the indivisible 'in-between' of two universals or of a unique-and-double universal. On this terrain of universality and mediation, Difference is a concept of unsurpassable effectiveness and rigor; it relays spatial-temporal extension through intensity as the superior form of universality. But the One then remains chained to tasks that are external and transcendent to its own essence. Difference remains within logic in general and within the logic of the primacy of Being over the One in particular. Yet is the essence of thinking to be found within logic? Or rather in the vision-in-One?

CHAPTER SEVEN
Theory of Philosophical Decision

FROM THE UNDECIDABLE TO THE THEORY OF
PHILOSOPHICAL DECISION

1. The systems of Difference, above all those of Finitude, have posed the problem of the essence of the philosophical act, of its power and powerlessness, its techniques, its calculation, its strategy. And also of what would limit these: the incalculable, the non-evaluable, the non-strategic, the an-economic, etc. But none has been able to pose, outside the always un-decided or inhibited decision that is Difference, the problem of a *real logic of philosophical decision* and the status of a real – that is, non-philosophical – *principle of choice* within philosophy. Now that we have conquered the real or transcendental point of view of the One beyond Difference, a point of view rendering possible the elaboration of a logic – none other than real – of philosophical decision and decision in general, the moment has come to pursue not the simple 'analysis', but the individual or unary 'vision' – we will explain this – of the themes that, surrounding Difference, would both announce and conceal this logic: the 'finitude' of thinking, its constraints, its weakness and its force, the long-term identification of metaphysics and technology, etc.

We have already encountered the problem of a real principle of choice within philosophy in various restricted forms: do we have a *real* criterion for deciding between Hegel and Heidegger? Nietzsche and Heidegger? Heidegger and Derrida? Is Finitude a criterion, and of what kind, capable of constraining us to the choice against absolute Idealism? etc. It is not a matter of knowing empirically or even ideally why we choose such and such a philosophy, the criterion must be transcendental or real and possess a power that would be at least that of a sufficient reason for philosophical decision. Transcendental, meaning strictly and solely immanent: *yet precisely what immanence, doubtless not one and the same, is at issue in Hegel, Nietzsche, Heidegger or Derrida? We have at any rate experienced the sole radically immanent and transcendental point of view, that of the immediate or non-reflexive essence of the One.* And it is this criterion of the non-thetic (of) itself immediation of the One that we must now put forward in order to elaborate a theory of philosophical decision. It will proceed from this vision-in-One of the struggle among the systems of Difference or of the internal conflict of Difference, and consequently in a mode that will be no longer philosophical but 'real' in the sense in which we have defined the real by the One whose essence does not require any philosophical operation. This is a science and a critique, a description and a destruction of the illusions bound to philosophical decision, but these are grounded in the One and abandon the processes of Difference and of decision in general.

2. Difference has its own interpretation of its work, of the real that it posits and works upon, of its historicity and its decisions. Yet just as access to the thinking (of) the One would presume the total abandonment of the classical operations of Difference and of transcendence (reversal, reversion, re-affirmation, turning, etc.), in the same way access to the non-reflexive or non-thetic essence (of) the decisions and techniques of Difference in particular and of transcendence in general would presume – for this task and for it alone – the abandonment of their self-interpretation as allegedly 'real', of their *Transcendental Illusion.* But this abandonment is less an operation and a decision than a simple effect. If the real is by definition the Unconstituted, the Unproduced, the Undecidable, every theory of decision would from the very beginning have to install itself in this problematic of the real and its 'undecidable' essence. *It is from the Vision-in-One, its immanence (to) itself without transcendence that the element of*

absolute transcendence may be thought as grounding, at the heart of meta-physics-and-its-overcomings, the very possibility of a philosophical decision. The 'order' of ideas requires that we would go from the Undecidable to decision: as much for the real foundation of decision as for the critique of its illusion of being real.

THE (NON-)ONE AND THE CONTINGENCY OF PHILOSOPHICAL DECISION

1. What then will be the effects of the One upon philosophical decision? They will be of two kinds. The first is the manifestation of the hallu-cinatory or non-real character of this decision, and of Difference in particular, rejected at once in a radical contingency that is the correl-ate of the One.

In general, a philosophical decision is a cut – repeated or relaunched – with regard to an empirical singular, or more generally, some given and, at the same time, an identification with a idealizing law of this given, itself then supposed as real, a transcendence towards the verit-able real. It is a relation and it modulates itself each time as a function of the real assumed as given and reduced, and the real assumed as attained and affirmed. *Yet the One henceforth prohibits the reflection in itself of this relation or this mixture in view of its auto-foundation that would be destined to suppress its contingency.* A blockage, no longer empirical but this time unary, inhibits its auto-foundation and its re-ascension towards its essence. The hiatus between the empirical and the ideal, which we have posited the possibility of lifting (in the form of an *a priori* relation, before then lifting it really through the passage to tran-scendental essence), is now definitively re-opened and lets *a new kind of gap* be glimpsed that is no longer that of the empirical and the ideal, or of empiricism and rationalism. It is the gap that the unary real itself straightaway imposes upon what is not it, upon this relation as such that is philosophical decision. It affects and immediately entails the ideality of the relation as well as its empiricism. The reflection in itself of Difference, this realization that would withdraw from it any dog-matic and empirical aspect, is brought back to a contingency more profound than any empiricism which the One alone is able to impose upon it. We will call this radical contingency that transfixes philosophical decision itself the *(non-)One*. This is a contingency that is no longer merely that of empirical and/or *a priori* 'fact', that is, of their relation of 'difference', but a contingency, still more powerful, affecting this very contingency of 'fact'. *This new contingency is always, itself, inadequate to the requirement of an ideal law of contingency; it is a real contingency beyond empiricism that resists every law of contingency and every a priori idealization.* This is no longer the contingency of fact, but that of the very definition of the real through such fact or through *a priori* 'facts' and through the relations of these facts to the requirement of a law or a reason desired as both transcendent and immanent. This irreducible hiatus, of a new type, between the 'empirical' and the 'transcendental', or rather between two forms of the real, which ruins Difference's infinite process of unification from the inside, signifies that the radical contingency of *real* transcendence or of the (non-) One has not found, and must not find, any reason or essence that would take the form of a law or ideal regularity, that instead it finds its essence solely in the immanence of the One.

2. We call this dimension that 'unilateralizes' decision the *(non-)One* because it derives from the One as its effect, and it is the charge of weak negation of which the One is capable. We must conceive a real facticity of a new type, irreducible to the empirico-ontic facticity (which is raised and idealized) as known by Difference. In order to formulate it, we still employ the term 'transcendence', yet in such a way that we must henceforth think transcendence directly as a function of the One. *The operation of the (non-)One is not at all an 'objectivization' of everything that falls outside the One – in the sense of the self-dividing operation of a consciousness – but what would have to be recognized as a setting-into absolute transcendence, beyond objectivization itself since it bears on this latter as well, of Difference and of all the ideal and thetic elements which, in Difference, would come to add themselves to the One and which discover themselves in this operation as strangers to the essence of the One.* The One stupefies Difference and lets it fall into dust, places it at a definitive distance that can no longer be 'recovered', interiorized and mastered. Here we have an absolute and absurd transcendence incommensurable to the merely *relative-absolute* transcendence of Being and Difference. The non-positional immanence of the One

signifies that transcendence too becomes 'radical' as transcendence, meaning that it becomes straightaway absolute or loses its relative nature, its essence of relation or position with respect to some being that it would be responsible for illuminating. This is no longer an ecstatic-horizonal projection but an 'in itself' or unary de-jection, where the horizon of Being or ontological transcendence itself founders. What we are calling absolute, non-positional or non-objectivizable Transcendence is transcendence that is immediately in a unary mode. The identity of the absolute contingency brought by the (non-)One and its 'reason' is given immediately with the One and, as such, it cannot be so through Difference which is itself never a true immediacy. It is solely from the point of view of the immediate givens of a real *singulare tantum*, strictly identical to its singular = *individuale* 'reason', that the hiatus is opened through which the law of the identification of the diverse and the non-positional diversity itself or its transcendental root fall this time ir-reversibly outside one another, or at least the non-positional diversity outside its identification, henceforth affecting its identification instead of allowing itself to be interiorized by it.

3. The (non-)One is not strictly real, if it is not so through its essence. Yet it is what there is of the real in every transcendence, what of transcendence there may be through a radically finite subject. This is no longer anything of objectivized beings in and through transcendence, nor even transcendence itself as objectivation. It is a facticity that will never have tolerated any ideal transcendence nor formed any mixture with it: for this reason it affects the transcendence of Being with an absolute abandon and unilaterality. The real is the singular, but the singular is no longer or not yet a singularity (= the being of the singular); it is the individual implying the immediately absolute and no longer relative-absolute (Heidegger, Derrida) de-jection and de-position of Being and consequently of 'singularity' itself. The One casts, outside of the mastery proper to Difference, *and without positing it*, a diversity which is the residue of the unary destruction of Difference and which is neither ontic nor ontological. It is no longer a matter of an idealized diversity in general, but a diversity of the contingency that refuses itself absolutely to any idealization whatsoever, that is rather the presupposition of every idealization by philosophy in

general and by Difference in particular. *Diversity 'in itself' and non-thetic (of) itself, more profound than the 'Thing in itself' and testifying to an absolute contingency of Difference, even 'finite' Difference.* Heidegger would put forward the withdrawal of beings 'in themselves' in order to liberate Being as Being itself rather than of such and such an exclusive region, but Finitude would remain a relative-absolute transcendence: only the One accomplishes the de-jecting of the 'Thing in itself' in the form of an absolute transcendence – *of which the absoluteness is henceforth measured to the immanent essence of the One* – and no longer the form of a merely *relative*-absolute transcendence. Finitude would testify to a dereliction that the One alone would be able to carry to its form 'without return'. The (non-)One has for real content the phenomenal givens of what we call 'uni-laterality' or irreversibility. This absolute and not relative de-jection of ontological transcendence, which is no longer susceptible to being re-interiorized by Being and which derives from the upholding of the One in its radical immanence, without dissolving the irreducible mixture of the empirical real and the *a priori* that were the material and element of classical transcendental thought as well as of Difference, renders it uni-lateral or estranges it from the One irreversibly. This is because the real of the (non-)One by which it is affected is definitively inadequate to the idealizing relation of Difference and 'leaps' outside of it.

The (non-)One henceforth affects all possible ideality, and philosophical decision globally, with this extra-empirical diversity. This is more than an inversion of the classical domination of ideality over and against empirical diversity. The transcendence of the (non-)One does not only acquire a supplement of 'transcendence' beyond even the transcendence of Being and its horizon – that which Heidegger sought under the name 'finitude' but with inadequate means – it also affects this latter and entails it in an irremediable transcendental facticity. *The reason, but only in the last instance, for the struggles among the systems of Difference will be this extra-empirical multiplicity, which remains absolutely contingent for the philosophy of which it is the excess.* Its contingency feeds an interminable conflict and an indifference that are content to take their arguments from new experiences of the real that they believe naïvely to be finally *the* real. Yet the real par excellence, outside of the One, is a non-positional or in-itself diversity of transcendence itself, such as never falls under experience. It is a principial, non-objectivizable diversity completely determined as such, and not empirically 'given'. If it may thus 'sidestep' both the empirically given and 'horizonal' ideality, it is because the (non-)One totally escapes objectivization – it is a non-objectivizing or non-positional transcendence – and it implies the unilateralization, without recourse or return, of Difference, Being, etc. It is a radical de-position of Being by the One.

NON-THETIC TRANSCENDENCE (NTT)

1. The second sort of effects produced by the One are what we call *Non-thetic Transcendence (NTT)* in a precise sense. This is the real kernel of transcendence that is the basis of every philosophical decision. This is in any case a mode of the (non-)One, but, more rigorously than the (non-)One, it merits being called 'transcendence': although no more objectivizing than the (non-)One, it is however, in distinction from it, partially relative to the given that presents itself outside of the One, for example philosophical decision or the World and its attributes (History, Language, Power, Desire, etc.). But it is no longer relative to these in the sense at any rate of philosophical, that is, traditional (positing and posited), transcendence: *it supposes the simple 'support' or vehicle of this given without forming again with it any philosophical decision,* since it forms rather the condition of philosophical decision as such: its *Real A priori*.

2. The One upholds itself in itself without withdrawing or transcending properly speaking, it upholds-itself-as-real in its immanence of the immediately given and abandons Difference to its degeneration. But correlatively, it entails with itself, outside of Difference, a non-thetic element of transcendence that had been dissimulated there: non-reflexive transcendence *beyond* ideal transcendence or the transcendence of Being. In a general way, if the philosophical usage of the transcendental offers examples, indices and types of the real or the individual, but without being able to ground their concept, that of the individual or the *tantum singulare*, it is because it makes of these or begins by making of them – even in 'Finitude' – an idea that is simultaneously empirical-and-rational; the real is for it what is given at the

interior of ob-jective transcendence, as an object or an element sub-tracted from an object, in order to then possibly be carried outside objective transcendence. Here, on the other hand, the real stands straightaway, in an absolutely non-empirical manner, even less empirical than 'Finitude' imagines, outside of the horizon of ideal or ontological transcendence. Not only the One stands at any rate already outside of such a horizon, but, if the One upholds itself in itself and by the force of its immanence, thus without transcending still in relation to Being, *something non-reflexive in transcendence also withdraws outside of itself, ceases to be reflected in itself and takes another form that is no longer in any way what we call 'auto-position'* in the manner of Idealism where it designates the operation of the I and of Self-Consciousness.

The second effect of the One upon Difference and decision in gen-eral is thus the disengagement of the *A priori real* that conditions them. *A priori* that is no longer postulated by decision since it is that which commands decision globally and of which decision is no longer the master. We see disengage itself a kernel of absolute = non-reflex-ive transcendence which is at the basis of Difference and of meta-physics. This non-reflexive or non-positional (of) itself transcendence is stripped of horizon, of thetic or horizonal structure, and it is this which renders possible every 'essential' decision. This *A priori real* is a mode of the special real that is the (non-)One. It allows us to show that the conflicts internal to Difference are indifferent to a thinking of the One, that we no longer have to *choose* among Hegel, Heidegger, Nietzsche, or between Derrida and Deleuze; that this is itself the true content of reality in the conflicts and dialectics of Difference: a non-thetic essence of transcendence, upon which they draw a debt that they refuse to honour, in the name of which, but solely in the last instance, since it is a matter of the reality that they can only hallucin-ate, they combat or ignore one another, and in the denial of which they are reconciled to one another.

THE ABYSS OF PHILOSOPHICAL DECISION

1. The real critique of Difference modifies the possibility and the limits of philosophical decision. *It is in this abyss of an absolute contingency that*

can never be partially filled in or closed up that we must go to look for the ultimate reasons of philosophy in general in the strict measure that it takes the form of a decision – hallucinatory, at that – on the authentic real or the One; or of Difference in particular and the strange rapport maintained among its diverse systems. The struggles and conflicts internal to Difference are made possible – but not commanded – by this 'logic' of non-positional transcendence which is a veritable *principle of real choice*, more precisely: *of choice as such.*

Difference would no doubt already be a criterion of choice – a critique – as well as of indecision, among the multiple significations of Being. This would no longer be a criterion of exclusive choice, in the mode of an alternative, of one signification among others. It would also be, just as much and simultaneously, a non-criterion, the non-criteriological essence of truth that refuses choice and at the same time affirms indivision, hesitation, the *a priori* wavering between one decision and another. This type of criterion is thus already transcendental, but in a partial or divided mode, since Difference is always at once immanent no doubt, but also transcendent to the significations of Being.

It cannot at any rate hold for the essence of the One inasmuch as the One is no longer determined in an ontological mode, but in a mode non-thetic (of) itself, and since the One is in no way decidable, not even partially. Being of the nature of an immediate given, the One and the science that it founds have no need of any criterion of choice nor of any critique, since there is nothing to choose, no critical decision to operate and to limit, no 'reduction', no *Kehre*, no 'analytic' of significations. *The criterion of science or of truth, if it is radically transcendental or immanent, annuls itself positively as criterion or manifests itself (to) itself as 'immediate givens'.* The *veritas transcendentalis* may always receive multiple possible interpretations and serve as the object of an ontological hermeneutic bearing upon its significations. These interpretations supply the most diverse philosophies, among these those of Difference. *Yet its essence has nothing of being the result of a choice or a division among these interpretations, the effect of a selection procedure among them, and neither is it the affirmation of their indivisibility:* indivision as essence of the One is not to be confused with indivision as applied to the transcendence of sense, the sense of Being or of the One. If there is an essence of the One, it falls outside of philosophy, but philosophy does not fall outside of it, which does not mean – we are precisely no longer in the domain of ontology – that philosophy as metaphysics or ontology would be some kind of negative 'henology' . . .

To the extent that a thinking is naively transcendental, it thereby has no need to justify or legitimate itself: this is the case with science; it is not so with philosophical decision. Its criteria are immanent: not only does it produce them simultaneously with their functioning, as is the case already with Difference, but, with the One and more rigorously, it makes of the experience of the 'positive' absence of criteria, always more or less exterior, the only real transcendental 'criterion'. For example, nothing, no 'reason', either allows or requires any choosing between the essence of the One and the usage that Difference makes of it. For the One there is nothing to choose, *no multiplicity of significations or interpretations of the One*, no ontological or rational foundation that would be more powerful than it; the One does not choose itself: it is the Undecidable as immediate given. Of all the criteria put forward by various philosophies, none will be of use to us, since *either* these are always those in the last instance of a semi-transcendental and semi-transcendent style that precisely we must unarily destroy (critical vigilance, the requirement of the critique of Representation and its metaphysico-political modes, the maximum of immanence and autonomy in thinking, the acceleration and aggravation of Heideggerean or Nietzschean questions, the intensification of questioning, etc.); *or* they annul themselves as criteria once they become fully transcendental, 'immediate givens' or 'non-reflexive transcendental experience'. If Difference itself would hesitate necessarily in this *either . . . or . . .* , content to render it autonomous and to elevate it to the status of essence, of criterion of-choice-and-of-in?decision among the significations (and the signifiers) of Being – the essence of the One implies on the other hand the passage (the choice? the non-choice rather, it is an immediate given) to the second possibility and thus to the absolute annulment without remainder of the alternative. The immanent givens are *index sui*: index non-thetic (of) itself, and consequently they are hardly criteria, they do not serve as a constraint of any logico-empirical kind nor of any kind of Difference that, itself, places the *index veri et falsi* solely in the *et* of this formula.

2. What now becomes of this problem of choice once we pass from the One to NTT?

Does the relative criterion of Difference hold as well for the (non-) One and NTT? We are aware already that the answer is no. It is the (non-)One that holds for Difference. From this we gather the paradoxical 'logic' of immediate or non-thetic (of) itself decision. It is clear that *this diversity, radical that-ness or in itself, of NTT, a diversity that is absolutely indifferent, grounds, unlike the One, an absolute or indifferent choice and thus an absolute limitation of philosophical choice or a positive annulment of philosophical decision.* There is no possible decision *as regards* this diversity; it is too indifferent to offer any *reason* for choosing, too absurd and contingent in its existence even to offer a reason for its existence. But also too positively stripped of reason not to liberate decision and to ground choice in its radical absurdity: it is the very diversity of decisions. NTT is even an absolute principle of choice, the principle *of* choice. Not of any particular and exclusive choice, nor even of a choice auto-limiting itself when it comes to the Undecidable, un?deciding itself when it comes to the One, 'paralysing' itself in its own critical and analytical decision – in the way Difference practices its own decision. It is the essence of choice, of absolutely any choice possible whatsoever without any limitation. It is a matter of neither a strategy, nor a logic, nor an economy of choice, but of a transcendental possibilization that frees choice as possible, that absolves the possible of every 'horizonal', ontological and legal closure, that subtracts choice from every empirico-ideal criterion or constraint, on the contrary limiting all such since it forms a principle exceeding and containing all relations of ideality and the empirical.

3. Contingency and necessity – those of philosophy – are no longer only those of the 'transcendentals' in the Scholastic sense, of the superior and universal 'categories' that hold for every being. *These are the transcendental and 'individual' lived experiences that hold a priori not only for beings but for 'Being itself' and for Difference.* In the non-reflexive experience (of) the One, Difference becomes an absolutely absurd thinking possessing no other right than its effective existence for itself. The (non-)One and NTT destroy every auto-position of philosophical decision. Even the metaphysical fact of Being, even what it becomes as 'being-that-is', as nothingness-that-nihilates, as

language-that-speaks, even these sublime and modest tautologies inscribe themselves in the abyss that unary multiplicities impose upon them.

What we are considering as the (non-)One itself, and its mode partially relative to the World and to effectivity, NTT, manifest a contingency otherwise-than-empirical of the systems of Difference. 'Otherwise-than-empirical' because it is no longer the traditional empirical contingency that stands opposite a transcendental that is itself exterior and forms a system with it, but a contingency that unfolds in a new sense, non-thetic (of) itself, from the transcendental. It is a matter of a radicalization of the well-known and still too empirical 'transcendental contingency' of experience (Kant, Heidegger, Merleau-Ponty) inasmuch as this is elevated by the reflection that gives it its necessity. It is now a extra-empirical contingency affecting the philosophical type of transcendental itself, such as it is understood generally, that is, the Difference that combines *both* the empirical *and* the transcendental. There is an emergence of philosophical decision that is of an absurdity more profound and more radical – an absurdity of essence founded in the One – than any contingency of a Greco-Occidental *fact*, even a finite one. Here is the blind spot of all the critical, thoughtful and deconstructive vigilances; it is the contingency that affects in totality this primitive act of reduction itself that claims nevertheless to regulate its accounts with the 'transcendence' of the real: for example the supposedly accomplished interiorization of ideality to the One, the possibility, still partially there in Heidegger and Derrida, of a transcendental tautology without any 'empirical' remainder or, more rigorously, without any 'real' remainder. Even when the logos and phono-centrism are said to return upon the cut to suture differance in Difference, this does not prevent in effect the essence of the 'philosophical' operation, its extreme point, subsisting in a Turning or Re-affirmation that still claims to re-inscribe and re-interiorize as One this efflux of the logos. This latter, its insistence, is then treated simply and reductively as exterior 'finitude', it is not recognized as principial, but merely as necessary evil or constraint that philosophical technique must and can limit to inhibitory blows and actions of slowing, without any real recognition of its force, *its transcendental origin in the last instance and its positivity*, its more-than-universal universality and necessity, its contingency more radical than any 'facticity' or 'finitude' – *its status of 'principle', of second principle opposite the One.*

THE NIETZSCHE-HEIDEGGER CONFLICT AND
ITS INDIFFERENCE

1. From this, the resolution we may bring to the conflict dominating contemporary philosophy: the conflict between Nietzsche and Heidegger, between absolute and finite Difference. Plunged back into the abyss of the (non-)One and the NTT, these two modes of Difference both become, for the finite subject, possible and yet indifferent decisions. We have no reason from here on for choosing between two absolute decisions that are indifferent to one another. Between a philosophy that begins with a radical decision of suspension of the presupposed *all*, that renders itself indifferent to experience (Husserl, Nietzsche, Deleuze) in its claimed transcendence of the in itself and that closes the transcendental field in advance, assuring *a priori* the terminal possibility of this closure, and a philosophy that roots itself in non-philosophical inauthenticity as the index of an irreducible Other preventing the idealizing closure of the transcendental field, there is no longer any principle of choice. Posed philosophically, as a simple antinomy, the problem clearly implies a reason for choosing. Posed as absolute Difference, in Nietzschean fashion, the choice is already made in favour of Nietzsche; as finite, it is made already in favour of Heidegger. Yet this is still a point of view internal to Difference, to its games and its interminable war. If the Nietzsche/Heidegger conflict or debate is really indifferent to us, it is because it is always possible to draw out the thesis of real Finitude from its naïvete and to reduce it to being still a philosophical thesis but one of a new style, forming *with* the restricted philosophy that it grounds a new space but one the real unity of which is beyond it, in a non-thetic, absolute and contingent decision. And inversely, the *a priori* reduction of all inauthenticity and the expulsion of the principle of the in itself beyond the essence of truth, is solely – in this still classical type of philosophy – the denial of a presupposition, a denial that it is always possible to re-introduce into this system of the idealizing usage of Difference in

order to reconstitute an absolute decision. The problem of a choice between Husserl and Heidegger, Nietzsche and Heidegger or, among contemporaries, between Deleuze and Derrida, respectively, is no longer posed once one points out that each of the two attitudes relates itself necessarily, through a more or less accentuated denial, to a given of transcendence with which it forms – each in its own way – a new space of experience, more encompassing and more 'powerful' that is itself governed by *the logic of absolute Transcendence, non-thetic (of) itself.* Such transcendence is not deduced from real finitude, it is as much the condition of possibility for idealizing reduction as for finitude. It is a more universal trait that contains these two or three types of decision as well as others. It is an absolute decision, rooted in the Undecidable or the One: it conditions in general the mixture of Difference as 'un?decidable decision', and renders indifferent, at least for the finite human subject (of) science, the choice of one type of Difference rather than another.

2. At the interior of a philosophical decision, of an empiricity-in-the-Idea or of a telos of the singular or of the real – one may no doubt always invoke such and such a particular content, some 'object', some region or experience rather than another, one may prefer Heidegger to Hegel, and it is true that each time the definition of the universal or the corresponding *a priori*, thus its relation to the real, varies with this very relation, since it is the immanence of this relation, that is, an *a priori* fact, that begins by giving itself every philosophical decision. But precisely because it is a matter of a relation, transcendent inasmuch as relation, it cannot emerge globally, comprehending its terms, except through a gesture that is, itself, straightaway contingent and 'finite' to the extent that nothing could ever sublate or idealize this contingency in any 'transcendental necessity'. All these arguments: Kant's empirical affectivity, Husserl's categorial intuition, Heidegger's beings as given in the relation of toolhood or equipment, the ruptures of dynamical forms or 'catastrophes', Derrida's 'extended' signifier as arche-writing, Deleuze's multiplicities of desiring machines, the Other and its exteriority, etc., all these may be invoked as index of the real in order to ground different forms, finite or otherwise, of decision, *but the promotion of such givens and their insertion into the a priori facts rests upon a principial absence of sufficient reason*, the real holding itself still

beyond these facts, precisely in this absence, an absence of entirely positive origin, of reasons for choosing. The argumentation by the contingency and multiplicity of the real is still more contingent than it would have thought. The transcendental radicalization of these arguments accomplishes the tearing away of them from their empirical, or, for example, intra-historical, model. Metaphysics is not contingent as an empirical fact, nor even as an *a priori* fact; it is absolutely contingent and absurd beyond every historical insertion, every historical or perceptual model of contingency: it is not necessary except for itself and at the interior of its hallucination of the real.

Take the case of finite Difference: it cannot but continue always to slog down ever more intensively into the Greco-Occidental *a priori* fact, into what it has admitted as being the universal fact of any possible thinking, into a mode of thinking that is at once duel and unitary – Difference – of which it has admitted once and for all that it shall be the only soil that it will both mine and undermine. Such is the destiny of contemporary philosophy as endogenous paralysis: to 'furnish' the Greek earth. This is the sense of what it claims as its Finitude: there would be an *a priori fact* of metaphysics, a prior and unsurpassable reality, an irreducible shadow that would draw in advance the sites and neighbourhoods of thought, a facticity that will have decided upon the seriousness of every possible thinking and that will have been 'findable' no doubt in Greco-Occidental history, but also as its always-opening limit . . .

It is unable to see that this argumentation, since it is grounded upon the question *'quid facti?'* and upon an inventory of the *a priori*, is tainted by a contingency still more radical than anything it could imagine since it isolates a particular experience of the real in the state of *a priori fact*, even if finite. So much so that, measured in respect of this other contingency, the much-vaunted Greco-historial fact of 'the' metaphysics has – at least in the last instance – neither more nor less validity or pertinence than Text, Desire, Power: there is no reason to 'choose' Heidegger rather than Nietzsche or inversely. At the interior of this general way of posing problems and making use of the transcendental, no doubt there are differences of more and/or less, differences of degree perhaps, if not nature (finite or non-finite usage of Difference), according to Difference's respective criteria of usage. But measured against finite or 'individual' man who precedes philosophical decision, who affects it with a stronger contingency, there is neither more nor less absurdity in one choice than in another, but an equal absurdity, a equal absence of sufficient reason for the choice, an 'absence' that is the true 'sufficient reason' of philosophical decision and of the war philosophical decision wages against itself. *We must posit the equivalence of philosophical decisions.*

'Being' is thus not only, except in terms of a restrictive and vicious interpretation, a Greco-Occidental historial *factum*; metaphysics is no such historial fact, at once immanent to and transcendent of history, intra-and-trans-historical. In its essence it is a 'decision' that responds, *from the point of view of the One*, to no principle of choice whatsoever and is so absurd in itself – and with it 'Being' and ontology, the Occidental ontological decision, *the onto-Occidental decision* – that it acquires its true reality from none other than this very absurdity itself.

3. That metaphysics would be unsurpassable may thus be understood in a more general and less philistine sense than Difference would have it. In the sense that metaphysics would be a mode of NTT and the (non-)One and not merely an empirico-ideal mixture; in the sense that its essence has not only the contingency of a fact that takes the form of a universal presupposed by thought, but a contingency – and a necessity – otherwise-than-universal, more positive than those of a fact; more essential absurdity than Heidegger's philistine 'facticity' or Nietzsche's 'chance', still imperfect since it must be re-affirmed. The Finitude of metaphysics is no doubt an affirmation of contingency directed against autoposition in the sense of the subject's self-mastery. But NTT, which underlies this thesis of Finitude itself, possesses a more extended and principial sense than it: it is all of Difference, the fact it postulates and its finitude in an Other, that is a matter for this non-idealist experience of Transcendence.

'Finitude', 'facticity', 'dereliction' are interpretations marked by the empiricism of the Second Principle, which is no 'fact' but rather the transcendental principle – the *A priori real* – necessary in order for there to be such things as facts or a transcendent real at all. Difference thinks 'lavishly' or, at times, 'aristocratically', identifying itself with the Combat rather than the combatants and having struggle for its essence, the tearing that binds adversaries and conciliates them without reconciliation through their struggle. Yet the 'great politics' or the 'grand style of thought' form a system with a philistinism – of philo-sophical origin – of Culture, of Language and History which are pos-ited from the outset as presuppositions destined to be over-come, instead of being gone into fully to the point of their ultimate absurd-ity. Heidegger, through his interpretation of finitude as non-objectiv-izing/non-objective scission, no doubt would have known how to limit Occidental idealism and activism. But his means, which he takes above all from Kant and the Greeks, prevent him from granting to the One's essence and its priority over Being a sufficiently radical sense. He claims to guard the singular or the real, but what he guards is rather the ontico-ontological mixture of the singular and its singular-ity. Finitude or being 'in itself' remain idealizations, the non-objectiv-izable is adjoined to an objectivizing idealization, it is from this 'mixed' position of the problem that he keeps to his discourse of the failure *really*, or through the real, to have 'surpassed' metaphysics. Instead of recognizing that the essence of the One implies, at least for itself, the dissolution of mixtures, inasmuch as, preceding them without exiting outside them, it is content with what can no longer be other than a juxtaposition-in-becoming, a self-wagering, of the real *and* the ideal linked through their indivisible relation . . . One must oppose to this a non-thetic 'finitude' the reality of which affects thoroughly and without remainder thetic transcendence or Being, all ideality in gen-eral and its innumerable internal relations that are the very stuff of sense and intelligibility.

DIFFERENCE, DENIAL OF THE REAL

1. The modes of Difference, finite or otherwise, are symptoms of the two 'principles' that exhaust the real, and quite particularly of the second, (non-)One and NTT.

If Difference has nothing to fear from Hegelianism and the ambi-tions of the *Concept*, if for example, in its finite form (Heidegger), it denounces the illusion of the Concept – which consists in denying, beyond the vulgar belief in the existence in itself of objects, also its real origin, the existence in itself of the non-objectivizable real – it itself forms one body with a double-sided denial, on the one hand bearing upon the One, on the other upon the correlative NTT. The true sense of the philosophical type of Finitude may now appear and its destruction be achieved. We have steadily denounced the Heideggerean restriction of non-reflexive Transcendence, individual lived experience, at worst to a phenomenon of empirical and/or idealized facticity and contingency, to a facticity (of) the *a priori* (that of Greco-Occidental metaphysics), at best to a structure of alterity: it is obvious that this a prioric facticity forms a system with the central thesis of Finitude and that if Heidegger maintains a metaphysical or ontological *factum*, it is on the strict condition that it be finite, since Finitude alone is able to ballast it with a reality and a certain autonomy in relation to the thinking that relativizes it. Yet Finitude itself is a conception of the real, of its autonomy, its absoluteness, that still restricts these to being – even as Other – modes of thetic transcendence. On the one hand it restricts the real as One to being scission or rather withdrawal and forgetting, absolute transcendence; it projects onto the One the status of beings and thinks the One through the extension of the ontic concept of Finitude, thus also as a mode of thetic transcendence since Finitude *is* the couple of Being *and* beings. On the other hand, always victim of this mixture of Being and beings, of Difference in general, it inversely conceives transcendence as real, on the side of its ideal or ontological form. *Here then is a mixture to be dissolved, the most general, that of ideality and the real, amphibology par excellence, still more profound, more persistent than that of Being and beings.* This latter is a denial of the Second Principle, its refraction in the amphibological element of mixtures and its division into, on the one hand, a transcendence of the real 'in itself' and its empirical correlate, and on the other the *factum a priori* of the Greco-historial meta-physical fact which represents an idealization of empirical facticity, its partial suppression and its interiorization. Against the Idealism of Hegel, Husserl or Nietzsche, Finitude is a blunted weapon. It takes its pertinence, like all philosophical decision, from the NTT that it expresses and upon which it is grounded; but it remains insufficient in its inability to conceive this horizonless transcendence.

2. The denial of NTT in philosophical decision is operated in the form of an auto-position of the latter, an auto-position that grounds the sphere of mixtures or effectivity. Any transcendental analytic

whatsoever, whether existential or otherwise, so little suppresses the auto-position of the real that it is content rather to take this as a point of departure, a given from which it takes its impetus as though from a Mannerist repoussoir. Auto-position remains essential to every analytic method: analysis posits the given from itself or repeats it, even when it receives it. However, we should be more nuanced: auto-position is an *a priori* structure of effectivity. As against philosophy we do not object here to the determined content of its point of departure (presence? identity? logocentrism? natural thesis of the world?), nor even to its proceeding through auto-position, but to its believing auto-position to be *real*; also its believing real the illusion it must overcome: believing that such an illusion or appearance of the in itself asks to be reduced, partially (Heidegger) or totally (Nietzsche), that this auto-position of the real may even be critiqued in certain cases, whereas it takes its necessity and its possibility from a ground of absolute transcendence that, itself, is not self-positing. It postulates that dogmatism and scepticism, that inauthenticity or illusion exist beyond their effectivity and as *real*; it necessarily contaminates the *factum* with the *datum*, but nothing proves – *precisely here is a contingency that appears from another point of view than that of Difference* – that it would be necessary to make of this contingency an obligatory point of departure for transcendental research. Dogmatic and inauthentic appearance co-belong, according to relations to be more authentically determined, to the essence of truth, but this necessity remains too unclear in its origin to make of it a point of departure. Presence and Representation, Inauthenticity, Logocentrism, Gregariousness, Natural thesis of the world, etc., are posited *a priori* by the analytic method, so much so that transcendental truth, by definition, would never be able to save itself from them (even when they believe themselves to do so, as in the idealists denounced by Heidegger), but would limit its ambitions to modifying its relations to them, to reappropriating them to itself in view of its own ends, to acceding to its 'ownness' by way of its forever insurmountable dissimulation.

3. *Yet, this entire game is none other than a restriction, unself-comprehending, of the duality of the One and of non-reflexive Transcendence.* This latter registers not as the particular content of Finitude and its presuppositions,

but as its content of phenomenality or absolute reality. It is a more universal *a priori* trait than Finitude. Finitude characterizes Being in its relation to beings, to nothingness or to itself, it is identical to its relativity. But non-reflexive transcendence designates the contingency of the global system of an empirical given or of a transcendent presupposition in general, and the relativity of reductions or divisions, of the transcendental 'syntax', to this given: in short, the contingency of a philosophical decision. This is no longer any ordinary presupposition, some simple 'empirical' given of which one would seek yet again the possibility, it is the constraint making it globally necessary to posit an empirical as correlate of the operations of transcendental analytic and of 'differance' in particular. As for the presuppositions – once admitted – and everything belonging to the empirical, Difference declares that the game is (nearly) over; that these givens are already – apart from a repetition – included in the game of Difference which will not let itself be exceeded by them since it is the system of their remainder or the regularity of their excess. But concerning this Non-positional Transcendence, which cannot be deferred since it globally conditions the project and technique of Difference, Difference can do nothing. It is a determination more profound than any presupposition, because it is precisely this absolute and altogether particular presupposition which explains the possibility of philosophically seeking for presuppositions. It is this that Difference denies by hallucinating the real through itself.

It is thus in turn a presupposition, if you like, necessary to the philosophical usage of the transcendental, but unperceived or denied by philosophy which is content always to posit Being or Difference as the presupposed par excellence: Great Presupposed or Pure Mixture, Thing or Case, Locus or Body, that gathers all the possibilities of presupposition and forms a system with the very exercise of thought. But these are here and more profoundly the inalienable phenomenal givens of a law that is beyond the correlation of the empirical *and* the *a priori*, since it sustains the existence of this correlation, since it *is* its existence and self-legitimation, as well as its absurdity. The blind spot of Difference, and not only of it: Difference attacks Presence, Identity, the Natural thesis of the world, Logocentrism, the Gregariousness of desire's organization, but can no longer, and for good reason, reappropriate itself to itself through any possible critique of this more profound 'thesis' which decides that it is a critique, a deconstruction, an elementary or even intentional analytic, a schizo-analysis, etc. – a analysis in general: it makes one body, in its very existence, with this Non-Thetic Transcendence that exceeds it absolutely and by means of which it posits itself all while claiming surreptitiously to take its legitimacy from itself (auto-position). As mixture, Difference gives rise to a becoming, a history, but it remains relative to a more powerful matrix, that of the One and its Opening-without-position. Difference cannot reappropriate this to itself in the mode of their 'difference' in general, since it is the system that sustains and conditions its project, its critical vigilance, its operation of difference.

Difference is a mixture, indeed mixture par excellence. Yet because of this excellence, because it is the last possible degree of mixture, it cannot be said that it occupies the in-between of the One and its correlate, NTT, as if it were to develop itself between these two absolute boundaries. It is true that outside of itself Difference leaves what might appear to be a double absolute excess, but it is no longer possible to say that the One and NTT together form a common intermediate space that would be occupied by Difference. This would be surreptitiously to place them in turn in a relation, a relation that would be by definition universal, an economy, a simultaneity, in the form of a mixture. If the One is what, in essence and at least by its own account, does not enter into relations in general, does not leave itself through any transcendence, there is nothing universal, no locus if not that of the (non-)One, beyond the locus, the universal locality that Difference is able to constitute. Thus there is also an absolute emergence of Difference as mixture at the heart of the (non-)One which is the contrary or 'positive' absence of every genesis. The mixture of Representation has no justification other than itself, and it is this that it draws from the brutality or the absurdity of its existence that becomes manifest upon the ground of the (non-)One and NTT.

CRITIQUE OF PHILOSOPHICAL DECISION

1. It is the One in its immanence that makes non-horizontal Transcendence apparent as one of the two origins of Difference and that

denounces the objective absurdity of this last procedure of philosophy and of philosophy in general.

There is no possible critique of Difference – global and in principle – that would not place itself straightaway in the Absolute, inasmuch as its essence is not exhausted by the way in which Difference makes use of it. That the *veritas transcendentalis* would be identically the experience of truth – here is an Archimedean point or an *a priori* constraint of every philosophy that even Difference would be able to accept. But what it is no longer able to accept is that this immanence would be real and not ideal, that it would be non-thetic and stripped of transcendence; that the One or Absolute would no longer be a presupposition or a position that could be simply opposed, with more or less mediation, whether negative or not, to Representation. Such an Absolute is rather what rejects every philosophy, every universal, every 'metaphysical a priori' in the sphere of mixtures and effectivity and what makes radical contingency and then NTT appear as the real content of the 'presuppositions' of philosophical decision.

If it is no longer even from the point of view of Difference that we may expose what sustains it in existence and will never fall any longer in its grip, that it will never encounter any longer in its paths, if it is from a completely other point of view, how are we to define this?

This is no longer and never has been a philosophical decision. Transcendental truth is absolutely autonomous and does not form a variable and indissociable mixture with appearance or illusion. This point of view for which thinking would no longer have to divide a mixture of truth and appearance it would have first of all supposed as given in order to be able to proceed to various reductions, various bracketings always relative to this given – the name of this point of view is science. We do not claim to have 'exited' from Heidegger and from Difference in general except from the side of the Absolute which has no need to exit from what it has never engaged in the first place, which is no longer a 'side'; and from a truth the essence of which has the structure of science, that is, *a reflection or representation which is non-thetic (of) the real*.

2. We thus do not put Heidegger in parentheses: because the truth of Being goes already by leaping lightly from one parenthesis (to) the other, but above all because the essence of the One and that of

the non-positional Transcendence that is its correlate are never, themselves, accessible through any transcendent operation, be it of reduction, division, limitation, demarcation, contra-band, disregard, supplement and excess, turning, offhandedness, because the essence of the One is rather an immediate given that renders possible, as their real unmoved mover, these operations, but that, itself, gives rise to an immanent and rigorous description. Thinking that is none other than 'unary' is in a state of poverty that is practically absolute, it is stripped of all operation, all technique, all power. It is content with a description without intervention, a contemplation without decision. The One has need of neither repetition, nor reduction and suspension, nor turning, it clasps nothing of Being, contenting itself with unclasping Being or de-clutching Difference.

It is no longer a matter, as in Husserl or Nietzsche, of suspending all transcendent philosophical positions, but of indifferentiating, one might say, every operation of suspension, of rendering useless the reduction itself by rejecting it, together with the presuppositions inseparable from it, presence, logocentrism, the thesis of the world, gregariousness, etc., outside of the essence of the *veritas transcendentalis*. To presuppose them in order to differentiate them, deconstruct them, analyze them, precisely this is the essential presupposition of philosophical decision as such, and it is from this that we discover that it is a matter for a logic other than that of its interminable auto/hetero-affection. Supposing that there would still be some kind of suspension – but there is no longer one, at least for the truth and the One, if not for philosophy – it would concern no longer the content of philosophical theses, nor even theses in general and as such, but rather the very thesis that there would be nothing other than theses. Correctly understood, the thetic, the present, the gregarious, etc., exist, but where? certainly not in the truth or in its margins or at its centre: the truth is not a 'locus' nor even the locality of the locus or locus in general. There is a topology of Being; there is no topology of the One.

3. The essence of truth, if it is an immediate given, at least in the sense that science posits such givens, is on the other hand no longer dependent upon a labour of analysis over some claimed *factum a priori*, over a universal concept of experience and the real preliminarily disengaged. It no longer has need of a *metaphysical a priori* in general,

of a *universal transcendental field* of experience or of the Unity of experience, which always forms a system with the thesis that there will have been presuppositions that must be analyzed, divided, reduced. It has no need of any preparatory and/or accompanying reduction. It does not begin by presupposing, in order to be able to accede to itself, that evil exists and must be vanquished by philosophy, nor even that philosophy exists: it rejects all of that outside of itself, that is, in radical contingency, in the sphere of what claims to legitimate itself from itself, but which is absurd or unnecessary for the One. This is the global project of philosophical critique inasmuch as it remains relative to hidden presuppositions, an appearance, an amphibology, and forms a system with these, which fall as strangers outside of scientific truth which is non-thetic. This is, in a broader sense, all philosophy as technology (of reduction or the putting between parentheses, of division and demarcation, of analysis and synthesis, of reappropriation and turning/reversion/reversal) that is expelled outside of truth (upon which it depends, to be sure, but of which it is not constitutive) and rejected to the rank of the infinite games of auto-position that in the last instance non-reflexive Transcendence renders possible. The empirico-transcendental mixture of truth and appearance, this inalienable alienation posited by the unitary tradition, if in effect it even exists, no longer co-belongs to the essence of the truth and has no more legitimation, in the last instance, than that of its real contingency upon the One.

THE VISION-IN-ONE AND THE DECISION IN FAVOR OF 'DUALISM'

1. As a function of the results obtained, we must thematize our own approach to the real critique of Difference, that is, our 'decision' in favour of dualism as against Greco-Occidental Difference.

At the interior of the radical suspension operated by the (non-)One, Difference is thus unilateralized, rejected or derived without return. Yet the passage from the (non-)One to NTT supposes that we still place it (it is not in effect destroyed or dissolved *effectively* by the One) in the point of view of Difference without however giving up the experience of the One of which immanence serves as the main thread of every scientific and no longer philosophical description of philosophical decision. NTT is itself affected by the (non-)One and its indifference, but it supposes the validity, in its order, of a philosophical type of given: Being, Difference or whatever other 'effective' decision. The dual of the One and its mixtures of effectivity is accompanied by the duality of the One and the (non-)One and followed by the dualism of the One and NTT.

2. Difference, analyzed as pure mixture or superior form of mixtures, has henceforth the appearance of a contradiction, more exactly of a duality that it would deny. Not between the One and Division, the indivisible One and the divisible Idea – this concerns precisely 'difference' and not a contradiction. But between the essence of the One and the transcendent usage of the 'limit' that it makes of it and which grounds Difference, between its condition in the last instance and the image that it gives of it, that is not illusory in itself since it suffices fully for Difference, but that is so in relation to the essence of the One.

However this 'contradiction' is complex and must be thought delicately. It is not a contradiction for Difference itself, which moreover has nothing to resolve since it is rather its very essence. Neither is it any contradiction for the One itself and its truth since this implies in an immanent manner the axiom: the One and the immanent experience of the One are identical, and for it the problem does not exist. The experience of the essence of the One as solely immanent implies at least for it the inexistence of Difference and the refusal – (non-) One – of its claims to exhaust the reality of the One. Having to do with the One and with it alone, there is no distinguishing between its essence and its transcendent usage of Limit, and there is no contradiction. It is necessary on the contrary to measure by this criterion Being's usage of the One and to have taken this seriously (it is grounded upon its autonomy of All as such). Such usage appears then as a contradiction internal to Difference or to 'Being itself' of which one sees that it holds only through this doublespeak, that it is nothing other than this equivocity, or this defect in movement, of an unconditioned condition and a conditioned that claims hallucinatorily to condition its condition. The solution of this 'contradiction' is the disengaging of the *real a priori*, NTT. Thus only Difference or Being are capable, perhaps through an ultimate torsion or a desperate effort that they would only 'grudgingly accept' for themselves under the 'impetus' of the One, of distinguishing between their restrictive requisition of the One and the One's essence, and of thinking the necessity of NTT. *The dualism that analyzes Being or Difference is still the philosophy of Being, while the One for its account has neither a monist philosophy nor a dualist philosophy, nor probably any philosophy 'at all'.* What would be able to pass in all rigor for a contradiction (internal to Difference, but inasmuch as Difference is grounded in the One's essence that Difference would distinguish from itself) is *a dualist thinking that cannot be born except in the spirit of Difference or Being.* We must explain this.

3. Who in effect operates this confrontation of Difference and the One, that is, the operation that we have made from the beginning of the present study? This would be precisely the wrong question, since whosoever asks this – operating in the unitary mode of the 'Who?', of the Greco-Occidental type of philosophizing subject – cannot do otherwise than order the state of ensuing description to a question that is already a response. 'Dualism' excludes the unitary philosophizing subject and the unity of his or her decision, but it does not exclude, to the contrary, since it is founded on it, the immanence of the One in itself as the real, non-unitary essence of Being, of Difference, etc.: this transcendental act of the One in Difference, let us call it without further explication here the 'determination in the last instance' of Difference by the One. It is such that, without requiring that Difference be necessary in order to think the One whose essence is absolute and autonomous, it does not exclude any longer that, under this condition of determination in the last instance thus maintained, it would be possible *also* to be placed in the point of view of Difference, Being, metaphysics, etc. Upon all these complex 'relations' between the One and Difference, which are neither those of exclusion, nor of interiorizing sublation, nor (precisely) of difference – we are not about to elaborate here. But what is proper to this transcendentally grounded dualism and what requires the concept of 'determination in the last instance', is the capability, the necessity of being placed in Difference 'at the same time' that it necessarily takes – without there being any

exclusion – the non-reflexive transcendental immanence of the One for unique guiding thread of its examination of Difference and its critique of Difference.

Consequently, if up to now we have proceeded 'naively' in the critique of Difference, in producing in that way as residue the concept of NTT, we must now take account of the complexity of the real situation and recognize the non-exclusive totality of conditions that has rendered possible the elaboration of this concept in which we see the transcendental origin of metaphysics and of philosophical decision in general. Yet it is clear now that this element of NTT could not be obtained except from Difference or Being, except in presupposing consequently constituted metaphysics and its amphibology, at least by way of material already containing previously, in a restrictive form, their own transcendental condition.

In other words, the power of NTT is truly a transcendental power relative to the philosophical decision that takes root in it, but a transcendental power of another nature than that, more abyssal, of the One. While this latter proceeds as a 'determination in the last instance' unconditioned by that of which it is the essence, the former is, in effect, of a more 'traditional' nature, it is still partially relative to the empirically conditioned, contenting itself with transforming the *empirico-transcendental parallelism* without rendering it radically contingent as does the One on its account. This is why the dualism of the One and NTT does not have any sense or truth except for metaphysics – but in the 'perspective' of the One –, except for Difference and its own 'auto-positional' necessity: non-positional Transcendence and dualism in general, dualist decision, are thus affected by a certain irreducible *auto-positional* effectivity . . . The duality of the One in its essence and the One-limit (of the One and Being-Difference) is still a philosophy for Being: if not vicious in turn, at least contingent.

Every distinction between the One and its usage, for example of limit, is affected as such by metaphysics and by auto-position. It sublates not only the absolute contingency of the (non-)One or of NTT, but the still quite 'factical' contingency of Difference. Either Difference is an Illusion for the One (it is contingent in the (non-)One); or, *if* it claims to be real, it is so solely for itself and from its own authority (auto-position). If the One itself has no need of thinking something that would be its own usage of Limit and of Difference, this latter still thinks itself, posits itself, engenders itself in the most vicious possible way: precisely as auto-position . . . Auto-position is the sole operation proper to Difference but this is not 'its own' operation except for the reason that another logic, that of NTT, constrains, isolates and averts it in other respects. Confronted by the radical immanence of the *veritas transcendentalis* and the (non-)One, Difference cannot but avow its own vicious essence. It must recognize that it carries no legitimacy except from itself – this self that is itself in the last instance designated by the (non-)One and NTT – and that it is thus absolutely contingent. The transcendental type of argumentation utilized here 'against' Difference by positing always the 'identity' of the One and its immanent experience is obviously in turn *immanent really* to this experience of the One. But dualism is in turn implicated in the auto-position or metaphysics that continues irreducibly to affect its own dualist dissolution. In reality this does not provide any actual alternative, since everything at any rate takes place at the interior of radical contingency or the (non-)One.

Other works by François Laruelle

PHILOSOPHY I

Phénomène et différence. Essai sur Ravaisson (Paris: Klincksieck, 1971)
Machines textuelles. Déconstruction et libido-d'écriture (Paris: Le Seuil, 1976)
Nietzsche contre Heidegger (Paris: Payot, 1977)
Le déclin de l'écriture (Paris: Aubier-Flammarion, 1977)
Au-delà de principe de pouvoir (Paris: Payot, 1978)

PHILOSOPHY II

Le principe de minorité (Paris: Aubier, 1981)
Une biographie de l'homme ordinaire. Des autorités et minorités (Paris: Aubier, 1985)
Philosophies of Difference: A Critical Introduction to Non-Philosophy, trans. Rocco Gangle (New York and London: Continuum, 2010 [1987])
Philosophie et non-philosophie (Liège-Bruxelles: Mardaga, 1989)
En tant qu'Un (Paris: Aubier, 1991)
Théorie des identités (Paris: PUF. 1992)

PHILOSOPHY III

Théorie des Étrangers (Paris: Kimé, 1995)
Principes de la non-philosophie (Paris: PUF, 1995)

Éthique de l'Étranger (Paris: Kimé, 2000)
Introduction au non-marxisme (Paris: PUF, 2000)

PHILOSOPHY IV

Future Christ: A Lesson in Heresy, trans. Anthony Paul Smith (New York
    and London: Continuum, 2010 [2002])
L'ultime honneur des intellectuels (Paris: Textuel, 2003)
La Lutte et l'Utopie à la fin des temps philosophiques (Paris: Kimé, 2004)
Mystique non-philosophique à l'usage des contemporains (Paris: L'Harmattan,
    2007)

PHILOSOPHY V

Introduction aux sciences génériques (Pars: Petra, 2008)
Philosophie non-standard (Paris: Kimé, 2010)

Index

INDEX